A Brief History of Money

BEST

CHANAN STEINHART

A Brief History of Money

How We Got Here and What's Next

Chanan Steinhart

Market Street Publishing
San Francisco
2015

To Anat
With thanks for the friendship and support over the years

Published in 2015 in the United States of America by Market Street
Publishing

Cover design: Leana mippieArt. Cover image: Shutterstock

Library of Congress Cataloging-in-Publishing Data

Steinhart, Chanan.

A brief history of money: How we got here and what's next/ Chanan
Steinhart

p.cm

Including bibliographical references and indexes.

ISBN 978-0-990-84730-4

US History 2. World History I. Title.

2014920563

10 9 8 7 6 5 4 3 2 1

Stand Beside Her

Contents

Introduction...9

1. "And there was evening, and there was morning"
   How did all this come about? 11

2. "Big is Better," or Is It?...23

3. Cash or Credit?..43

4. The Secret Weapon: Not All Taxes Are Created Equal....57

5. The Birth of the Money Creation Machine 71

6. The Illegitimate Child: Lender of Last Resort.................97

7. A Sabre Dance—Gold and Paper 117

8. A World Off Balance: Between Two Wars 135

9. The Golden Dollar: the Bretton Woods System 167

10. Bye-Bye, Gold; Hello, Fiat Money 181

11. 2008: A Peek at Hell..249

12. What's Next?...283

NOTES...323

Acknowledgments 347

Introduction

My love of history was passed down to me from my grandfather. He was born in Germany, proud of the country that genera- tions of his ancestors had called home. In 1914 he and his four brothers gladly joined the German army to fight its war. He was wounded and one of his brothers was killed.

I am sure he never imagined that only twenty years later his nine-year-old daughter would be rushed out of the country with only the clothes on her body. She was being saved by the former enemy, the English, in what came to be known as the *Kindertransport*, a rescue mission of predominantly Jewish children organized in the lead-up to World War II. She would survive her father. He was killed in the Theresienstadt concen- tration camp, exactly thirteen years from the day I was born to his refugee daughter. Although I would never meet him, his and his family's fate made history a prime area of interest in my life.

When I was young, I was fascinated by the war and the Holocaust and read extensively about what had happened. As time went on, I became more interested in people than in events, trying to comprehend not what happens, but why. This question expanded the scope of my study well beyond WWII Europe. Human history is mostly the study of human group behavior. It is like an onion: examination of a layer inevitably leads you to another layer, deeper into history.

In the summer of 2008, a major financial event took place. I felt that the truth of the events was not being accurately and sufficiently represented by the standard media outlets. Thus I went out on a quest to better understand.

As I delved into the subject, I came to the realization that 2008 was much more than a periodical market downturn as the media and politicians often depicted it. Rather, the financial crisis was a watershed moment in the history of money, one characterized by intrigue, greed and innovation. I also concluded that you cannot really understand the world we live in without understanding the history of money, an amazing tool invented some 6,500 years ago. Without such understanding we are like the six blind men trying to figure out what an elephant is by feeling different parts of the animal and coming to wildly different conclusions.

Though history tends to surprise us with unexpected events, it is more because of our physiological makeup that we are surprised than for lack of information. Thus, painting a clear and comprehensive big picture of money, its history and where we stand today is the main goal of this book, if not for the generation that brought us to this point, then for the benefit of the growing one soon to face an uncertain future.

This book is not for economists and it is not about the bits and pieces of economic theory, though you cannot cover the history of money without touching upon some important highlights of economics. The book also does not strive to be an encyclopedia of money. Rather it is an overview, designed to give an idea of the big picture, of the elephant.

Chapter 1:
"And there was evening, and there was morning" How did all this come about?

Some 10,000 years ago a major event occurred: people took charge of their food production. As ice sheets melted, transforming desolate land into wet and fertile fields, people discovered the concept of sowing and slowly developed mass wheat cultivation. Wild goats were herded between steep hills. Eventually herding led to the first in-captivity pregnancy, and breeding proceeded from there. This revolution happened in a several places around the globe at about the same time period. The simultaneous yet independent nature of these revolutions is a mystery in and of itself, but between 9,000 to 7,000 BC the gears started turning and people were starting to form agricultural communities.

The Neolithic Revolution—which transformed mankind from tiny groups of hunter and gatherers to agrarian societies with cities, complex networks, infrastructure, and institutions—did not happen overnight. This process likely spanned a few thousand years, but once it was completed, it brought about notable changes that transformed the face of the earth and touched almost all of its habitants forever.

The first and most important immediate effect was the substantial growth in food production. If in a hunter-gatherer model a given size of land could yield a certain amount of food and thus support a set number of people, the same size of land could now, after the discovery of wheat cultivation and animal domestication, produce 5 to 10 times more food and thus support 5 or 10 times more people. This considerable growth in food production and the surpluses it created had growing impacts on human society, one of which was population growth.

During hunter-gatherer times, there were clear limitations on the pace of reproduction, among them the limitation imposed by the nomadic lifestyle. Hunter-gatherer mothers were generally tasked with carrying around children that could not yet walk. Thus, people could not practically have more than one non-walking child at any given time. Given that it takes children 3-4 years to develop the ability to independently walk through varied terrain, the reproduction rate was set by nature at around one child per 3-4 years.

Once people began settling down in one place, the reproductive pace could slowly rise to one child every two years, or even less. The surplus in food availability enabled this growth in population, creating a positive feedback loop: a larger population meant more manpower in the fields, which meant more food surplus to go around, which meant the ability to further grow the population.

Production and food surpluses were key to many more developments as we will soon see, not the least of which was the ability to save and invest.

A society that must consume everything it produces or catches has nothing left over for investment and cannot accumulate wealth; that is, you cannot grow a herd if you have to eat every cow. However, if you have surpluses of cows and food to feed them with, you can allow the excess cows to live, reproduce, and even create new products like milk and cheese. Here we see a simple but lasting lesson: societies with excess goods can invest and, over time, become richer, leaving them with a growing amount of capital which they can invest again and become even richer. Societies which must (or decide) to consume all they produce are ultimately consuming their future.

Population growth, the sedentary nature of the new communities tied to their fields, and food surpluses permanently altered the social structure and setup of human communities.

As the agricultural communities grew, so did the fundamental need for organizing those communities. The food supply afforded the creation and support of organizations that were dedicated not to food production, but rather to administrative duties. Why, though, did humans need organization? Why not live as a group of individual farmers the same way that groups of hunter-gatherers had lived?

The creation of organizations dedicated to serving communities was fundamentally an economic decision. In simple terms, the return on investment for getting organized was significant. The resources used for creating these organizations—manpower, time, food, energy—created a bigger positive impact than if they had been applied to more agricultural production. In almost every aspect of their lives, early agricultural communities found value in grouping together. Creating these function-specific organizations was the best way to bring to life big projects such as building an irrigation system, gathering a force to defend food and production assets from rival communities, and sharing and advancing knowledge. The organization of society proved perhaps most critical when it came to defending food supplies and production assets.

Now that food was no longer a moving target, but rather "low-hanging fruit," it had to be defended against those who believed that the simplest way to get their daily calories was to take it from others. It is not hard to imagine that the first organization occurred organically when the strongest and perhaps socially smartest guy in the new community, offered to take it upon himself to protect the community's goods. While he would not be contributing productivity per se, he would be preventing members of rivaling clans from helping themselves to the community's crops. Although he would depend on others to produce his food, the tradeoff for the community was clearly worthwhile.

Organization led to a social structure wherein some people specialized in different aspects of communal social and economic life, such as defense, irrigation, knowledge, information

13

distribution, craftsmanship, trade, and so on. Still, the vast majority were occupied with the core task of food production. As populations grew to a size in which its members no longer knew one another personally, concepts and rules started to take the place of personal connections and networks. Trust and myths replaced personal relationships and firsthand knowledge.

Slowly but inevitably, the previously voluntary layer of organization transformed into a layer of professional management, dedicated to the administrative and non-food-producing duties of the community. This management, knowing full well that working in the fields is a much harder way to gather calories than say, planning irrigation, had to start investing in maintaining ongoing legitimacy and acceptance of their authority. Retaining such acceptance could be accomplished through several, non-mutually exclusive means like delivering results, distributing benefits, propagating myths—like claiming to be chosen by a higher power—and of course, fear and coercion.

Still the overall returns on organization, labor specialization, and professional management were positive. As a result, sometime 6,000 years ago (some 4,000 years from the beginning of the Neolithic Revolution) we start seeing the first cities consisting of more than 10,000 residents. Along with these cities come sizable layers of specialized laborers and professional management.

Funding this social structure necessitated the invention of taxes. But before we get to taxes and money, there is one more point we have to really understand: specialization. The Neolithic Revolution brought on not only labor specialization (i.e. an irrigation engineer or soldiers), but also the specialization of crops, livestock, and other products. As we know, different land is better for different types of crops due to weather, altitude, soil type, and water availability. While it's a good idea to grow bananas in Costa Rica, it's not quite as logical to try to grow them in Sweden. The same logic applies to types of livestock and their foods. The new farmers from the Neolithic era eventually understood this lesson and, after much trial and error, specialization became king.

This new phenomenon of specialization opened the way for trading between people and across markets. When different people and territories produced different products and became better and better at it, trading was the next natural step: "Give me some of your bananas in exchange for some of my goat milk. We don't have wood here but we surely can give you some wool that will keep you warm through many winter nights."

The stage was now set for one of mankind's most significant inventions: money. But why did people really need money in the first place? What issue was the invention aiming to resolve?

The conventional wisdom that "money" came to replace barter trading might be correct, though it is extremely limited. Bartering probably came about naturally as the means of trading favors and priorities, even in hunter-gatherer societies. Nonetheless, bartering had some significant limitations; attempting to trade and negotiate 2 sheep for 1 cow for 5 hours of irrigation work for 3 bushels of wheat could get confusing and burdensome quite quickly. The complications of having multiple products coming from multiple parties with no standards for value created a need for one unified "language." There was a need for a unit of accounting that would be accepted and used by all traders.

But as much as this unit-of-account reasoning for the creation of money makes sense, it is just the tip of the iceberg. The ingenious invention of money goes well beyond making the life of a merchant simpler.

The revolutionary concept behind money and the real power of this invention was its ability to easily move surpluses in food output across geographies and even across time—that is into the future and even into the past! Geographical movement is easy to imagine: I need to pay 100 pounds of wheat for protection services, at this stage probably managed by a central organization like the city or state, but the payment station is located 20 miles away. It's quite clear that carrying these 100 pounds on my back is not the most enjoyable or efficient use of my time. Thus, if I could just condense these 100 pounds into something that can be easily carried in my pocket, it would be a huge relief.

But equally important is the ability to move surplus through time, like by gathering wealth when I am young and strong to support me in later years when I am older. Food surpluses (or wealth) are not only limited to moving into the future. Wealth can also effectively move backwards from the future! Let me explain: if I just got a new piece of land but need seeds to sow it, what do I do? I know for a fact that these seeds will yield crop in the coming spring and that this crop can feed me and my family and even create a new surplus of food. However, what if I don't have the capital to buy the seeds today, before they give me any value? How do I bring some part of those future crops into the present and use them to buy the seeds I need now? We who are so accustomed to the concept of money think the answer simple: with a loan against the future crops. It wasn't as clear 6,000 years ago. The need to transport food surpluses through space and time led mankind to come up with an ingenious concept—a physical object that has no entrenched value in and of itself (it cannot be eaten) but which is accepted by all as representing and reflecting value. Based on this social agreement and belief, the object derives value as if it were the crop itself. In today's world where we swipe plastic cards in return for virtual points usable in non-physical digital worlds, the concept seems almost naïve. In those early times, however, a valueless object representing the real value of a tangible asset was a huge breakthrough, on par with learning to control fire.

Can you imagine the face of a farmer asked to exchange the crop he toiled months to create for a piece of some metal that cannot be eaten? Think of the farmer agreeing to forgo his only protection from death by starvation just for the promise that somebody he doesn't even know will be willing to one day exchange this metal back for the same amount of food! Thus, it is reasonable to assume that this transition probably did not happen overnight, or totally voluntarily.

The material representing the products, soon to be known as money, gained its value entirely from peoples' trust that it truly represented and reflected the product and could be exchanged

16

back and forth at will. After all, the moment that the belief in the representing material is lost, it goes back to being nothing more than a worthless piece of metal or paper.

Though the first coins found are about 2,600 years old (around 600 BC), it is clear that currency existed well before that period. Genesis 23:16 tells about Abraham's purchase of a grave lot for his wife: "And Abraham weighed out to Ephron the silver that he had named [...] four hundred shekels [a weight measurement] of silver, accepted by the merchant." Scholars and believers may debate when and if Abraham existed, but if he did indeed exist it was probably around 2,000 BC. This was about 500 to 1,000 years after the people of Mesopotamia, the most advanced culture at the time, began using silver as a form of exchange and as a tool for wealth preservation.

In order for this new invention, now known as money, to address the issues of moving goods through space and time, it had to function in at least two ways. First, people had to be willing to exchange and accept the otherwise valueless metal in return for their real consumable products. In other words, the money had to be a widely accepted means of exchange for which people were willing to exchange their real products and services. Second, money had to also keep the value of those exchanged products over time; otherwise, why would a farmer agree to exchange 5 bushels of edible wheat for a piece of metal if a few months or years down the line that same metal would only give him 1 bushel in return?

These two characteristics—means of exchange and store of value— are still the keys to having otherwise meaningless materials function as money. There were several other qualities that needed to be satisfied in order for this concept to function, most of them physical:

> › **Scarcity:** money had to be made of something rare and limited. Otherwise, the market would be flooded by that money and in turn its value and status as a means of exchange would evaporate. For example, if for some

reason readily available pebbles were chosen as a form of currency, then everyone would go to the seashore and pick up as many of them as they wanted. As a result, nobody would be willing to exchange real edible goods for these unlimitedly available pebbles! As such, money had to be made of a rare material which was both difficult and expensive to find and bring to the market.

> **Size:** Money had to be small and condensed in size. It had to be easy to carry around, hide, store, guard and exchange.

> **Objectivity:** Money had to be easily and objectively measured and split into equal subunits. This quality is critical for the ability to transact, count and trade. Thus, money had to have a numeric mathematical value, where 2 units are inherently twice more than 1 unit, and 8 units can be easily given as change for a two unit purchase made with 10 units. For this reason, diamonds, for example, could not function as money.

> **Endurance:** Lastly, money had to have fine physical endurance to stand the test of time and not easily fall apart or erode. At the same time, money had to be relatively easy to shape into equal size units and to melt and reconstruct into fairly identical pieces.

Of the 98 naturally occurring elements, only a select few pass all these tests; some are too rare, others have too high a melting point, some erode and rust, and others are not rare enough. Of all materials in nature, only two really fit the bill: silver and gold.

We don't know exactly how, but around 5,000 years ago silver emerged as the solution to the question of money material in the developed world of the Mediterranean and Mesopotamia. It is likely silver's beauty and rarity that attracted people and transformed it in a short period of time from an aesthetic object into a measure of exchange and value storage, i.e. money.

We are not sure if Mesopotamian cities actually created something like coins from those evenly shaped pieces of silver since none have ever been discovered, but we do know that the first discovered coins date back to somewhere around 600 BC in the kingdom of Lydia, currently western Turkey.

But why coins? And why did kingdoms get involved in the first place? How did money, a free market invention created by traders from materials available only in nature, become a state issue? The reason is simple: fraud. Until Archimedes, the well-known Greek physicist, mathematician, engineer and astronomer, stepped into his bathtub around 2,250 years ago and discovered what's known as Archimedes' principle, there was very little way to fight fraud when it came to gold or silver. As the story goes, Archimedes was hired by the king to check if the gold the king had donated for a temple crown had actually gone into the crown or if some of the gold had made its way to the goldsmith's pocket and been substituted by a cheaper material. While taking a bath, Archimedes realized that his body was pushing the water upwards and that the water was rising. After some hard thinking in the tub, he figured out that this water displacement had a formula to it and that the same would apply to the crown. Thus, Archimedes was able to calculate the crown's metallic makeup. Archimedes was so excited, so goes the story that he took to the streets naked crying "Eureka!" (I have found it). Aside from giving a nice little city in northern California the name Eureka, this story demonstrates one of the main problems of money: people trying to chip, debase (melt and mix with other cheaper metals), counterfeit and otherwise infringe upon its integrity.

The solution seemed simple: move the production of money into the hands of the city-state. The ruler would set up a minting operation which was much more complex than individuals could reasonably replicate while simultaneously imposing severe punishments on those trying to compromise the integrity of the money coins. In return, the ruler would charge a service fee and use the coins as a very powerful means of promoting himself and building legitimacy for his regime. In a world with no methods of mass communication, coins were one of the very few ways a ruler could be in front of his subjects every day. Indeed coins were often dominated by slogans and images promoting the ruler, his powers, and military victories. Still even with rulers' involvement in these early days, money was a hard currency made of silver or gold. Regardless of which ruler was minting the currency, it was valued for the gold or silver content.

It is important to remember that there is nothing inherently valuable in gold and silver. Rather, the two metals were granted value as means of exchange by shared belief and social agreement. It is only the trust of the users that eventually enabled an otherwise worthless piece of metal to reflect products and be exchanged for the hard-earned fruits of people's labor. As we shall see time and again, once this trust and social agreement is achieved, it can take years, hundreds of years sometimes, to erode. However, once the concepts underpinning its existence falter, once the money does not store value and does not serve as a medium of exchange, the social agreement is broken and the money becomes worthless.

Such a large scale exercise in trust took place in China around 1279. Kublai Khan, the grandson of Genghis Khan, concluded the conquest of China and established the Yuan (Mongol) Dynasty. He proceeded to significantly increase the use of paper money, which had been originally introduced in China some 400 years earlier. Khan also issued a decree that enforced the acceptance of the paper money he issued. Paper money had many practical advantages, including its ability to be easily moved across large distances, which earned it the nickname "flying money." When Marco Polo, a fourteenth-century Italian merchant and traveler, visited China, he was awed and wrote in his journal: "All these pieces of paper are issued with as much solemnity and authority as if they were of pure gold or silver. [...] And the Khan causes every year to be made such a vast quantity of this money, which costs him nothing that it must equal in amount all the treasure of the world."

And this, making "vast quantity of this money, which costs him nothing" was exactly the problem. Over the next 160 years, more and more paper money was created and, as a result, its value steadily dropped. By 1448, the Ming paper money notes had lost 97% of their value and eventually people lost trust. Without the trust of the people, the money was no longer an accepted medium of exchange and reverted back to being just worthless pieces of paper. In 1455, the paper money system was abandoned and China returned to gold and silver money, which prevailed all the way into the 20th century.

Chapter 2:
"Big is Better," or Is It?

"Society will develop a new kind of servitude which covers the surface of society with a network of complicated rules, through which the most original minds and the most energetic characters cannot penetrate. It does not tyrannise but it compresses, enervates, extinguishes, and stupefies a people, till each nation is reduced to nothing better than a flock of timid and industrious animals, of which the government is the shepherd."
— *Alexis de Tocqueville in Democracy in America, vol. 2 (1805–1859)*

It was around 10,000 years ago that what are called agriculture's "founding crops", 8 basic crops including wheat and barley, were domesticated by farmers. This advance sparked what is now called the Neolithic Revolution. The first signs of such agricultural communities were found in the Middle East just south of the Taurus Mountains in what is today eastern Turkey. The Taurus Mountains are the source of two rivers which shaped the region and the world, the Euphrates and the Tigris. These rivers lie in the heart of the area called Mesopotamia (from Greek: *Meso-Potamos*—the land between the rivers), today mainly Iraq and small parts of Syria and Turkey.

One of the first such farming communities was excavated in today's northern Syria along the Euphrates Valley. Around 11,000 years ago, in a place called Tell Abu Hureyra, now covered by Lake Assad, a handful of the world's earliest farmers cultivated and grew plants and later created pottery and other tools. These early communities were small in size, 50 to 100 individuals, and lived off of what they could grow, find, fish or hunt in their surroundings.

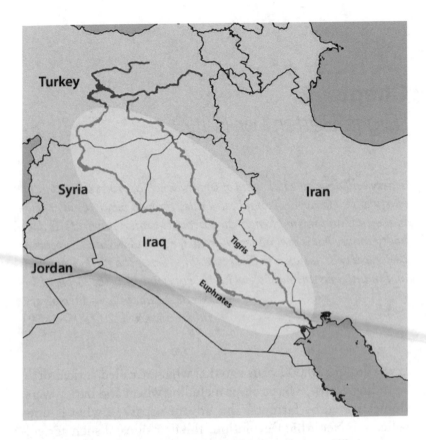

The area of Mesopotamia that is today Iraq, Syria and Turkey

In the days of hunting and gathering there was no advantage to organizing in large groups. On the contrary, large groups proved a disadvantage because of the limited amount of food available in the space people could cover each day. As all people were on the move, they accumulated very few possessions. Few possessions also meant that there was typically little to steal or loot from each other. All of this changed with the Neolithic Revolution and the shift from a hunter-gatherer society to an agricultural one.

Size started to matter and the population grew not only because of the abandonment of the nomadic lifestyle and the resulting removal of the child-bearing limitation, but also because there was a demand for more working hands.

In the 5,000 years since the days of the tiny and primitive agricultural community at Tell Abu Hureyra, four major developments took place. First, the communities gradually grew in size. Second, the communities learned to domesticate a few types of edible animals and to sustain significant numbers of them. These animals also became sources of products and help in hard labor. Third, people migrated to what became the southern part of Mesopotamia, making it the dominant area, and fourth, the communities became progressively more and more organized.

The first large human communities grew along rivers, particularly along the Nile and the Euphrates/Tigris. Both these rivers carried significant amounts of water essential for drinking and growing crops. These rivers also accumulated large amounts of silt and sediment that they dumped where they met the sea. This sediment buildup created vast plains of fertile land ideal for agriculture. The rivers were also habitats for fish and other wildlife and offered a relatively easy means of transportation between settlements along their banks.

With such optimal land and climate for agriculture, economic and social opportunities were ripe for the picking. The newly founded agricultural communities had the means to become richer and bigger, to produce and enjoy more and better food, and to develop a better lifestyle. In order to undertake these drastic improvements, however, the population had to be large enough to support specialization and organization. The community of 100 families whose members spent their days in the fields was no longer as beneficial as a society of tens of thousands. The benefit of becoming larger and organized was clear: large and organized communities could create, trade, and protect much more wealth.

Defense and irrigation were the first and most important tasks. With the transition to sedentary communities storing food and domesticated animals came the risk of theft, looting, and takeover. People and rival communities could now act on the basic human impulse of wanting to live off other peoples' work.

The top priority of the natural leadership, therefore, became to protect against unwanted visitors. To succeed in such a mission, an organization had to be established and versed in weapons and defense concepts. Here, once again, size did matter: only a large enough community could support such specialization.

Irrigation was another fundamental task where people saw exceptionally positive returns on human investment. The rivers, with all that they provided and enabled, still had to be harnessed in some way. For irrigation, water had to be carriedto far away plots of land. In the case of southern Mesopotamia, the land was vast and extremely fertile but saw very little rainfall most of the year. Long and sophisticated networks of irrigation canals made all the difference in taking advantage of the land's fertility. The creation and maintenance of such an irrigation system required a highly organized and knowledgeable society. Here again a society of thousands was able to create, innovate, and execute much more quickly and efficiently than a society of hundreds.

As communities grew and different types of occupations emerged, another critical need arose. Rules had to be established to define the rights, hierarchy, and conduct of the individuals in their ever-growing community. A clan of 20 hunters and gatherer needed few rules. Like in many other groups of mammals, hunter-gatherers basically lived by the law of the jungle. Once communities began growing to the thousands and even tens of thousands, things became much more complicated.

All of this societal organization required an infrastructure: buildings, weapons manufacturing, irrigation planning, tools, a bureaucracy, and a professional class. In short, society needed an administration, and at the top of the administration, a "chief executive."

There were two options for obtaining the extensive resources required to maintain an administration: take resources from the producing part of the population or loot resources from other communities. Even if looting were chosen as the primary strategy, it could come only after the creation of a militia, making the first option the only viable first step. So, to make sure that

26

all individuals "paid their fair share" for the growing organization, the collection of resources was naturally delegated to the nascent administration. Thus, taxes were born.

Although participation in these new large and organized communities, soon to be known as city-states, wasn't total voluntary, and nor were the "chief executives" chosen or fired at will, it is reasonable to assume that people cooperated with the new super-community more out of a desire to do so than due to coercion. After all, the bureaucracy delivered critical and essentials protection from enemies—foreign and domestic—and orchestrated the building and maintenance of a critical infrastructure. These were the basic preconditions for life and the economy to flourish, and indeed they did.

By 4,000 BC the area later known as Mesopotamia was dotted with relatively large urban centers managed by full-time administrations.

These new societies led to a revolution in human life. This era saw the creation and development of stone temples, palaces, musical instruments, writing, bookkeeping, jewelry, stone masonry, terracotta mosaics, math, astronomy, literature, and poetry. A legendary tale, the *Epic of Gilgamesh*, is a story of a king from around 2,500 BC and is considered one of the oldest surviving pieces of literature.

Among these large urban areas, with their growing culture and structure, was Uruk, likely the source of the name *Iraq*. Uruk grew to around 2.5 square kilometers, about 615 acres, and was home to tens of thousands of people.[1] Together, Uruk and similar city-states formed the civilization known as Sumer. Sumer thrived for an unprecedented 2,000 years before it was conquered and merged with the relatively short-lived Akkadian Empire, which eventually was conquered and united around 1894 BC with Babylonia, the state and culture which dominated central and south Mesopotamia for the next 1,200 years. As they continued to grow, the nation-states saw great scientific progress and achievements that enabled more prolific and efficient food production. Excess meat, grain, palms, vegetables, leather, and other products were produced and traded to cities eager for resources and products they lacked.

Trade practices advanced and extensive trading networks developed. Throughout its 3,300-plus years of existence, Mesopotamia was in contact with the world around it. Merchants traded and interacted east to the Indus valley, west to Egypt, north to Assyria and up to Armenia, and south, sailing the Persian Gulf. Extensive systems of dirt roads were constructed allowing the trade of wood, metals, ivory, and silver to flourish further. These roads did not only facilitate trade, they would also come to serve marching armies.

These developed societies were the grounds on which many new and competing social interests and desires were born. Many new institutions and concepts arose, such as property ownership, family and inheritance rules, and rules to ensure stability in leadership through succession. Financing this society—its armies, stone palaces and temples, professional bureaucracy, judiciary and executive courts—demanded resources, and a lot of them.

A society that invented money managed easily to invent taxes, which came in different shapes and forms: duty fees on merchants, percentages of harvests, individual poll taxes, and many others. One tax was especially painful, and was often referenced to simply as the "burden." This tax required individuals to enlist for work or military duty in the government service with no compensation. These duties included digging canals, working the fields owned by the state, and participating in military campaigns. These taxes, like many other activities in ancient Mesopotamia, were recorded on clay tablets. Almost a million of these tablets have been found, and some 30,000 of these tablets are exhibited in the University Of Pennsylvania Museum Of Archaeology. Among these tablets is one that deals with tax payment. Taxes were even levied on donations given to the temple and a special person was appointed to collect this tax.[2]

In order to organize, instruct, collect, record, and enforce this massive tax system, the Mesopotamians had to develop sophisticated tools including mathematics, record keeping, communications, laws and a law enforcement.

Babylon's most famous king was Hammurabi, who reigned around 3,750 years ago. The Code of Hammurabi, a lengthy engraving of 280 laws on a 7.5 foot stone, excavated by French archeologists in 1901 and still residing at the Louvre, covers a large array of topics such as criminal law, family law, and also deals heavily in tort law and liabilities. In addition, the code includes what can be considered an advanced commercial law section addressing the new economic system developed in these growing communities. The code covers subjects like property rights, inheritance laws, taxation, trade, and debt. Reading through these laws, you would be astonished at how closely the lives and issues of ancient Mesopotamians 3750 years ago resemble our own.

Some interesting laws include:

50. If anyone borrows money upon a cultivated grain field or cultivated sesame field he shall receive the grain or sesame which is grown upon that field. He shall pay back to the person making him the loan the money borrowed, with interest.
51. In the event he is unable to repay the loan or money borrowed, he shall deliver to the lender grain or sesame [equal in value] to the amount of the sum borrowed, with interest, in accordance with the rate of interest provided by the royal tariff [legal rate].
52. In the event anyone borrows money upon a field and fails to raise grain or sesame whereby to repay his creditors, his indebtedness is not extinguished.
221. If a doctor heals the broken bone of anyone or diseased soft parts, the sick one is to give the doctor 5 shekels.
273. Anyone hiring a laborer shall give him [for his services] from every new year to the fifth month [at the rate of] 6 Grochen of money per day and from the sixth month to the end of the year he is to pay him [at the rate of] 5 Grochen per day.[3]

Mesopotamia is justifiably called the "cradle of civilization." There, human society transformed over a span of 4,000 years from tiny, poor, and primitive agricultural communities to large, developed city-states. In these city-states, humans learned to overcome some of nature's most crucial limitations and invented some of humanity's most important inventions, many of which are still in use today. Along with their inventions, our ancestors built magnificent cities. Berlin's Pergamon Museum offers an awe-inspiring glimpse at one of these cities. Many social institutions, some great and some terrible, like slavery and servitude, also originated in Mesopotamia. The Mesopotamians invented the foundations of math, astronomy, and law, and transformed human society to what it is today: an organized structure composed of very large communities that dominate and exploit our surroundings, rule by written law, innovate in technology, art, architecture, and war, and operate vast trading economies.

But by 500 BC a new power rose, and Babylonia was absorbed into the Achaemenid (Persian) Empire. Thus, the torch of Western civilization was passed west to Greece and later to Rome.

Benjamin Franklin's statement that there is nothing certain except death and taxes became true the day that taxes were first instituted far back in Mesopotamia, and from that day on they tended to constantly grow unless checked by the people's strong push back. But why is it so? In modern democratic societies, this phenomenon can probably be explained by the ongoing need to buy constituencies or at least fulfill their expectations fueled by campaign promises. In ancient autocratic society, however, what was the reason for governments' needs for ever greater financial resources? The marvel of insatiable tax appetites can be explained with a few different reasons, with varying relevance.

The first reason for this appetite is the need to buy legitimacy: every government, including autocratic ones, needs to achieve some level of legitimacy and respect from its subjects. This task

30

can be achieved through coercion, by delivering achievements, through bribes, and via splendid building and entertainment projects, or through a combination of all of the above. Yet these conditions cost money. Even relaying on coercion alone is costly. The Stasi, the secret police arm of the Communist and ironically named Germany Democratic Republic, employed up to 91,000 employees for the purpose of maintaining a tight grasp on its citizenry.

Another reason for tax growth is war. Throughout history, war and excessive defense spending have managed to bring down nations and bankrupt empires time and time again. War is an immense destroyer of wealth. War's return on investment is almost always negative. Wars rob societies' excess food and materials, or even worse, they rob productivity of food and materials from the future via war debts which linger for decades and sometimes centuries. Wars exchange food and other products for guns, which are then consumed along with the young potential laborers to whom the guns are assigned. In the early days, the riches and spoils robbed from the adversary were supposed to offset the costs of war. Still, even in ancient days, war did not have an ongoing positive return on investment in most cases.

The final key reason for governments' insatiable appetites for funds derives from their relentless tendency to grow. Like a force put in motion, organizations, especially the most powerful in society and with no profit or loss accountability, continue growing well beyond their founders' original intentions. Even once they have accomplished their initial purpose, these organizations constantly find new tasks to legitimize their own existences. In his fascinating book *The Collapse of Complex Societies*, Joseph Tainter gives a more comprehensive view explaining that as societies develop they tend to build ever-growing complex systems. While hunting and gathering parties had only dozen or so networks and information flows, as societies and economic activity matured, these connections and intertwined activities grew exponentially, requiring more and more institutions and laws.

31

He further claims that as societies become more complex the cost of maintaining that complexity grows since it requires information management, control, information processing, coordination between the different parts of the complex society, as well as people to perform those tasks. Needless to say, growing complexity requires increasing resources to be diverted to its maintenance, placing a constant and rising burden on each productive member of society.

Yet this growth and investment in complexity tends to yield diminishing returns as the system grows but the kinds of projects that would benefit from its existence fall. At a certain point, the benefits to society of organization and complexity start to decline. Over time, the rate of decline accelerates. Ultimately, society invests more and more resources into systems that generate less and less value, until eventually the return on investment becomes negative and complexity yields more cost than benefits.[4]

By that point however, there are so many bureaucratic layers and public mythologies vested in the complexity of the system that just attempting to reduce this complexity becomes a colossal challenge. Thus, the government continues to grow as long as taxes can be collected in order to support all of its activities, even though their value is in rapid decline.

From here stems the never-ending tension between the producer and the taxman: while the taxman (the government) represents unconditional ever-growing demand for taxes, the producer (the subject) is willing to go along as long as he feels this investment is affordable and actually yields positive returns for him.

In his book, Tainter lays out the case of the Roman Empire. At the early stages of the empire, its successful military campaigns financed its growth and continuous expansion. When, however, the costs of expansion and defense began outweighing the benefits brought in by plunder, the financial burden fell on the supporting population, mainly peasants and others doing hard physical labor. Throughout the first century, taxation grew. Meanwhile, the currency's debasement continued. Still the empire managed to deliver relative prosperity and peace over what during what became known as the Pax Romana. The price the population paid, then, was still worthwhile.

Over time, the cost of maintenance increased and so did the burden, while the value derived for the supporting population constantly declined. As political, economic and social the pressures grew, so did taxes. Tax collection too became a brutal exercise that included crop confiscation, which led to starvation and child enslavement when taxes quotas were not met. Eventually a critical mass of the Roman population became indifferent to the fate of the empire. Too much of its production infrastructure had become useless and too much of its social fabric destroyed. The returns on complexity grew increasingly negative until eventually the empire reached a point where it lost both its legitimacy and its ability to survive.[5]

Ruling the seas for a shorter period of time, the British Empire experienced a much lighter end than the Roman Empire. Nevertheless, it also suffered from increased war spending, an ever-growing government bureaucracy, and ongoing investment in complexity. In his well-known work *Parkinson's Law*, British naval historian and prolific author Cyril Parkinson (1909–1993) tries to formulate a mathematical equation defining the rate at which bureaucracies expand over time. His writing is full of numbers and observations. One especially amusing observation concerns the increase in employees at the Colonial Office that occurred at the same time that Great Britain's empire was shrinking. Parkinson provides two simple explanations for this phenomenon: "An official wants to multiply subordinates," and "Officials make work for each other."

The concept of increased spending on wars and an ever-growing government, which constantly draws resources from its subjects, is a reality many American readers can instinctively identify with. There are many examples from modern-day America that show that not much has changed from the days of Rome. The big difference is that today, the US government is spending money it does not have which will presumably have to be paid back by future Americans. The following are only a few "samples" of the thousands of wasteful projects the American government is undertaking.

Wars, as mentioned, were, historically, the greatest drain on governments and national resources. Still, the following example is a record high! The US Air Force has been buying planes from Italy at $50 million dollars a plane, only to retire them immediately in Arizona's Aircraft Boneyard. Furthermore, even after the Air Force announced its decision to mothball these planes, there were still 5 more in production on the assembly lines in Italy, expected to be delivered after the project's cancelation. Like the rest of the order, these planes would be delivered directly to the huge boneyard without flying a mile beyond their travel from the factory to their final resting place. The total cost to the US taxpayers of this aviation travesty weighs in at about half a billion dollars.

As we look deeper into the world of aviation, we see that it is not only fighter jets that target taxpayer money. Unused civilian airports, like the one in St. Cloud, Minnesota, are just another item on a long list of tax-dollar drainers. St. Cloud is a small city located 65 miles northwest of Minneapolis with a population of about 65,000. The city sits along Minnesota's main highway and is just a one hour and twenty minute drive from the Minneapolis-Saint Paul International Airport. Interestingly enough, however, St. Cloud's small airport has received over $24 million dollars in public funding since 2000. In November 2013, the number of monthly (yes monthly!) scheduled flights for this airport was...9! In December that monthly figure dropped to 7 flights (so not even 2 flights a week)! An equally disturbing twist to this story is that all of these flights were operated by one small carrier that flies to and from a small airport in Mesa, Arizona. The Mesa airport is located 27 miles from the Phoenix International Airport.[6]

Complexity, however, is not about taxes and wasteful projects. The latter are simply the products of complexity. Complexity is about the policies that it creates and about the exponentially growing bureaucracy that follows, which, together, have lasting and deep damaging effects.

We all know sugar to be sweet, but for sugar growers in America the true sweetness comes from government intervention in the market. The US sugar program is long-standing and quite complicated. For special interests, this is ideal: most people, representatives, and the press get lost in the details and lose the money trail which leads from the federal government to the sugar growers and from the sugar growers to their supporters in Washington, D.C.

We will end our small taxpayer scams sampler with the sugar case, one that demonstrates the web of unlimited appetite for taxes. The sugar program as we know it started in 1934 when the Sugar Act of 1934 was enacted to control the sugar market. The act seized control of the import, growth, and workforce of the sugar industry, and started the tradition of allocating direct subsidies to sugar growers. In 1976, the Sugar Act expired and as a result, lower cost sugar entered the market, so sugar growers knew it was time to get the government gears turning again. Shortly thereafter, President Carter introduced a payment program of subsidies for sugar growers in cases where the imported sugar drove prices below a certain support level. A little further down the road President Reagan introduced an import quota in order to keep market prices above those support levels with the Agriculture and Food Act of 1981. In 1990, President Bush approved a bill which imposed allotment on sugar determining who can grow and sell, which President Clinton later amended. In 2008 the Farm Bill was enacted though a Congress override of President George W. Bush's veto. This bill moved the sugar game to a whole new level.

According to the bill, the sugar business is made of four components: first, a price guarantee which promised growers a minimum price for their sugar. This price is significantly higher (almost double) than the global going price. You might ask yourself how this price serves any national interest. But no answer

35

can be found on the record! In order to achieve that minimum price guarantee, the government imposes import restrictions that severely limit the importation of cheaper sugar. As a second component, the federal government imposes growing limits and quotas on each and every producer to prevent too much local production at the guaranteed inflated price. This action completely abolishes any chance for production improvement through competition. The third component of the bill ensures that if this Soviet-style central planning doesn't work perfectly (as it never does) and surpluses are created, the government commits to buying that excess supply from the growers so that the price will not go down below the set guaranteed prices. The fourth component of the bill, the heart of this market planning and control, is a loan program sugar processors get from the government that uses sugar as collateral. The loan is calculated roughly based on the growing allotment multiplied by the guaranteed selling price, which should equal the sugar growers' total annual guaranteed income, hence advancing their guaranteed annual income. After harvest season, the sugar processors can either sell the sugar on the market at the guaranteed price or above and return the loan, or pay back the loan or parts of it by giving the government the physical sugar. Once the government gets the sugar it then turns around and sells it to the ethanol plants at a significant loss!

So how much does this Soviet Union-style sugar market planning orchestrated in DC cost the US economy and tax payers? The first cost is the higher cost consumers pay for their sugar in sweets, ice creams, cereal, and other consumer goods. This cost is estimated at around $2 billion a year.[7] As for the cost of the direct subsides, in 2013 the Department of Agriculture gave out $1.2 billion in loans to sugar companies, about $170 million of which have not or will not be paid back.[8] From the amounts paid back in sugar the government lost about 80% of the loans when selling this sugar to ethanol plants at a price which was some 20% of the official loan value. Overall, analysts estimate that the sugar subsidy program cost $280 million in 2013 alone.[9] The longer-term estimated cost is in the billions. This cost doesn't take into consideration the damage to exporting industries impacted by export retaliation, especially on the part of Brazil, due to the import restrictions on their half-priced sugar.

It is amusing that when this program was passed, supporters in D.C. sold it as a "no cost to US taxpayers" solution.[10] You would think that elected officials in the highest chambers of the legislature would have at least the memory, if not the intellectual honesty, to remember the US's prior stance on central planning and government-controlled markets when it came to the Soviet Union.

In the summer of 2012, bipartisan Congressional efforts to curtail this program remain unsuccessful. This sugar story is especially baffling because there is not even a supposed reason for continuing this ongoing program which costs taxpayers and the US consumers billions of dollars year after year. And this is one of hundreds of programs and pet projects weaved into the monstrously complex federal government budget and legislation.

According to complexity theory, growth in complexity is the natural and inevitable result of an evolving society. Therefore, unless energy is constantly invested into reducing such complexity, society will inevitably continue to grow more and more complex. This growth in complexity will force society to divert increasing amounts of resources in order to maintain the expanding structure. Given that these resources are diverted from investments, production, and other essential activities, the direct cost and indirect burden of complexity will eventually end up bringing society to financial ruin.

A good manifestation of the Complex Society Theory and the actual cost of such complexity can be demonstrated through the history of bridge development in the US. Given the US's geography, bridges have for years served as critical components for the development of modern and urban life. Without bridges, a real integrated and modern economy is impossible. Thus, the value of bridge construction is enormous. Building these bridges, however, is no simple undertaking—it requires high levels of organization and technology. Many of the US's landmark bridges were built in the 1930s. One great example is the San Francisco-Oakland Bay Bridge (aka the Bay Bridge), which spans the San Francisco Bay connecting San Francisco to Oakland, Berkeley, and beyond. Today, the Bay Bridge carries around 240,000 vehicles a day to and from San Francisco. This 8.2 mile long bridge was opened on November 1936 after three-and-a-half years of building and two years of planning. Its construction finished well ahead of schedule and under budget, at a cost of $78 million (around $1.3 billion in 2014 dollars).

In 1989, the Loma Prieta earthquake hit the San Francisco area. The bridge suffered some minor damage in the quake and one part of the bridge collapsed along with a single car. In one month, the bridge was fixed and reopened to traffic. In the aftermath of the earthquake, a study concluded that the eastern span of the bride should undergo a retrofit. Such a project was estimated to cost $200 million. However, in the days to come and after some review, it was suggested that replacing the 2.2 mile span, rather than fixing it, would cost just a few more hundred million dollars and would deliver a more lasting structure with lower ongoing maintenance costs. Thus, the authorities set out to design and build a new eastern span of the Bay Bridge, a quarter of the length of the original full-sized bridge. By the mid-1990s, the project's estimated cost had climbed to $1.5 Billion and its completion date was moved to 2003. With marginal value compared to the building of the original bridge, considerations and goals of the project now moved to, as one official stated in a planning meeting: "The tower and cables are world-class, but you only see it for about 20 seconds when you're traveling across the bridge. [...] The remaining 85 percent has no class." Another official added, "It's not a dignified and exciting entrance to the East Bay.[...] I like the idea [...] where you can actually see the hills."[11]

The design also required that the new bridge span withstand an 8.5 magnitude earthquake, even though only 4 such quakes have hit America in known history, with 3 of them in Alaska and only one (in 1700) in the lower 48.[12] Such a magnitude earthquake happens in all the US, on average, once every 500 years.[13]

This time around, the bridge design took 5 years compared to the 2 years it took to design a bridge four times the size in the 1930s. Additionally, no fewer than 13 regulation agencies were involved in the approval process of the new bridge; in 1930 there was only one. The actual cost of the project came out to be more than 4 times the $1.5 billion estimate, swelling to around $6.4 billion, with some estimating it actually cost $7.2 billion. Considering the fact that this time only about 2.2 miles of bridge were built, compared to 8.2 miles in 1930, the inflation-adjusted cost per foot came out to almost 20 times higher. The 1936 bridge cost (inflation adjusted) was $30,000 per foot, while the 2013 project cost $550,000 per foot. The new span of the bridge, originally planned to be completed by 2003, opened ten years late in late 2013.[14] And while in the 1930s the bridge was American-made, this time around significant parts of the bridge were built in China and assembled by Chinese companies. CNBC quoted California officials contending that "the US does not have the manufacturing capacity or the workforce to build such a project on its own."[15] As if all the above were not absurd enough, the bridge was completed with serious quality concerns. As detailed at a hearing before a State Senate commission, the bridge suffers from: "cracked welds and other subpar work, and myriad construction mistakes which could lead to costly future repairs."[16]

The Bay Bridge is not an exception; many projects nationwide have suffered a similar fate. When the New York Port Authority attempted merely elevating the deck of the existing Bayonne Bridge in New York to allow higher cargo ships to pass below, it took six months just to find a federal agency that would agree to serve as the leading agency for the environmental review required by law. Then the review itself took more than four years and was made of more than 5,000 pages of mandated studies, which included archeological and historical building surveys of every building within a 4 miles radius. Along the way, 55 government agencies on federal, state, and local levels gave their input, and 47 different permits had to be issued. In addition, 50 Native American tribes, some residing as far as Oklahoma, were invited to give their input on the project, and the final report included 307 comments and rebuts from organizations and individuals. The project is eventually expected to cost around $1.5 billion.[17] For comparison, the Ben Franklin Bridge was actually built, at less than a *third* of the cost of the estimated Bayonne Bridge project, and in the time it took just to complete the studies for the elevation of the Bayonne Bridge deck. When completed in 1926, after 4.5 years of construction, the Ben Franklin Bridge was the longest suspension bridge in the world at 1.57 miles in length (the Bayonne Bridge is 1.1 mile in length). Still standing today, the bridge carries 100,000 vehicles and 40,000 rail commuters a day, connecting Camden, New Jersey, and Philadelphia.[18]

As we can see, the web of bureaucracy grows exponentially, resulting in significant increases in cost and time necessary for project completion. Over a short eighty years, the US has not only lost the manufacturing capacity and the workforce to build such projects like the Bay Bridge, it has also "complexed" itself out of being able to afford and execute them in any meaningful timeframe, at manageable cost, or scale.

Bridge construction is, of course, not the only case in which complexity impedes efficiency. Consider, for example, pharmaceutical drugs. Less than three years passed between the discovery of insulin's function and its use for the treatment of diabetics and its full commercialization by Eli Lilly in early 1923. It also took less than three years to conduct all clinical trials for penicillin and produce it in large enough quantities for use on wounded D-Day soldiers in June 1944. Today it takes an average 12 years for a drug to move from the lab to pharmacy.[19] The process costs at least $350 million—not counting the cost of unsuccessful drugs—and requires an FDA application that typically contains more than 100,000 pages.

Drugs are part of a larger industry, healthcare. Almost everyone who works within or regularly interacts with this industry is aware of its extremely problematic nature—including its "coding departments," heavy paperwork, gross inefficiencies and fraud—resulting in its excessive costs to the American economy: costs that are at least a third or more than in countries like Germany or Australia. These costs are rolled-over. Childbirth for example, a common medical procedure, costs in the US more than twice than in Switzerland the second most expensive country, and almost four times than in the UK.[20] A study published in 2010 found that most doctors in the surveyed hospitals spent four to five hours a day on documentation and clerical duties while only few spent as much time on direct patient care. The time spent on paperwork has doubled since 1988.[21]

Yet the current attempt at repairing the system—the Affordable Care Act, a.k.a Obamacare—has not led to the system's simplification. Instead it has yielded 20,000 new pages of law and regulations on top of the 2,262 existing state laws already addressing varying aspects of healthcare insurance coverage. As if a web of complexity can be solved with even more tens of thousands of pages of complex regulations.

All of this complexity doesn't come free. On top of the ongoing indirect drag and inefficiencies, there is the direct cost to society. This cost comes in the form of hundreds of different direct and indirect taxes, levies, fees, wasteful occupations, widespread waste, fraud and abuse and debt imposed on the entire US population and on generations to come. It seems we have become accustomed to these taxes and requirements, as if they were all an unavoidable law of nature. Our burden is a heavy one: from federal and state income taxes to employment taxes, from capital gain to property taxes, from sales to inheritance taxes, and all the many other taxes in between, all on top of a massive debt and ongoing deficits. In short, we are all paying the price for a grossly overly complex society.

This omnipresent tax burden includes, for example, more than 22 types of taxes and fees on air transportation.[22] The

International Air Transport Association (IATA) charges its members $2,671 for a CD which includes the list of ticket and airport taxes and fees which lay out the "requirements for collection, filing, ticketing, remitting, interlining of various ticket and airport taxes, charges and fees." Featured on the CD are more than 1,500 different international airline related taxes and filing requirements.[23] These taxes and filing requirements add sizable sums to the cost of air travel tickets, something between 20 and 35 percent depending on destination, ticket cost, and method of calculation.

Of course, air travel is just one little segment we have chosen to dive into. Hundreds of other targeted taxes and fees rear their heads in all parts of the economy. There are specific and additional taxes on pets, fuel, cigarettes, alcoholic beverages, sweet beverages, sports booking, bagel slicing, hotel occupancy, car renting, property transfer, motor vehicles, fur clothing, wine production, fresh fruit vending, litigation, medical devices, cell phones, gas emission, toll bridges and roads, well digging, boats, fishing, hunting, business licenses, business operation, business closure. The list goes on. For the most part, these taxes, levies, and fees unnecessarily burden consumers and businesses and further complicate economic activities while adding yet more layers of complexity and cost through compliance, enforcement, and collection.

This complex society, its direct and indirect costs, the tax burden it imposes, and the social structure it creates, are deeply interconnected with the general subject of money: its creation and allocation as well as the usage of resources in society. It is this relationship that we will explore to better understand how we got to where we are today, and what are we facing in the years ahead.

Chapter 3:
Cash or Credit?

Once the concept of money had been invented in Mesopotamia's growing societies, another well-known institution started becoming necessary. Surpluses were being created, but they had to be stored somewhere. Furthermore, people had the desire to lend these surpluses out to others who could put them into use to cultivate new fields or raise new herds. Naturally, palaces and temples acted as the first centers of such activity; they became places where grain, and later silver, were stored and deposited. Over time, these deposits were also lent out, and the practice spread across the lands. As we saw in Hammurabi's code, the institution of lending for investment in agricultural activities was common by 2000 BC: "100. Anyone borrowing money shall, on the day of settlement, repay the same to his creditor, with interest, according to the memoranda of his contract [for payment]."

Amazingly, we even know by name one of these early banking institutions. Some 1700 clay tablets tell the story of the house of Egibi from 700 BC, located in city of Babylon. The Egibi family was involved in trading real estate, slaves, and cattle, and their banking arm accepted deposits for safekeeping, financed trade, and gave out loans.

As the center of western civilization transitioned to Greece, so did money and banking. We saw that the first coin was probably minted around the seventh century BC in the kingdom of Lydia, Asia Minor (today's Turkey). Signs of the first Greek bank appear around the 5th century BC, also in the Lydia area, with many more banks sprang up in the coming years. The first known banker in Greece itself was Philostephanus of Corinth from the fifth century BC. Among his many important customers was Themistocles, a prominent politician and general who fought in the battle of Marathon and rose to fame in the early years of the Athenian democracy.

Another early banker had a special rise to prominence: he started his banking career for one of the known banks as a slave working at a money-changing table in a port near Athens. Pasion by name, he was later granted his freedom and became the most famous and wealthiest banker of his time in Greece. He was engaged in all aspects of banking, including deposits and lending. He also owned many ships and the largest shield factory in Greece.[1]

As banking grew, the island of Delos soon became the Wall Street of ancient Greece. Located around 100 miles southeast of Athens, the island was the host of the sacred temple of Apollo. The temple and the island's harbor, into which merchants' goods and slaves poured in, became centers around which a trading and financial center developed. It was here that the first Roman merchants also became bankers, eventually spreading the trade to Rome itself. Interestingly enough, banking in Rome never became as important and dominant as it was in Greece. Rome, in contrast to Greece, never set up a state-run banking system, and the Roman emperors focused on mints and coinage as their main monetary tool. As a result, private banking in Rome remained in the shadows.[2]

The most commonly used and widely known banking activity in Rome was money changing; it was a critical part of trade due to the large variety of different coins and the widespread practice of coin forgery. This "retail" side of banking did not involve lending and was conducted around public buildings, ports, and temples. A group of these money changers gained lasting notoriety when they found their way into the New Testament. These money changers would typically conduct their business around or behind a table, and in the case of the Greeks, behind a trapezium-shaped table. Hence the origin of the name *trápeza*, which means *bank* in Greek. This name is quite similar to the root of the word *bank*, which came from the word bench—*banca* in Italian.

Of course, banking also had a much more exclusive and lucrative side to it. This was the side devoted to financing mining activities, merchants, and most lucrative of all, international trade, which included adventurous voyages to distant lands that yielded exotic and precious goods.

As we saw in the Hammurabi's code, money lending was a means of starting a new business activity "upon a cultivated grain field or cultivated sesame field" from which new gains could be created and used to pay back loans. Words similar to the word *interest* in the ancient languages of Mesopotamia, as well as in Greek and Latin, came from the word for newborn. Indeed, interest was seen as the share of the capital in the "newborn," created with the help of that capital. These ancient bankers probably also saw interest as a way to compensate and balance the risk the lender was taking.

The interest rates on agricultural loans were quite stable for many hundreds of years in Mesopotamia, Greece, and Rome. The rates, however, did fall from one society to the next: around 20% in Mesopotamia, (but 33% for grain debt), 10% in Greece, and 8.3% in Rome. Some historians explain these rates economically as being representations of the yields the fields and agricultural activity could produce— the more yield the lender could expect from his field, the higher the rate he was willing to pay. The drop in interest rates from Mesopotamia to Greece and then from Greece to Rome is explained as a result of the drop in the rate of productivity growth. While in the early days the growth rate of agricultural productivity was much higher due to new technologies and production systems, as these advancements become widespread the growth rates dropped and as did the interest rate.

This explanation, however, does not manage to explain why the rates stayed stable for so many hundreds of years. Why were changes in growth rates over 2,000 years not reflected in the interest rate, which stayed stable for so long? And why did interest rates differ from one society to another while still remaining stable at their respective levels? Dr. Michael Hudson offers a different explanation for interest rate behavior in those times. According to Hudson, the interest rates were influenced by the number systems of each of these civilizations, and especially by the way they calculated numerical fractions.

In Mesopotamia, a base 60 system (sexagesimal) was developed. This system originated from the number of days in a month (rounded to thirty multiplied by two), and widespread because 60 is a number with many factors (30, 20, 15, 10, 6, 5, 4, 3, 2 and 1). Part of this ancient system still thrives today: our 60 minute hour comes from the Mesopotamian system. The standard measurement for weight (including silver) was mina (about 1.25 pounds). The mina was divided into 60 shekels, and the interest was set at one silver shekel per silver mina per month, which totals 12 shekels per mina per year. Given that a mina was made of 60 shekels, this rate came out to 20% annually.

The same concept of interest calculation was later imported to ancient Greece and to the Roman Empire. The big difference in rates came from the fact that the Greek and Roman weight systems were different. In Rome, for example, the weight system was based on fractions of 12. The basic unit was the libra (with the abbreviation lb. is still used today). The libra was divided into 12 uncials, which made the rate of 1/12 equal to 8.33%.[3]

An alternate explanation for the nature of interest was given by a nineteenth-century economist, Eugen von Böhm-Bawerk (1851-1914). Eugen von Böhm-Bawerk was an economist, lawyer, and finance minister of the Austro-Hungarian Empire, and one of the founders of what came to be known as the Austrian school of economics.[1] Böhm argued that, in principle, people prefer goods sooner rather than later. The owner of capital can use his money to go out and buy goods right now. If, instead, the capital holder decides to invest the capital in a partnership with an entrepreneur, he is delaying the satisfaction of consuming goods in return for having that capital grow, which will enable him to purchase even more goods later. The level of tolerance for such a delay in satisfaction defines the cost of the capital, i.e. the interest rate. In a society where the owners of capital have no such tolerance—let's say where they need that capital immediately to buy food for their families—the owners' ability to delay the usage of the capital will be next to nothing. Due to a scarcity in capital, the price thereof will skyrocket. On the contrary, if the owners wish to use their capital years down the road, they will be receptive to a much lower payment for the delayed satisfaction, i.e. they will accept lower interest rates.

Today's capital markets have morphed into something entirely different. Interest rates today are set by central banks as a means

---

[1] The Austrian school of economics is a school of economic thought (not a physical school) which originated in the late nineteenth and early twentieth century in Vienna (then the capital of the Austro-Hungarian Empire). Carl Menger's 1871 book, *Principles of Economics*, is generally considered the progenitor of the Austrian school. Menger was followed shortly after by Böhm-Bawerk and Friedrich von Wieser. Menger and his followers were classical nineteenth-century liberals who promoted the view of economics as the sum of individual choices. They saw government intervention as an attack on market economic forces which would eventually fail to deliver the government's intended results. In the early years of the twentieth century, Ludwig von Mises and Friedrich Hayek became the prominent public theorists and speakers for the Austrian School. Mises and Hayek were also the first to identify credit expansion as the key reason for business cycles. In fact, many years later, in 1974, Hayek won the Nobel Prize in Economics for "pioneering work in the theory of money and economic fluctuations." The two left Austria in 1930s and Hayek found himself in Britain, where he became the primary ideological opponent of the rising star John Maynard Keynes. Both Mises and Hayek wrote extensively on the topics of economics and were harsh critics of socialist and Marxist theories. Mises moved to the US where held a position as a visiting professor at New York University until his retirement in 1969. He died in 1973 at the age of 92. In 1982, the Von Mises Institute was established in Auburn, Alabama, with the mission of "advancing [...] the defense of the market economy, private property, sound money, and peaceful international relations, while opposing government intervention as economically and socially destructive." You can learn more at http://www.mises.org.

of controlling the amount of money in the market as well as to achieve other goals. We will touch upon this information later.

When we closely examine the relationship between lender and borrower there is one more key issue we have to discuss: while the lender may be taking a higher risk by parting with his money upfront, the borrower is the one with a pressing need for the money. While for the lender the loan represents a potential opportunity for profit, for the borrower the loan can represent life itself. After all, the borrower could need the money to sow the field that will feed his family. This gross imbalance not only has the potential to push the price of money—the interest, higher—but it can push the borrower to acts of desperation. A borrower may have to act on optimistic assumptions and take significant risks. If the "good" scenario doesn't pan out and he cannot repay his loans, the borrower is slowly sucked into a never-ending cycle of debt and misery. Unlike today, personal bankruptcy did not exist in the ancient world, and an inability to pay a debt led to things like slavery (aka debt-slavery) for the borrower, his wife, and even his children. Though debt-slavery was limited to three years in some periods in Babylonia and debt slaves could be freed by repayment of their debt, the practice of debt-slavery was nonetheless a key source of local slaves.[4]

This was the background against which the Old Testament enacted a progressive rule forbidding the practice of interest: "you shall not lend him your money at interest, nor give him your food for profit" forbids Leviticus 25:37. The law didn't abolish interest completely, but did limit it, stating that "you may charge a foreigner interest, but you may not charge your brother interest" (Deuteronomy 23:19-20). With these words the concept and term usury was born. Though Merriam-Webster defines usury as "the practice of lending money and requiring a high amount of interest," in a world where interest is forbidden, any interest is considered usury. The concept of usury moved from the Old Testament to Christianity, though the term usury appears only twice in the New Testament (Matt 25, Luck 19)

Still, influenced by the Old Testament, almost all early Chu... fathers and church councils condemned the practice of usury.

Usury, however, became quite insignificant as the collapse of the Roman Empire in 476 AD took a huge toll on both lending and borrowing. The Dark Ages (6-11 centuries AD) engulfed Europe and saw the total collapse of its vibrant economic life. As a result, money lending, interest, and usury became but faint memories for the next 600 years. The practice came back to life only as Europe emerged from the Dark Ages. Popular opinion regarding usury, however, remained the same. In 1139 the Second Lateran council, overseen by Pope Innocent II, issued a canon condemning the practice and banning usurers "from every comfort of the church [...] including a Christian burial." The final church council addressing the issue was the Council of Vienna (1311), which declared usury heresy and proclaimed that a person engaging in its practice was "to be punished as a heretic," which meant death by burning.[5] Still, the repeated appearance of the issue of usury indicates that market forces brought it to the forefront again and again. Canon law, however, did not apply to Jews. This ruling, together with other restrictions imposed on Jews, made money lending in Europe's early Middle Ages a "Jewish trade."

As Europe advanced from the Dark and Middle Ages into the Renaissance, Italy became a growing trading center. As we have previously mentioned, trade requires finance, and finance needs a return on the risk of capital (i.e. interest). Thus, pressure on the Church's harsh usury laws was mounting. Initially, people invented sophisticated workarounds. For instance, a loan was still given at no cost, but if the borrower defaulted on the loan then there was nothing preventing the lender from charging him a payment for the damages caused by that default. This payment was called *inter-est* which in Latin means existing between one thing and another. This term referred to the difference "between" the situation where the creditor's money is returned and the situation where the lender failed to pay. This payment could be for the losses the lender suffered or even for potential profits he forewent as a result of the loan.

Over the course of the 15th and 16th centuries, the church's grip on life in Europe loosened and the usury doctrine crumbled. As time went on, people invented even more "kosher" interest payment models to sidestep the usury clauses. Some examples included defining usury as rent or as an insurance payment to guarantee the loan return, and even hiding the interest within exchange rates. By the early years of the 17th century, interest was approved by scholars and received papal silent approval, though canon law had not yet been officially amended.[6]

In the aftermath of the Protestant Reformation, interest payments became legal and subject to state-regulation. In 1553, the king of Bavaria issued a civil code permitting lenders to charge 5% interest. Three other Protestant states—Saxony (1572), Mecklenburg (1572), and Brandenburg (1573)—followed suit. In England, Henry VIII's Parliament of 1545 legalized interest payments of up to 10%. This rate was later reduced to 8% in 1624, and to 6% in 1651.[7]

Italy's city-states were not only gaining status as centers for trade and culture, they were also building up their military might. Between 1494 and 1559, a series of wars between the city-states created a surge in demand for money and credit. The institutions that sprang up as a result were not only called banks, but were starting to resemble what we know as banks today. For this very reason, the Italian banks of the 1500s can be considered the founding fathers of modern banking.

The debate around which bank was truly the "father of banks" is still raging. Venetians are fervently convinced that the honor belongs to the Bank of Venice. Established in 1171 by the government of the Republic of Venice and named the Chamber of Loans, the Bank of Venice was created to manage interest payments on mandatory war bonds the government had "sold" to its citizens. Over time, the Chamber of Loans got involved in taking merchants' deposits and issuing notes payable on demand as well as other small quasi-banking activities. It wasn't until 1587, however, that the Venetian government established the Bank of Venice, called the Banco della Piazza di Rialto (Bank of Rialto Square). This bank was named after the famous Ponte Rialto, which is one of the oldest bridges across the Grand Canal in Venice.

Across the sunny Mediterranean, Spanish historians claim that the Bank of Barcelona was the first real modern bank. Founded in 1401 by the city of Barcelona, the bank received deposits from customers and merchants with the city's property pledged as security for the deposits. Unlike its Italian counterpart, the bank did not issue notes nor were its customers able to use checks or discount bills (a debt note issued at a discount which is paid in full upon its maturity date).

Just a few years later, in 1407, the Republic of Genoa in Italy founded what many consider the first modern bank, the Casa delle compere e dei banchi di San Giorgio, or the Bank of Saint George. The republic, located on the shore of the Mediterranean Sea in the northwest corner of Italy, was an epicenter of commerce, trade, and culture that rivaled even Venice. The city-state had partnerships, settlements, and commercial colonies all over the Mediterranean and as far as the northern Black Sea.

After years of war with Venice, the Republic of Genoa was quickly running out of money, so in 1407 the city-state authorized the setup of a bank aimed at helping repay the republic's debts and raising money from investors. The bank was lending money to the government at a 7% interest rate in exchange for the right to collect taxes and customs. Over time, the bank also got involved in deposits, bills of exchange, and other banking activities. Furthermore, the bank had capital stock that was owned by the public and was run by eight protectors, chosen annually by the stockholders.[8] One of the bank's well-known customers was a proud native son of Genoa named Christopher Columbus. In fact, a copy of his letter addressed to the bank dated April 2nd, 1502, was put up for sale in New York in the late 1800s for the price of $2000.[9]

In the 14th and 15th centuries, Florence, Genoa, and Venice were Italy's major trading centers and powerhouses. As such, we shall end the story of early Italian banking with the story of the family responsible for Europe's most powerful banking institution of the time: the Medicis. In 1397, Giovanni de' Medici, a Florence native who had settled in Rome and there entered the world of money and politics, moved his banking operation from Rome back to Florence and set up the Medici Bank. The bank issued loans, accepted deposits, changed money, and handled bills of exchange (a written order binding one party to pay another a fixed sum of money at a set future date). The bank had, at its height, some 10 branches in which the manager was a type of a partner. The bank was very internationally oriented, partly due to its biggest customer, the Pope. As the bank to the Pope, Medici handled the transfer of funds and taxes from the church's branches all over Europe to the Vatican. The extremely profitable branch in Rome was not more than a traveling desk that followed the Pope to wherever he was going. This operation was so profitable that in the early years, almost half of the bank's business came from the Vatican. This papal connection translated into power and also brought in new customers and business. In one incident, the nomination of a new bishop was held up until his father—a cardinal—paid his debt to the Medici Bank.[10]

Europe's leading merchants in those days were Italian, and the bank was not only responsible for financing them, but was itself also deeply involved in international trade. This trade included lucrative and unique goods like silk. In 1478, however, Medici Bank lost the Vatican's business to a rival Florentine clan. This huge loss together with some unsuccessful successions pushed the bank into a downward spiral. By 1494, the bank had closed most of its branches and eventually the Medici family was forced out of Florence. This collapse marked the last time an Italian institution or family would dominate Europe's banking and financial markets. Financial power would now move north to Amsterdam, Hamburg, and eventually to London.

Without today's golden parachutes, being a banker in those times could be a very dangerous business. This was especially true if your main debtor was an all-powerful borrower, such as a king. In their 2009 book *This Time is Different*, Carmen Reinhart and Kenneth Rogoff list 16 cases of default on external sovereign debt (debt owed by the king or state to out of state lenders as opposed to debt owed to their citizens) in Europe between 1300 and 1799. Probably the most hideous of these cases was that of King Phillip IV of France, the most populated and potent European power of the time.

In his first years on the throne, Phillip the Fair, who ruled from 1285 to 1314, initiated a war to challenge the mighty Edward I of England, also known as the "Hammer of the Scots". A 10-year conflict ensued, which drained the crown's resources without bringing military success. The Order of the Knights Templar was King Phillip's primary banker, to which King Phillip owed a large debt. The Knights Templar was a powerful military order that became prominent in the Crusades (1095-1285). After the conquest of Jerusalem, they set their headquarters on the Temple Mount in Jerusalem from which they got their name, the "Soldiers of Christ and the Temple of Solomon" in short—the Templars. Though the members made vows of poverty, the organization grew to be very wealthy.

The Templars' infrastructure in Europe as well as in the Holy Land proved very powerful and enabled them to act as a bank between the two locations. Pilgrims and other travelers could deposit money with the order in Europe and withdraw it from their branches in the Holy Land. These pilgrims were de facto withdrawing the first traveler's checks.

The Knights Templar were not only the king's largest creditors, they were also big asset and property owners in France. These riches made them a very tempting target. At dawn on October 13, 1307, French troops arrested all the leaders of the French Templars and many regular members. King Phillip delivered the final blow by bullying Pope Clement V into authorizing the prosecution of the leaders of the Templars.

In medieval trials, confessions were treated as queens of evidence and typically were extracted through torture. Templars underwent some brutal torture including beatings, starvation, teeth pulling, and hanging with weights. This treatment would end with a confession or when the torture victims died. 112 leaders succumbed to the pressure and confessed to crimes like spitting on the cross. Some of these men later recanted their confessions and were declared heretics and consequently burned at the stake. This fate awaited the Grand Master of the Templar Order, who was brought to Paris for a public confession, and instead recanted his confession. As the flames engulfed his body, so the story goes, he called out for both King Philip and Pope Clement to join him before the judgment seat of God. Before the year was out both were dead. Meanwhile, on earth, the order was dissolved and the Templar's properties outside of France transferred to the Hospitaller Knights, as were many of the ranking surviving Templars. The assets as well as the debt within France became property of King Phillip the Fair.

Through time also the nature of debt changed, until recently, debt was undertaken for two main reasons—war and investments. The concept of "consumer credit" (individuals borrowing money to buy goods and services they consume) was unheard of until the beginning of the 20th century. Mortgages, a subsection of consumer credit, hardly existed before the 1920s. Even states barely took out loans, spare the occasional war. True or imaginary threats, external or internal, were practically the only reason states ran up significant deficits and took out loans. Such debts were typically paid off after the war.

The main reason that debt was historically associated with investment was the basic nature of debt: if debt is something that has to be paid with interest, the activity for which the debt is taken on has to produce more returns than that interest plus its principle. Taking on debt to pay for a vacation in Disneyland doesn't create new wealth from which the debt and interest can be paid back. Our ancestors understood one simple principle: that debt creates an extra burden—the interest—and that without a way to create constant extra wealth to cover that interest, debt will eventually be impossible to pay back.

It is important to note that until the 1700s, the amount of possible debt was limited, set, and mostly equal to the amount of silver and gold money available. That is, one person's debt was another person's silver or gold. It was at this tipping point that mankind began working on a new invention that would expand the possibilities of debt dramatically. To discuss this next part, our story must move to Amsterdam, Holland, and Stockholm, Sweden. Before we cross these borders, however, let's cover one topic critical to the bigger picture: the impact of the creation of money, also known as inflation.

Chapter 4:
The Secret Weapon: Not All Taxes Are Created Equal

"Lenin is said to have declared that the best way to destroy the capitalist system was to debauch the currency. By a continuing process of inflation, governments can confiscate, secretly and unobserved, an important part of the wealth of their citizens. By this method they not only confiscate, but they confiscate arbitrarily; and, while the process impoverishes many, it actually enriches some. The sight of this arbitrary rearrangement of riches strikes not only at security, but at confidence in the equity of the existing distribution of wealth.

Lenin was certainly right. There is no subtler, no surer means of overturning the existing basis of society than to debauch the currency. The process engages all the hidden forces of economic law on the side of destruction, and does it in a manner which not one man in a million is able to diagnose."

—John Maynard Keynes[1]

Merriam-Webster defines inflation as a "continuing rise in the general price level usually attributed to an increase in the volume of money and credit relative to available goods and services." This is a simple definition and a great launching pad for our discussion of inflation. As we dig deeper to better understand inflation, how it came about, and who it benefits, we will find a fascinating web of human interests, weaknesses, corruption, and deception. Inflation, as we will soon see, is the culmination and end result of these behaviors.

As we previously saw, money was made of rare metals (silver, gold, and sometimes copper) for the majority of its existence. One of the fundamental characteristics of these metals, also known as commodity money, is their limited quantity. Finding and mining precious metals was (and still is) hard and expensive, and thus the amount of the metals circulating in the market is necessarily limited in volume. It seems unbelievable that the total amount of gold mined in the world since the Egyptians began mining gold 4,000 years ago would only take up the volume of three Olympic-sized swimming pools or about one-third of the Washington Monument.[2]

The power of this ancient commodity money was threefold: it was unified (all societies used the same money), it was difficult to forge, and it was scarce and thus available only in small and limited quantities. As mentioned, gold, silver, or copper money have very limited intrinsic value. They cannot be eaten and they have very limited other practical uses (though silver is used in some industrial processes today). Thus, the value of money comes strictly from the willingness of people to exchange goods they possess for that money. The value of the money is derived from the goods, contrary to what we impulsively think. The goods are what set the value of the money, and not vice versa. If in a certain city no goods are available to exchange, even a pound of gold would be valued at zero. In the Nazi concentration camps, the price of a gold ring was a few slices of bread. If nobody is willing to trade goods for gold then the owner of the gold is not rich, as we would instinctively assume.

Given that goods define the value of the money, they create equilibrium between the two. Theoretically, if we had a set amount of goods and also a set amount of money, the goods and the money would settle on an agreed ratio (i.e. price) between them. This ratio would be determined by the market participants' priorities and tastes, and would not change as long as the desire and preference for specific goods stay the same.

In the real world, however, the amount of goods is always changing, even in times when the amount of money does not.

58

This condition exists simply because people consume and create goods regularly and the amount and type of goods available fluctuates. Some examples include a year with better harvests than another, or a breakthrough in technology which enables the production of more products and new products in less time. As the quantities of goods fluctuate, so do their prices in terms of money. Prices have an inverse relationship with supply: fewer goods relative to the set amount of money means their prices go up. The goods are now more scarce, and the set amount of money is dedicated to fewer goods. In other words, we have more money "available" for each good. On the contrary, when more goods are produced (given a set amount of money), then the price of goods (in money) goes down. The set amount of money is now dedicated to more goods and thus we have more goods "available" per each unit of money.

To simplify this model, let's look at an example. Imagine we are on an island with only two things: 1,000 gold coins and 1,000 identical cows. Naturally, the price will settle (assuming people want to trade) around one coin per cow, or one cow per coin. Suddenly, a disastrous storm hits and half of the cows freeze to death. Now our island still has 1,000 coins, but they are now going after 500 cows. The price of a cow will go up to 2 coins. In the next year, a miracle happens and all the cows give birth to triplets; now we have 2000 cows. This occurrence is great news from the perspective of food production (which, after all, is quite important), but the value of a cow has now dropped to half a coin. The reason is clear: the 1,000 gold coins are going after 2,000 cows, meaning that for each coin we can now get two cows.

The same concept comes into play when we increase only the amount of money. Let's say the people of our island (reset to 1000 coins and 1000 cows) go out and loot a neighboring island, leading to a total money supply of 2,000 coins. Now we have 2,000 coins available for trade on the island, but we still have only 1,000 cows. The price of a cow will consequently go up. With double the money going after the same amount of cows the coin- to-cow ratio will equal 2 coins per cow. We can clearly see that the increase in the amount of money increased the price of the cow. Interestingly enough, each individual participating in the looting was hoping to come back home with one coin of newfound wealth, since when he left home a coin could buy him a cow. With the influx of coins, paradoxically, the looters actually created inflation which perfectly negated their newfound wealth. With more money going after the same amount of goods, the price of the goods rose accordingly. This relationship of money to goods stays true as long as the amount of goods is set. Now, if in some way, our island is able to increase the amount of goods—by importing cows from a neighboring island, for example— then the new coins actually do hold value.

Simply put, prices go up when the amount of money increases or when the amount of goods decreases, as in both cases we have more money chasing fewer goods. Prices go down when the amount of money decreases or when the amount of goods increases since in both scenarios we have less money per available good.

Ironically enough, this simple formula isn't so clear to many politicians and people. When a nation discovers large oil and gas deposits that markedly exceed the nation's needs, the discovery elicits feelings of true luck and bliss. Many times, however, the result of these riches is not so different from the 1,000 coins looted from the neighboring island in the above example. When lots of oil money is spent locally, the costs of local products that are limited in supply (like real estate for example) shoots up. Although there is now a lot of money to spend, it can buy you little more usable product than before. The price of the object does not reflect the quantity. Simply put, there's just as many cows even if now they are worth two coins instead of one. In Norway, where large deposits of oil were discovered in the 1990s, for example, housing prices jumped almost six-fold between 1992 and 2012.[3] This jump delivered few tangible increases in housing benefits to those living in the same, now six times more expensive, houses, while at the same time making housing much less affordable to the younger generation.

The big question, then, is whether more money eventually leads to the creation of more products. We will later examine this question in detail and the many historical experiments that can provide the answer.

Emperor Nero ruled Rome from 54 to 68 AD and was faced with a problem common to many rulers: he needed more money. Debt, to his chagrin, was not an option as Romans did not believe in taking on debt. So Nero came up with a unique solution—instead of further taxing his subjects, an act that could have negative consequences and would not necessarily yield more money, why not just "create" money?

Money in Rome in those days was made of silver and gold, and sometimes copper. The most commonly used coin was the silver denarius, with which the empire paid its soldiers. Twenty-five silver denarii were worth 1 gold aureus. In the times of Julius Caesar, 50 years prior to Nero, the weight of such an Aureus was set at 1/40th of a Roman pound, which is equivalent to about 8 grams.

The silver denarius was made of pure silver, so Nero figured that if he could reduce the amount of silver in each coin then he could make more coins from using the same amount of silver. For example, if he reduced the silver content to 90%, then he could make 1 new coin from every 9 coins he "fixed." Nero was sure that no one would notice this trick and that he could easily create more coins to pay his soldiers and to cover other expenses he had incurred on subsidies and building projects.

With his master plan figured out, Nero went forward and reduced the denarius's silver content by about 11%. This act enabled him to make around 11% more coins with the amount of silver he had on hand. It also consequently increased the money supply (the amount of money in circulation). The increase was nonetheless gradual, and thus the impact on the market was gradual as well. With more money in circulation prices slowly crept up over time without people realizing that the coins they owned were worth less than before. This trick is now called debasement.

Nero is infamous because he is rumored to have started the Great Fire of Rome, a blaze which burned for almost a week and destroyed large parts of the city. The real fire Nero started, however, was his currency debasement scheme. It raged for centuries past his violent departure in 68 AD. Silent and corrosive, it's what eventually brought the Roman Empire to its knees.

The next 150 years saw some 15 emperors sitting on the throne, all but four of whom continued the debasement of the silver denarius. By 211 AD, the silver coin consisted of only 58% silver. In an attempt to stop the downward spiral, Emperor Caracalla minted a new coin in 213 AD, valued at two denarii. Unfortunately, the introduction of this new coin could not stabilize the value of the denarius as long as the debasement continued.

As a result of the continuing debasement, prices were constantly ascending, which in turn also caused government expenses to rise. To try to make up for this shortage, new taxes were imposed and debasement continued. By 265 AD the new coin created by Emperor Caracalla 50 years prior consisted of a mere 5% silver. Meanwhile, the empire was rapidly approaching a severe economic crisis as a result of inflation, government deficits, and instability.

In 301 AD, Emperor Diocletian tried to put an end to the downward spiral: he issued a decree which set maximum prices for nearly one thousand products and a cap on wages. Merchants were also restricted in shipping goods to other outside markets. These rules, known as the Edict of Diocletian of the Edict of Maximum Prices ordered the death penalty on "profiteers and speculators" who were blamed for the inflation. As we will see, little has changed in history in this regard: placing the blame on "profiteers and speculators" has always been a popular political escape, and today is no different.

The story of the Roman Empire does not get much better. The debasement of the denarius continued—the silver that once went into one denarius now produced 150 of them—and the amount of coins in circulation kept climbing. The Edict of Maximum Prices was all but ignored and prices continued to climb, though a few unfortunate "profiteers and speculators" were indeed executed. For example, at the time of the edict, a pound of pork was fixed at 12 denarii. A hundred years later, this same item cost 90. In Egypt—the "grain basket" of the empire—a unit of wheat rose from 6 drachma at the time of Nero in 65 AD to 200 drachma in 276 AD, to 9,000 in 314 AD, and to more than 2,000,000 in 334 AD.[4] As a result of the skyrocketing prices, practically all fortunes and savings held in the Roman currency were wiped out.

The tumble of the Roman Empire was the first known case of hyper-inflation in history; this hyperinflation was a direct result of the empire's constant debasing of its currency. Reducing the amount of silver in the coins and using the "saved" silver to create more and more new coins eventually led to the complete devaluation of all coins.

To make matters worse, a lasting plague caused a drop in population, and the burden of supporting the administration now fell on even fewer shoulders. The dire ongoing economic situation, which translated into a drop in food production, did nothing to help the society recover from its population crisis. The shortage of manpower to support the military and the empire's production needs had become dire. As a result, harsh laws were issued which forced sons to assume the same roles as their fathers, from soldiers to civil servants to farmers. These laws laid down the foundations of serfdom, which eventually became the basis of society in most of Europe following the fall of Rome.

In an attempt to save the Empire and raise the needed resources, the government sharply increased the tax burden. The tax on property and the one on people—also known as the poll tax—were now two to three times what they had been in Rome's heyday. On top of this, new taxes were also introduced. In 444 AD, the government inaugurated a 4% sales tax, which required all sales to be conducted in the presence of a tax collector.[5] The heavy taxation levied on communities brought about starvation and widespread land abandonment. The empire's ability to withstand outside pressures, mainly from Germanic Barbarian tribes, was crumbling. The once-proud far outpost of Britain, with its mighty Hadrian's Wall, was abandoned by 410 AD, followed by other territories in the west. On September 476 AD, nearly 1229 years after Romulus allegedly established Rome, the last Roman emperor (incidentally also named Romulus), was deposed.

The role the debasement played in economic collapse of the empire and hence the fate of the Roman Empire did not quite manage to serve as a lesson to future governments. At least 19 cases of currency debasement occurred in Europe between 1258 and 1799. As with Rome, these cases saw the content of silver in currencies reduced between 12 and 91%, with many cases spanning hundreds of years.[6] Among history's most infamous debasers was Henry VIII of England. Between Henry VIII's reign and his son Edward VI's, the pound lost 83% of its silver content.[7] The record, however, probably belonged to the French King John (Jean) II whose need for financing for his ongoing war with England was so great that during the first year of his reign, from 1350, the currency went through eighteen debasements. In the coming decade it would be debased a further seventy times. This process harmed and eroded commoners' purchasing power, who held and used coins for their daily transactions. Meanwhile, the nobility was affected to a lesser degree since it tended to store its fortunes in gold and silver items.

It is important to note here that debasement and inflation are not exactly the same thing. While debasement is the act, inflation is the typical result. Inflation, however, does not have to be the result of increasing the money supply through debasement or money printing. If, for example, the economy's growth rate is greater than the increase in the amount of money due to debasement, then the inflationary price increase caused by debasement would be absorbed in part or in full by the price decline created by the economic growth. That is to say, it is possible for inflation to be hidden by greater economic growth and sizable increases in goods availability due to such growth.

Still, regardless of the inflationary results, traditional debasement (reducing the content of silver in coins) and modern debasement (money printing) are both, when boiled down, a form of tax on society. The reduction of the currency's value is essentially a way of transferring purchasing power from the people to the government. This ability to slyly tax and default on debt has been the ultimate motivation for debasement throughout history. When a government creates new money and uses it to buy things, it dilutes the money of all other players in the marketplace. As we have seen, when new money is created and the amount of goods stays the same, the cost of each good will go up given that more money is going after the same amount of goods. The net result is that the value of money goes down. By printing money, a relatively effortless action, a government can buy real new goods for itself while decreasing the value of the money held by others. This tactic is equal to taking over some of the resources and wealth in the marketplace; in other words, a tax. The difference between this seizure of wealth and a traditional tax is that a tax is typically targeted and noticed, while this process is arbitrary and subtle. It is for this exact reason that rulers came to love currency devaluation so much.

Nobody likes to pay taxes, and when taxes get too high it can have serious consequences for the authority exacting them. France and England's monarchs learned this danger firsthand during the Hundred Years' War (1337-1453). A succession of steep tax increases made to offset the drain of resources caused by the war led to social unrest and a series of brutal revolts in England and in France. Furthermore, when a tax burden becomes too heavy it fails to bring in more money. In essence, the total cost of collection plus the lost revenue from people trying to avoid higher taxes altogether can negate the additional tax revenue collected. Debasement and money printing is therefore a perfect solution: it is a convenient tax that is silent, hard to measure, and which very few people understand or are aware of.

Inflation offers rulers one more crucial benefit: if a ruler is in debt, paying back the debt with devalued money is the same as partially defaulting on the debt without bearing the shame of officially defaulting. In the period from 1500 to 1799, no less than 14 European states partially defaulted through inflation. This list includes France, Poland, Italy, Spain, Sweden, the Netherlands, and Britain. This number grows to more than 50 if you expand the range to 2008 and include the rest of the world. Among the partially defaulted economies are the US in 1779, Japan in 1819, and China in 1947.[8] The attraction of this practice has not vanished: in November 2014, Benoît Cœuré, an executive board member of the European Central Bank, candidly admitted on an interview to Bloomberg TV: "low inflation is as bad as deflation in terms of the capacity of our economy to grow out of debt. [...] Low inflation is a concern."

It is painfully clear that this secret weapon doesn't come without a price. We have already seen what constant debasement did to Rome, and will soon see what slow, deep, and subtle money printing can do elsewhere, but first we have to understand a key requirement for that hidden tax to work

The official name of the currency of the state of Israel was, until not long ago, the "New Israeli Shekel" (NIS). The *new* is there to distinguish the currency from the older shekel. The old shekel came after the Israeli lira, which was the state currency from 1948 until 1980. In the 1980s, Israel suffered from hyperinflation which forced it, among other steps, to change the name of its currency. This name change also came with a not-so-small adjustment: at first one zero (from lira to shekel) and then another three zeros (from shekel to new shekel) were slashed off the end of the numbers printed on the bills. 10,000 (old) shekels became 10 new shekels, 20,000 became 20, and so on. For the most part, the same notes were even used, just with a few zeros removed. Below you can see a 10,000 old shekel bill and its successor, the new 10 shekel bill (at a ratio of 1:1,000).

As a result of these changes, the monthly salary of a junior bank clerk, originally around 100,000 old shekels, dropped to 100 new shekels overnight. Prices, debts, and bills all dropped along with salaries. Everything was simply noted in new shekels, 3 zeros less than prior.

This change, however, had no real effect on actual real pricing. No civil unrest broke out, no merchant felt poorer because the value of his inventory supposedly dropped by 99.9%, and no employee felt threatened that his salary had gone from 100,000 to 100. The amount of money in the economy dropped by just about 99.9% (NIS was 1/1,000 of the old shekel) and no depression or contraction in the economy took place. In essence, nothing really happened except that day-to-day calculations became easier. Was this some sort of miracle? Not quite.

The reason nothing changed is simple: when the amount of money changes overnight and all players in the economy know about it, nothing is lost or gained. An individual does not feel poorer or richer because of the number of zeroes on his bills. If he or she knows that everyone else has gone through the change and that everything is relatively the same then nothing has changed in practice. Remember that the numbers behind prices are set based on the *value of the goods* as they reflect the preferences of the buyer. Whether the measure of currency is an old shekel with 3 zeros or a new shekel with no zeros, it makes no difference. As long as the change in the amount of money in the economy, in this case a 99.9% drop, is equal for everyone, i.e. evenly occurring and with full knowledge by all market participants, then there is no impact on people's wealth, purchasing power , or purchasing behavior.

A similar occurrence took place sixteen hundred years ago when Dionysius I (432 – 367 BC) was the king of Syracuse, today's Sicily. Dionysius had a reputation for being cruel and vindictive. When his subjects asked him to repay money that he owed them, he devised a plan. He demanded that all subjects hand over their coins and proceeded to stamp all the coins with a new value, making all one drachma coins into two drachmas ones. Now with the new two drachma coins, Dionysius paid off his debt at a nominal value with coins "worth" twice as much. The frightened subjects were probably happy to get away with their lives, but most understood they hadn't really been paid back in full. The subjects understood that the new two Drachmas was really worth one, and that what they got back was the right nominal sum, just with half of its original value and purchasing power. Accordingly, all the prices on the island adjusted to the new amount of money.

Let's quickly hop to an island neighboring Syracuse and assume that the island has one remote village to which the story of the Dionysius's mischief has not yet arrived. A few opportunistic merchants arrive to the village with the new 2 drachma coins and the villagers, not knowing what the king has done (and thus not aware that the real value of the new 2 drachma coins is equal to 1 old drachma) are happy to sell their products at the old prices, treating the new 2 drachmas as if they were 2 old ones. Without the right information, the villagers have no idea that the money they get from the merchants is worth half what they think, and thus will buy them only half of what the "old" money did outside of the village.

As we can see here, the key to exploiting the effects of new money creation lies in the knowledge of the creation activity. When everybody knows that the amount of money has doubled or has been reduced by 99%, nothing happens. The market simply adjusts everything accordingly to the change and moves on. When the information is not available to all and travels slowly from its origin, however, the impact is very different. When Nero's soldiers got paid in the newly debased denarius, they didn't know that they were receiving what was worth in terms of silver content only 90% of the previous currency. The merchants or prostitutes whom the soldiers paid also had no idea they were getting coins of lower value. Thus, it took time for prices in the marketplace to slowly adjust to the new money supply. As the devalued coins traveled through the economy and increased the amount of coins in circulation, prices naturally crept up.

It is exactly this covert aspect of money creation that made it so popular with rulers and politicians. Not only do rulers get to secretly tax the people, they can do so with little chance of taking any blame. Under constant yet bearable inflation it is very hard to figure out what exactly is going on with the value of money. People see their salaries increasing (even if buying power has decreased) and see their 401(k)s growing (even if in net value they are not), and they don't even realize that they are paying taxes (capital gains) on inflationary profits which actually result in net losses in terms of real purchasing power.

The fact that new money traveling through the economy generates economic activity complicates the issue further. In the 1930s a British economist by the name of John Maynard Keynes came up with the idea of intentionally using money creation to ignite economic activity. This idea became a mainstream economic thought that remains strong to this day. You are likely familiar with its modern name: stimulus spending.

Very soon in our journey through the history of money we will attend to the unintended consequences of such stimulus and to what happens behind the scenes while this newly created money travels through the economy.

Chapter 5:
The Birth of the Money Creation Machine

"Banking was conceived in iniquity, and was born in sin. The bankers own the Earth. Take it away from them, but leave them the power to create deposits, and with the flick of the pen, they will create enough deposits to buy it back again."
—*Josiah Charles Stamp, British economist and banker, director of the Bank of England*

Despite their usefulness as money, gold and silver were heavy, inconvenient, and, most importantly, dangerous to carry around. To remedy these inconveniences, the early banks we mentioned developed notes that represented the gold and silver deposits stored physically in the bank. These promissory notes could be transferred between merchants as payment instead of the actual metal. As this practice spread, however, the number of different promissory notes rose and their legitimacy came into question. The need to simplify the world of currency and promissory notes led to the establishment of the first exchange bank in Amsterdam in 1609.

The bank allowed merchants to open accounts where they could deposit coins and notes and have these accounts run in standardized currencies. It also allowed merchants to transact between these accounts, paying each other by debiting and crediting accounts as needed. This practice allowed people to complete transactions without the need for coins or even notes altogether. At this stage of banking, the legal relationship between the bank and the depositing customers was simple: the bank was a guardian for the depositor. It took care of the money in return for a fee. It is important to note that the depositor retained full ownership of the deposits; the deposited money was for the owner's use, and not the bank's. The exchange bank was a relatively safe institution because as long a natural disaster or a robbery didn't occur, the gold and silver money was safe in the exchange bank's vault, a much safer location that the road or an individual home. Even though the depositors used only a small part of the actual gold or coin deposits, the unused money was kept in the bank's safe untouched. Loans, on the other hand, where made by another type of bank. Those banks used money invested by the bank's owners to make loans in return for interest payment.

In 1656 a Dutch merchant named Johan Palmstruch arrived in Sweden from Amsterdam and petitioned the king to allow him to open an exchange bank similar to Amsterdam's. It would also then be the country's first bank. His first two petitions were rejected, but after promising half of the bank's profits to the crown, the third petition was approved. Thus, on November 30, 1656, King Charles X Gustav signed two charters, one to create an exchange bank and one to create a bank for loans. The exchange bank would operate like other similar banks that had been opened in Europe: it would take deposits of silver, gold, and, another popular Swedish currency, copper, and safeguard them for a fee. The loan bank, which opened almost two years later, would offer interest-bearing loans from funds provided by the bank owners. All in all, these two banks were not very different from the Italian and Amsterdam banking practices of the time. It was only a short time after the establishment of the two banks that they were combined into one institution. Stockholms Banco was thus formed with Palmstruch appointed as general manager. Given that Stockholms Banco was the first and only bank in Sweden, Palmstruch's loan business was flourishing.

Very soon, the number of borrowers outweighed the invested capital that was available to be loaned. Shortly after gaining his new position, Palmstruch observed that while his ability to lend was limited by the capital and funds provided by the bank's owners, he still had large amounts of money in the form of deposits sitting essentially unused in the exchange bank. We do not know exactly how and when but Palmstruch soon started, though not in a systematic manner, to use the deposits in the exchange-savings bank to finance the booming loaning business. At the beginning all went well as the owners of the deposits hardly ever asked for their money in cash. Even when a few depositors did ask to withdraw their funds, Mr. Palmstruch kept enough cash reserves to satisfy such demands. This smoothly sailing business hit a rough spot in a few short years, though, when, in 1660, the crown debased the main coin, the daler copper coin, by lowering its copper content.

The Banco had deposits of old dalers, which had a higher content of copper and were thus worth more than the newly debased dalers. As a result, many of the customers started to request their daler deposits back. That's when things took a bad turn, as the bank was unable to return the depositors' dalers because they had been loaned out to other customers as long-term loans. The situation could have resulted in the first bank run in history, but Palmstruch was blessed with ingenuity and devised a second plan. As he was convinced that these loans would eventually be repaid, and that he would thus have the resources to pay back the deposits, he figured he could cover the gap by convincing depositors to accept paper notes, essentially promising to pay the original deposit in (old) copper daler or silver daler coins upon the holders' request. The first banknotes (*Kreditivsedlar*, which translates literally to credit note) were issued in 1661 and became very popular substitutes for copper coins, which were bulky and inconvenient to carry and store. Pushed by growing demand, more and more of these notes were issued. The most popular of these were called "Palmstruchers."

What started as an emergency and limited solution developed into a much larger strategy. Palmstruch concluded that if only a very small portion of deposits are needed to manage the ongoing operational needs of the exchange bank, and people are using and trusting the notes as if they were money, why not systematically lend out the unused deposits using the new banknotes as mechanisms of payment for the depositors and borrowers alike? This mechanism would also enable him to lend a much larger amount of money based on a much smaller amount of physical silver and gold reserves. The actual physical gold and silver in deposit would be leveraged and multiplied many times with the usage of the notes. Thus, if, let's say, the bank's ongoing operations only required 10% of the silver and gold in cash to safely meet withdrawal needs, then the bank could lend out ten times more the physical money using bank notes. In other words, the bank's entire store of gold & silver cash deposits would now become the 10% cash reserve needed to meet withdrawal demands, while the loans given via notes would be 10 times this amount.

By 1666 the amount of notes issued well exceeded the amount of coins and gold in the bank's vault and the notes had infiltrated far beyond the realm of merchants. Probably without him even realizing, Palmstruch had created a new and very significant invention that is known today as fractional-reserve banking, meaning that banks keep only a fraction of deposits as reserve for withdrawals. This invention is probably the single most important factor in shaping today's financial world and monetary system.

We do not know exactly how many notes the Banco printed and what reserve ratio (the amount of physical money kept per notes issued) the Banco kept, but by the end of 1666 there were so many banknotes in circulation that the Banco could no longer honor requests by depositors for cash. Under pressure, the bank ceased operating, hence causing the first classic run on a bank. Following the bank's crash, the government was forced to take over the bank's operation and undo the mess. In 1668, Palmstruch's charter to operate the Banco was revoked and the bank's business was transferred to a new bank, operated by the parliament. This new bank was later renamed Sveriges Riksbank and, as of the early 1900s, became Sweden's central bank, one of the first of its kind in Europe. Mr. Palmstruch, on the other hand, was a little less lucky than the new bank he created. Two years after the foundation of Sveriges Riksbank, Palmstruch was put on trial and thrown in prison. Though he was released two years later, he died shortly thereafter.

Neither the Palmstruch's nor his bank's fate could halt his invention. Fractional-reserve banking was just too tempting for bankers, rulers and depositors alike. In the words of a 20th century economist, "surprising though it may seem, banking has one characteristic in common with alcohol consumption, drug taking, and prostitution. No matter the strictness with which officialdom tries to restrict and control it, banking—the operation of a deposit taking and lending system with a reserve of well under 100%—is irrepressible."[1] Fractional-reserve banking not only changed the face of banking, it also changed the face of money. For the first time in history money was being legally and officially created out of thin air. The mechanism can be reviewed in the sample below, but the principle is simple, and involves multiplying the gold/silver cash on hand many times over when giving out loans.

Stockholm's Banco first credit notes
The first paper money in Europe

75

How does fractional reserve banking actually work?

Banker		Keeps 10% cash reserve, and then lends out:	Bank's balance sheet	
			Assets: Loans made + cash reserve	Liabilities owed to depositors
Day 1	Gets $1000 from depositor 1	$900 Loan to A	$100 in cash (from deposit 1) $900 in loan made to A	$1000 (to 1)
Day 2	Gets the $900 loan A back as deposit 2 (as loan is used and circulates)	$810 Loan to B	$100 in cash (from deposit 1) $90 in cash (from deposit 2) $900 in loan to A $810 in loan to B	$1000 (to 1) + $900 (to 2)
Day 3	Gets the $810 loan back as deposit 3	$729 Loan C	$100 in cash (1) + 90 in cash (2) + 81 in cash (3) Plus $900 in loan A $810 in loan B $729 in Loan C	$1000 (to1) + $900 (to 2) + $810 (to 3)
Totals			$ 271 in cash $2439 in loans Total: $2710	$2710

These three rounds made the $1,000 initial deposit turn into $2,710 in circulation. The bank has $271 cash on hand plus $2439 in loans it made, totaling at $2,710 in assets. On the other side, the bank has against these assets $2,710 in liabilities owed to the different layers of depositors. This example could have continued until it reached the x10 mark (assuming 10% cash reserves). In the process, the amount of "new" money created by fractional reserve banking equals 9 times the initial deposit.

Despite mounting contrary evidence and plenty of historical failures, the fractional-reserve banking model is still considered viable, with the reasoning that generally the bank only needs a fraction of its cash deposits to meet its obligations to its depositors. Since this condition is true in the normal course of business (say, 99% of days), why not use the excess reserve as capital for lending, which will yield interest and stimulate business? After all, lending benefits the banker and the depositor alike. The concept of letting the depositor earn money—interest— on his deposits rather than pay money for the deposit guardian's services grew wildly popular. So did the notion that bankers could profit from interest on a significantly higher supply of money than would have been available if only the bank's capital were in use.

Fractional-reserve banking fundamentally changed the legal relationship between the depositor and the bank, likely without most of the depositors even noticing. While prior to fractional banking the depositor was the owner of his deposit, with the advent of fractional banking, the depositor lost ownership of his deposit. In return he received a claim, a right to get the money back from the bank. This was a "claim" because his money no longer existed in any specific place. The money, in fact, turned into fractions of loans given to third parties. The cash in the bank's vault no longer belonged to individuals, but rather was pooled together to represent only a fraction of all the money lent and deposited by the bank's clients. This change in ownership status is meaningful. While ownership trumps almost any other claim, the claim to one's money in the bank is just as valid as the claims of all other people with deposited money. Thus, if the bank issues 10 times the cash deposits (of silver and gold) in banknotes, each one of these banknotes represents a claim that is just as valid as all the other ones. Everything else being equal, and assuming no other preferential claims, the holder of the claim has a right to only a small part of the cash he deposited. This position was made clear, if any doubt existed, in an 1848 ruling by Lord Cottenham, British Lord Chancellor:

Money, when paid into a bank, ceases altogether to be the money of the principal; it is then money of the banker, who is bound to an equivalent by paying a similar sum to that deposit with him when he is asked for it. [...] The money placed in the custody of the banker is, to all intents and purposes, the money of the banker, to do with it as he pleases; he is guilty of no breach of trust in employing it; he is not answerable to the principal if he puts it into jeopardy.[2]

This change in ownership and the fact that the banks were now holding only a fraction of their deposits in cash were the root of the forthcoming bank runs.

Although fractional banking sparked a huge growth in banking, it also carried with it inherent instability. As we saw, under a fractional-reserve banking system, the vast majority of a bank's assets which could cover the bank's obligations to its depositors are not more than money it is owed by those it made loans to. Thus, if and when the soundness of these loans comes into question, so does the bank's ability to repay its depositors! Furthermore, even if the bank's loans are sound and backed by good collaterals there is a critical time gap since the money comprising the loans is still tied up in long-term loans and cannot be retrieved immediately. Given that banks promise their depositors their money upon request, a run on the bank spells disaster even for a good bank with a good loan portfolio, since it cannot possibly make all of its assets/loans liquid immediately and therefore cannot make good on its obligations to its depositors. Thus, as fractional-reserve banking grew in popularity, so did bank runs when terrified depositors rushed to be first to the banks' limited cash on hand. As a result, bank bankruptcies, which bring down banks and their depositors alike, became not uncommon occurrences. As we will soon see, it was one of these periodical bank runs that led to the creation of the Federal Reserve.

While during the Roman Empire rulers could debase the money in order to create more money, fractional-reserve banking enabled an unlimited number of private institutions to create money. And they could now create sizable quantities at a much faster pace. When money was made in gold and silver money, then the total amount of money in the marketplace (be it in gold and silver or in promissory notes representing deposit amounts) could not exceed the amount of physical money available. With the invention of fractional-reserve banking, deposited money becomes only a percentage, a fraction, of the total money on loan, and the banks become cash creation machines. In essence, fractional-reserve banking changed the nature of money: prior, money was tied to the physical amount of a commodity (gold, silver or copper) and thus, inelastic. In the aftermath of Palm-struch's invention, money was tied to the ever-changing reserve ratio and its quantity much more elastic as a result.

There was one more drastic change we must highlight in our fractional banking discussion. As the nature of money changed so did the nature of almost every financial asset. The deposit that had previously been stored in a vault was now no more than an IOU given by the bank. This IOU's validity depended on the solvency of the organizations and individuals the deposited money was lent to over and over as the money circulated. Changing the nature of most financial assets from a hard asset to a chain of back-to-back liabilities and assets (every asset is somebody else's liability) had some detrimental consequences as we shall soon see.

It is important to note that under a commodity money system (i.e. when money is based on gold and silver); the amount of money created by fractional-reserve banking couldn't have grown endlessly. Since every lending stage reduces the amount of "new" money for fractional lending, the lending process is finite. In the 10% reserve example, the process would end at creating and lending 9 times the original total amount deposited. However, if the base amount of money is elastic, i.e. the initial amount of money deposited can grow infinitely, then fractional banking will constantly grow the amount of money in the market as long as the banks find borrowers for that money, hence acting as a huge accelerator for money creation.

The development of paper money and the increase of the amount of money in circulation due to fractional-reserve banking had an inevitable impact on price levels. One of the first to realize and write about this consequence was Henry Thornton. Born in England in 1760 to a family of prominent merchants and bankers, Thornton was elected to parliament at the age of 22. Thornton served as a member of parliament for the next 30 years until his death. In 1797, the Bank of England suspended the convertibility of its notes to gold due to the long and costly Napoleonic Wars with France. This suspension catalyzed Thornton's thinking about money and its role in the economy. In 1802, Henry Thornton published *An Enquiry into the Nature and Effects of the Paper Credit of Great Britain.* The book attempted to explain, among other things, the ratio between money quantity and prices. Thornton put forth the idea that the Bank of England could control the price levels in the market through the quantity of paper money. This theory, now known as the quantity theory of money, explains that the supply of money is the core determinant of price levels in the market. It posits a direct, proportional, and measurable relationship between the two.

The quantity theory of money states that the actual amount of money in circulation is composed not only of the sheer amount of money in the economy, but also of the speed at which this money is used. In practice, the higher the frequency of money usage, the more money there is in the market. Money's usage speed is known as its velocity. If, for example, people stash 25% of their gold coins under their mattresses, the amount of money in circulation is 25% lower. The same effect holds true if they use the coins to buy a set of goods once a week as opposed to once a day.

It was an American economist of the early 20th century, Irving Fisher, who put the ratio in an easy-to-understand formula: $MV = PT$ where:

M = Money Supply (the amount of money)
V = Velocity (how many times the money changes hands)
P = Price Level
T = Number of Transactions

The two sides of this equation also equal to total GDP (Gross Domestic Product), as the number of transactions multiplied by the price of those transactions is the total value of all the finished goods and services produced in a market (the definition of GDP).

The relationship between the actual money supply (M) and its velocity (V) is key to understanding the ratio between price level and money quantity. If the velocity is fixed, i.e. people generally use money at the same frequency regardless of the amount of money, then an increase in money supply will result in an immediate increase in pricing. If the velocity dramatically fluctuates (for example, if increases in money supply lead to a decrease in the use of money), then the increase in money supply by itself will not necessarily bring about price increases. Changes in velocity are therefore able, in some conditions, to counteract the effects caused by changes in the money supply.

Arguments about the relationship between money supply and its velocity lie at the base of the debate between Keynesians and Monetarists. We will review Keynes and his theories later in this book, but regarding the relationship between money supply and velocity, Keynes argued that there is no proof that when the money supply increases people actually use that extra money. Keynes suggested that an increase in money supply could be offset by a reduction in its velocity as that extra money could be used to "speculate" in assets such as the stock or bond market, which would increase the prices of those assets alone but not overall market price levels. The dominance Keynes had on economic thinking for 40 years, beginning in the late 1930s, blocked any real challenge to this notion. It was not until the 1960s that a forceful, undeterred, and brilliant opponent emerged.

Born in 1912 to a family of immigrants in New York City, Milton Friedman joined in 1946 the University of Chicago as a professor of economic theory. He would work there for the following 30 years assisting in the creation of the intellectual group known as the Chicago School of Economics. Friedman insisted that empirical evidence demonstrates that velocity is stable and claimed that "inflation is always and everywhere a monetary phenomenon in the sense that it is and can be produced only by a more rapid increase in the quantity of money than in output." Friedman was the founder of the school of thought that came to be known as monetarism, an economic worldview that became popular in the late 1970s and 1980s.

According to monetarism, inflation was always a result of "too much money chasing too few goods." Friedman's argument went further still: he claimed that even though the amount of money is the cause of inflation, central banks and governments cannot hope to be able to closely "turn on and off" the tap on the money supply to achieve growth or to slow down the economy because they can never manage the timing of the impact of the change in money supply. Thus, according to Milton Friedman, the key to economic growth and stability is stability in the creation of money (for example, in tandem with population growth) which can be effective even if done by a robot. Friedman was a staunch believer in the free market and in limited government intervention in economics. His school of thought became so popular in the '70s and '80s that Harvard Professor of Economics and Secretary of the Treasury Larry Summers said that "if John Maynard Keynes was the most influential economist of the first half of the 20th century, then Milton Friedman was the most influential economist of the second half."[3] In the 1990s, however, monetarism began to fall out of favor as the stability and predictability of velocity became increasingly subject to doubt.

Fractional-reserve banking also creates an inherent conflict of interest between bank management and shareholders, especially in large banks owned by many shareholders. Given that a bank's profits are a percentage of its loan portfolio, the bank has an inherent desire to grow that portfolio. The simplest way to increase the amount of loans is to decrease the cash reserve ratio (i.e. the ratio between the loans and the cash reserve), thereby multiplying even more the amount of money available for lending. But as the bank reduces its reserve ratio, it increases the risk of being unable to absorb loan failures and satisfy the demands of depositors for cash withdrawals. As a result, bank managers are rewarded for engaging in increasingly risky behavior. As long as the bank makes money, bonuses skyrocket, even though this increase in profit inherently means an increase in risk. So while the burdens of risk are carried by shareholders, and increasingly also by taxpayers, the benefits go disproportionately to management.

This inequality became clear to Lehman Brothers' many shareholders in September 2008 when their holdings became worthless as the company filed for bankruptcy. Lehman Brothers' CEO, on the other hand, walked away with around $71 million in compensation in 2007. In fact, his 5-year compensation prior to 2007, when the risky assets were accumulating in the banks' loan portfolio, totaled $354 million dollars.[4]

In reality, under fractional-reserve banking, bank crashes are an inevitable outcome and not merely freak coincidence. What's more, because the hysteria associated with a run on the bank tends to spread from bank to bank, once the process is set into motion it leads to a general financial crisis. Though bankers like to paint such large-scale crashes as rarities, the truth is that since 1800 almost all countries have experienced them, including: 12 in the UK, 15 in France, 11 in Italy, 11 in Brazil, 8 in Canada, and 13 in the USA.[5]

Due to the inherently risky nature of fractional-reserve banking as well as banks' continual quest to expand their lending practices, the burden of these gambles was gradually pushed squarely on the shoulders of taxpayers. And though it took some 350 years, eventually fractional-reserve banking risks ended up taking a toll on the same people as they had back in Sweden, as we will soon see in detail.

Fractional-reserve banking begot another phenomenon which contributed to the general destabilization of economies: the exacerbation of the boom and bust cycle.

The cycle of boom and bust is as old as civilization itself. One of the first such cycles is graphically recorded in Genesis 41:

Pharaoh had a dream: He was standing by the Nile, when out of the river there came up seven cows, sleek and fat, and they grazed among the reeds. After them, seven other cows, ugly and gaunt, came up out of the Nile and stood beside those on the riverbank. And the cows that were ugly and gaunt ate up the seven sleek, fat cows. Then Pharaoh woke up...He fell asleep again and had a second dream: Seven heads of grain, healthy and good, were growing on a single stalk. After them, seven other heads of grain sprouted—thin and scorched by the east wind. The thin heads of grain swallowed up the seven healthy, full heads. Then Pharaoh woke up; it had been a dream.

As the story goes, Joseph helped Pharaoh decode the dreams and prepare for a cycle of 7 boom years and 7 bust years. This cycle was said to have resulted from ups and downs in weather and agriculture production.

In agrarian societies, climate and harvest were indeed the main contributors to booms and busts, and the ability to save for an *un*rainy day was critical to surviving it. As society became less dependent on a single year's harvest, the nature of and reasons for booms and busts morphed and changed.

While Joseph's interpretation helped save Egypt from the consequences of a weather driven boom and bust cycle, the latter can sometimes bring nations to their knees, especially when they involve playing with the fire of money creation. Such was the case of France and John Law.

A Scottish financier and economist born in 1671, John had a few innovative and unique economic and financial ideas. Law wrote his ideas in a few books and pitched them to Scottish authorities. After they were rejected by the Scottish parliament, John moved to France. At the time of Law's arrival in 1714, the French crown was plagued with debt and the country's economy was depressed. These conditions made France a fertile ground for Law to test his ambitious theories. Through some personal connections, Law was granted a license to open a bank in 1716.

Thanks to Law's persuasiveness, the bank was allowed to issue bank notes (paper money), a totally new concept for France at the time. The notes would be supported by gold and silver, meaning they could be exchanged for gold and silver kept in the bank's vaults.

One of Law's ideas behind the bank was to make it a tool for financing the crown's debt. This proved a very persuasive argument when presented to the bankrupt king. Persuasive, yet completely unheard of in France, though this was the very reason for the creation of the Bank of England some 20 years prior. As a next step, Law's bank allowed the public to buy its shares and pay for them with sovereign debt (IOU notes they got from the king). The bank also bought some sovereign debt itself. In return, the bank's paper money was accepted as legal tender, which allowed the currency to be used for payment of taxes owed to the government and to settle debts. At this stage, the bank still kept a reasonable reserve ratio of about 50% gold/silver to paper money in circulation.[6]

Law's grand plan relied on three facts: The crown had a high debt that it wanted to get rid of, the public had gold and silver money that it was holding onto instead of spending, and France had unexploited lands. One of the most promising of these lands was the vast and unsettled Louisiana territory. It stretched some 3,000 miles from the mouth of the Mississippi River all the way to Canada. As an overriding philosophy Law had a belief that what was holding the French economy back was the limited amount of gold and silver money in circulation. Law speculated that if these commodities were replaced with larger quantities of paper money then the result would be an increase in economic activity, trade, and employment. If this sounds all too familiar, it's because it is. There is no question that Law was the first economic thinker to conceive of money as a tool for economic stimulus rather than just as a means of exchange. So Law set out to consolidate all those elements while simultaneously reviving France's economy and cementing his name and legend forever.

In 1717, a new John Law company was set up and named Company of the West. This company, originally formed and named the Mississippi Company, was granted a monopoly on commerce in the Louisiana territory. The company's capital was set at 100 million livres (the French currency at the time), and shares were priced at 500 livres each. The shares were offered to all members of the public, French and foreigners alike. The investors could pay for shares with sovereign debt, thus transferring some of that debt from the crown to the company. Shortly the company was granted more rights, further boosting its appeal. It was given trading rights with other territories, the right to collect certain taxes, and a tobacco monopoly. Most shares, nonetheless, were paid for in gold and silver money. Relying on shareholder money and profits from the exclusively granted activities, the company agreed to lend the crown 1.2 billion livres in 1719. This sum would cover the crown's entire debt.[7] Thereafter, all tax collection duties were granted to the company.

At the same time, the bank Law operated was dropping its reserve ratio and creating paper money which was by that point legal tender and widely accepted. Law believed that France and its lands and assets, rather than gold, would be better backing for his new paper money. As the Company of the West grew more and more powerful, it continually issued new shares, raised more money, and used this new money to acquire even more exclusive rights from the crown. Some of these rights included the operation of the royal mint and trading rights with China.

The consistently high level of activities ensured the escalation of the company's share prices. To guarantee the continued excitement and assist with trade, the company established a new outpost at the mouth of the Mississippi River. This settlement was named New Orleans after one of Law's best friends, the Duke of Orleans. Publications about the riches of this new promised land soon followed. When investors wanted to invest in new rounds of share offerings, they could get a loan from Law's bank using the newly bought shares as collateral. When Law had to pay dividends on outstanding shares, it was done with paper money issued by the bank.

The excitement was nearing its peak. An eyewitness described the company's offices as: "crowded from morning to night. [...]

Princes, dukes [...] were selling estate and pawning jewels to purchase shares."[8] The price of the shares eventually reached 10,000 livres per share. In as little as a year, the shares had experienced a twenty-fold growth!

In early 1720, however, things started to take a turn for the worse: investors started to cash out their huge profits, while new investors were just not coming in, and the price of shares started to tumble. In an attempt to cool down the situation Law offered to buy some of those shares and paid for them with more paper money created by the bank. This paper money, after all, was legal tender and was "backed" by France's lands and riches. But the uncontrolled creation of new money was flooding the market and created rapid inflation. The buying power, and value, of the notes was rapidly declining and people started to panic. As people tried to exchange their paper notes back to silver and gold, the state proceeded to ban the export of gold and silver and the production of gold and silver objects.[9]

By this point, nothing could stop the inevitable: the price of company shares plummeted from 9,000 livres to around 900 livres in just a few months. People's trust in the paper money vanished simultaneously. Law fled France by the skin of his teeth, penniless and shamed but at least alive. Law left behind a devastated society, individuals that had lost everything they owned, and a nation scarred for generations.

Law's boom and bust was much more than just another company's stock bubble like so many through history. His system was intertwined with much more fundamental ideas regarding the place of money in the economy, its true nature, its right quantity and the appropriate backing necessary to instill trust in it. Though ridiculed after his colossal failure, scholars and historians of the late 20th century tend to see Law and his theories in a different light. Many see Law not as a failed scammer, but as a forefather of the theories underlying and guiding economic thought around the world in the 20th century, and whose thinking contained many parallels with the Keynesian economic theories.[10]

Indeed, Law was a serious economic thinker and writer. He wrote extensively about money supply and its impact on the economy, and about paper money versus commodity money. In fact, some of his writings sound as if they were written just recently by renowned economists. Law was the first economist to come up with the idea of a paper money system, not because it facilitates transactions, but because it enables the state to easily increase the money supply. He theorized that increasing the money supply would in turn increase economic activity and employment. In his very detailed proposal to the Scottish parliament titled "Money and Trade Considered: With a Proposal for Supplying the Nation with Money" he laid out a system which resembles a modern central bank: "To supply nation with money it is humbly proposed that 40 commissioners be appointed by parliament, answerable to parliament [...] that the commissioners have power to coin notes: which notes will be received in payments."[11] He saw that organization as responsible for the creation, distribution, and management of paper money which would be the money of a nation. Law believed that the increased activity ignited by the new money would also absorb the newly created money, and thus the money creation would not have any inflationary impact. In fact, he was the first economist to use the term "demand for money" in his writings.[12] It is quite accurate to label Law as a kind of founding father of stimulus spending, a practice used excessively by all western central banks in recent years. In his writings, Law saw money as more than just a medium of exchange; he saw it as a product in and of itself. Law truly believed that an expansion in the money supply would achieve positive social goals, like increasing employment and economic prosperity. Law's trial failed miserably. The success of current trials of his theories remains up for debate.

Given the growing popularity of fractional-reserve banking, it comes as no surprise that an opposing view of the impact of money creation via credit emerged. Ludwig von Mises was born in 1881 in the Austro-Hungarian Empire in Galicia, now Lviv, Ukraine. Later he moved to Vienna where he attended the University of Vienna and took classes from the leading Austrian economists of the time. Mises went on to become a post-doctoral student of the Austrian economist Eugen von Böhm-Bawerk. In 1912, he finished his first important book *The Theory of Money and Credit*. In his book he claimed that increases in money supply created through bank credit, i.e. through fractional-reserve banking, not only cause inflation but also significantly contribute to boom and bust business cycles.

Mises, along with his student and future colleague Friedrich A. Hayek developed what's known as the Austrian business cycle theory. According to this theory, business cycles of boom and bust are a result of increases in the money supply. Increases in money supply are both a result of fractional- reserve banking and low interest rates. While fractional reserve banking is a mechanism for money creation, it is low interest rates that motivate borrowers to put this money into use, and borrow it. This newly created money enters the market in the shape of loans taken for activities which otherwise (without the new money) did not make sense since the market wasn't originally willing to allocate resources for these activities. These new undertakings, as we shall see, end up not only taking resources from other parts of the economy, but also creating products the market doesn't really need. If the market had really needed these products they would have been created without the added push of new money and loans.

To understand the above we need to remember that economic activity is the aggregate thoughts, priorities, and actions of millions of individuals and businesses. These aggregate behaviors and preferences translate into pricing, i.e. what people are willing to pay for specific products. This is what Adam Smith, the founder of free market economics, called the price mechanism. Pricing is the means by which the decisions taken by millions of consumers and businesses interact; these aggregate decisions deliver bottom-line critical information without the need to understand or analyze all the information they embody. This bottom-line result comes in the form of pricing, which helps represent the market's preferences given limited resources split between competing options. Pricing is therefore a critical signal which allows individuals and businesses to decode aggregated preferences, and react accordingly in terms of what they will produce, sell, and invest.

Newly created money distorts this critical information by pushing up demand and pricing. New money creates the illusion that more resources are available than actually exist, and thus drives new economic activity. But this new money causes what Mises and Hayek called malinvestments: unneeded investments from the perspective of what the market is really willing to pay for. These false investments, and the activity tied to them creates a boom. The boom is not sustainable, however, because the market is not actually willing to allocate resources for these new activities. Once the newly created money is absorbed in the market, the activities that owe their existences to that new money end, bringing about the bust.

To make this clear let's revert to a simple example which will demonstrate what market information is and how distorted information can lead to unsustainable decisions and false economic activity. A small town has 10,000 residents and three restaurants. Each day an average of 9,500 residents eat at home and 500 eat out, more or less evenly split between the restaurants (around 160 per restaurant). Imagine that a battalion of 300 soldiers comes into town. This battalion has no canteen, so all of the soldiers will be eating at the restaurants in civilian dress such that the townspeople do not know that they are soldiers. The arrival of the battalion is well coordinated with the mayor of the city, who is aware of its existence and plans. Our three restaurant owners, however, have very different connections with city hall. Owner A is the mayor's bother, owner B is a remote relative of the mayor's secretary, and owner C is an old rival of the mayor's because the mayor stole owner C's girlfriend in high school. As the soldiers start coming into town to eat, they start visiting the three restaurants. Around 100 soldiers go to each restaurant, significantly increasing the demand for meals.

90

Now, how will each restaurant owner handle this growing demand? Owner A just met his brother the mayor for drinks last night and was told that these newcomers are nothing more than a battalion visiting town for no more than 3 months. Armed with this knowledge, owner A will probably make very few changes to his restaurant's arrangements. Maybe he will rent the open lot next door, put up a canopy, and bring his wife and sons to help in their free time. Under the canopy he will start selling food targeted at the soldiers at a reduced but still profitable price. He has a 3 month window and he will try to maximize profits with as little investment possible. He will surely not take out bank loans or any other type of large or long-term investments. Owner C interprets the signals from the market in a very different way. He has no idea that the new customers are just temporary guests in town and thinks the new crowds are a result of his new chef's wonderful cooking.

Owner C is so happy he goes to the bank the next day and mortgages out his house for a loan to enlarge the restaurant's seating area and to buy new equipment for the kitchen. He also rushes and hires new employees and invests in training them and even increases the pay of the existing ones. Owner C is even considering pre-buying crops from farmers to insure his food supply for next year. He and his wife are exuberantly happy; life never looked so promising.

Owner B also does not know what is going on. She is a little confused and does nothing. Her regular customers are not happy because the restaurant is now very crowded so she decides to visit her remote relative, the mayor's secretary. She figures that maybe the secretary has heard something. However, visiting a remote relative is not something that happens on a whim, so after a little gift, a little excuse, and four weeks of waiting, the two finally meet and owner B learns that these new guests are soldiers that are probably leaving town soon. By now it's a little late to do anything so owner B decides to close the restaurant to new customers at rush hours seeking to restore and protect her relationship with the loyal patrons. Ten weeks later the battalion leaves town.

Now let's look at each of our restaurant owners. Owner A is definitely happy: he made a bundle while incurring very few expenses and with no real new investment. His canopy restaurant operated by his wife and sons served those temporary customers and his old client base was left intact. Owner C is very unhappy and is on his way to bankruptcy because he misallocated his assets. His house—his main asset—will also be foreclosed on by the bank as he made significant investments under the assumption that the influx signaled a permanent change in demand for his product. Eventually the bank takes over the restaurant and a receiver will be managing it under receivership hoping to recover some of the bank's losses. Owner B is unhappy because of the missed opportunity and the unhappy customers. She will need to work hard to win them back, which will probably result in discounts, happy hours, and other tricks that will be hard on her cash flow.

So what really happened here? The three owners had different information about the increase in demand for their product, and thus they interpreted the market signal—the surge in demand—in very different ways.

Leaving aside the evil mayor, this is essentially what happens when a surge in demand occurs due to a temporary surge in the supply of money. The newly created money creates demand for products and services which in turn ignite a flare of activity known as the boom. But eventually, these activities are not needed based on people's real desires as they are reflected in the pricing mechanism. This flare of activity shrivels away as the new money is absorbed into the economy. The bust comes once the new money is absorbed and the unnecessary swell of activity ends. The cycle brings us to a worse place than we would have been without the injected money because now all those misallocations will be going through a reallocation process, which will mean losses on false investments and people losing their unneeded jobs, as in the case of the investments and employees of restaurant C.

Newly created money doesn't enter the market evenly. For example, if it's in the shape of mortgages, then the entrance point will be around housing. Thus, new money will have different levels of impact on different places and people in the economy. The new money causes prices in the place of entrance to rise, because there is now more money going after the same amount of products. As prices start rising, the participants in that sector misinterpret those price changes as changes in customers' preferences. The misled participants are convinced that it is smart to engage in activities like investment and borrowing that wouldn't have made sense in the "old" price structure, thereby bringing the boom. As the newly created money makes its way through the economy, it shifts priorities, resources, and employment, not because the new activities make sense economically, but because they seem to make sense under the impact of the movement of the new money and the price changes it creates. Eventually if no more new money is created the entire market will adapt to the new quantity of money and new price levels will be established all over. Boom activities will again make no sense and the bust will follow.

But a bust can be due even before the money creation comes to an end as the enhanced activity will eventually lead to overproduction, creating products people do not really need or want, and have no interest in at the newly established price levels. We will see some examples when we take a close look at the events of 2008, when millions of unoccupied houses were built.

The creation of new money has one more significant and painful impact: it arbitrarily selects winners and losers. The hidden power behind the creation of money is its ability to enrich some people and institutions while impoverishing many more others.

Imagine I secretly have a printing press which can print perfect dollar bills. Now let's say that in my town there are 100 houses on sale at a price of $250,000 each. One day I want to buy a house, so I go to my basement and print $250,000. Now I go out to the market and buy a house I like. The price of the home will be $250,000. My kids and siblings also want houses so I repeat this action many times. My whole family now owns houses and they cost us about $250,000 each. But something else has happened as a result of my housing shopping spree. As the amount of money in the market going after a fix number of homes increases (for the sake of this simple example we assumed no new sellers) so does the price of homes. My shopping spree has led to a new price for homes, let's say $300,000. Now I have a $300,000 home, but the people who sold us their homes at $250,000 now have only 83% of the value of a house (250/300). The new money I created made me richer while the people downstream became poorer. This is an intrinsic property of the creation of new money: it makes the people closer to the supply of the new money (typically the rich) richer, and those who are far from it (typically the poor) poorer.

Richard Cantillon was an Irish gentleman who was a close witness to the story of John Law and the French paper money experiment. Not much is known of Cantillon's life, though we do know that he was likely born in Ireland and that he died at the age of 54 as a result of mysterious murder. Cantillon spent most of his adult years as a banker and trader of exotic merchandise. Cantillon's only surviving work was a book he authored in French, *Essay on the Nature of Commerce in General* (*Essai sur la nature du commerce en général*). Even this book was lost and forgotten for many years. In it, Cantillon addressed issues relating to trade and money and was clearly revolutionary in his thoughts and ideas. These included observations on the impact of increased money supply, on the nature of interest, and more.

Following the increase in the amount of gold and silver in the aftermath of the discovery of the Americas, Cantillon pointed out that such increases in silver and gold supply do not affect all prices equally or simultaneously. Rather, Cantillon explained, the place where this money enters the economy will see prices increase first and its effects will ripple through the economy as the money travels through the market. He showed that when money, in the shape of newly discovered gold, enters the market, the prices of goods demanded by gold mine owners will rise first. Cantillon explained that although the money will eventually travel through the whole economy and cause prices to rise all over, the owners of the new money will benefit most in the

94

meantime as they are able to buy first and more "cheaply" with their new money. That is to say, the owners of the new money can buy goods at the old prices before prices increase. Thus, the new money entering the market will, in essence, transfer purchasing power from the owners of "old" money and assets to the owners of the newly created money.

This phenomenon of new money entering the market and impacting money and asset owners differently based on their location in the chain of money movement is known as the Cantillon Effect. It describes the change in prices and the transfer of wealth that occurs in the time between when new money enters the economy and when the entire economy adjusts to that new money through an overall price increase.

The Cantillon Effect: the higher and closer to the
money injection point you are, the better.
Image: Alexander Klink

The Cantillon Effect is one of the key reasons the income gap in America grows in periods of huge growth in money supply. We will examine this closely later when we get back to the messy world of fractional banking and money creation in future chapters. Before that, we will need to jump to 1913 and spend some time with a direct descendant of Palmstruch's Stockholms Banco.

Chapter 6:
The Illegitimate Child: Lender of Last Resort

"It is well enough that people of the nation do not understand our banking and monetary system, for if they did, I believe there would be a revolution before tomorrow morning."

—Henry Ford

If there is one thing that shaped the financial world we live in today it is fractional-reserve banking. We shall therefore make a quick leap forward from 17th-century Stockholm to 20th-century USA and follow how this invention led to the creation and operation of the most powerful financial institution in the world, the Federal Reserve. As we saw in the previous chapter, fractional-reserve banking became a big hit among bankers and depositors alike. We also saw that it inevitably led to bank runs when concerned depositors tried to be first in line to access the relatively small cash reserves banks had in their vaults. As the practice of fractional-reserve banking grew, so did bank runs in terms of both size and frequency. Furthermore, bank runs wreaked havoc on the economy at large due to their ripple effects and disruptions of financial systems since, by this point, banks had already become the veins through which the blood of the economy—money—circulated.

For the bankers, however, bank runs did not make sense. If they had reliable long-term assets—loans owed to them—backed by good collateral that covered their entire outstanding obligation to their depositors, why would banks be vulnerable to the public's random and rare irrational panics? After all, it is just a time gap between the short-term obligations payable on demand to depositors and the long-term obligations from the debtors. This confusion on the part of the bankers, called by them a liquidity problem, brings us to the next chapter in our story, the birth of the Federal Reserve.

The Federal Reserve was one of the last central banks to be set up in the West. The Bank of England already had a 300-year headstart! Nevertheless, within 30-something years of its inception, the Federal Reserve had secured its throne as the most powerful central bank in the world. Our story of how this newcomer became king will begin in New Jersey.

On a dark November evening in 1910, a handful of Wall Street bankers and a prominent US senator quietly gathered at an isolated rail station in New Jersey. Cloaked in anonymity, they boarded private train cars heading south. After two days of travel they arrived at a small beautiful island off the Atlantic shores called Jekyll Island, near the border of Georgia and Florida. There they gathered at a private club frequented by some of the world's wealthiest people. This lavish and secluded club was partially owned by none other than banker J. P. Morgan. In a club cottage on Jekyll Island, the group spent over a week working on a bill that would bring into being the most powerful financial institution in the world and one of the two most powerful institutions in the US. But who were these people? And why did they travel in secrecy by train from New Jersey all the way to southern Georgia to draft a bill that would serve as the foundation of the Federal Reserve?

The meeting's chair, and the person who had summoned the attendees, was a prominent US senator from Rhode Island. Nelson Aldrich (1841 –1915) was for some time the leader of the Republican Party in the Senate, where he served for 30 long years. Aldrich also served on the House Committee of Transportation and Infrastructure and on the Senate Committee on Finance. From his position within the Finance Committee, Aldrich helped create an extensive system of tariffs and taxes that sheltered American manufactures and farmers from overseas competition. He also served as chairman of the National Monetary Commission between 1908 and 1912. While serving in Congress, he became rich from well-made investments in the railroads, rubber and banking. His good fortune was further compounded when his daughter married John D. Rockefeller, Jr., John D. Rockefeller's only son.

Another one of this clandestine gathering's participants was Paul Warburg, a Hamburg native born into a family of bankers. Warburg had married Nina Loeb, the daughter of Solomon Loeb, founder of New York investment firm of Kuhn, Loeb & Co. In 1907, the *New York Times* published Warburg's article "Defects and Needs of Our Banking System." In this article he passionately claimed, "The United States is in fact at about the same point that had been reached by Europe at the time of the Medicis."[1] He argued for a central banking institution that would make it easier for the excess reserves of one bank to bolster the insufficient reserves of another. Warburg concluded the article with this call: "I think we are greatly mistaken if we believe that our country is so entirely different from all others that we should be obliged to continue to do the opposite of what is done by them, while the system of all other important nations has proved to be excellent."

Frank Vanderlip, president of the National City Bank and the previous assistant secretary of the Treasury, was part of the ensemble. Vanderlip's National City Bank, founded in 1812, was one of the first banks in New York and is today known as Citibank, one of the top three largest banks in the US. In 2008, Citibank was, ironically enough, saved from collapse by the Federal Reserve Vanderlip had helped establish nearly a hundred years prior. Henry Davison, too, was part of the group. In 1909, Davidson became a senior partner at J.P. Morgan & Company, a banking partnership founded in New York in 1871. A mere century later, J.P. Morgan would merge with Chase Bank to form JPMorgan Chase & Co., one of the world's largest banks.

There is something about this meeting that sounds inherently off to almost any listener. Negative sentiments towards banks and central banking run deep in American history and culture.

It was no less a figure than Thomas Jefferson who said, "I believe that banking institutions are more dangerous to our liberties than standing armies." Later presidents shared Jefferson's sentiments. Two prior attempts at establishing a central bank in the United States ended in dissolution. The second was the Second Bank of the United States, which existed for twenty years but whose charter President Andrew Jackson refused to renew when the time came to do so. In his veto, Jackson addressed Congress and stated:

> One Congress, in 1791, decided in favor of a bank; another, in 1811, decided against it. One Congress, in 1815, decided against a bank; another, in 1816, decided in its favor. Prior to the present Congress, therefore, the precedents drawn from that source were equal. If we resort to the States, the expressions of legislative, judicial, and executive opinions against the bank have been probably to those in its favor as 4 to 1. There is nothing in precedent, therefore, which, if its authority were admitted, ought to weigh in favor of the act before me.... It is to be regretted that the rich and powerful too often bend the acts of government to their selfish purposes. Distinctions in society will always exist under every just government. Equality of talents, of education, or of wealth cannot be produced by human institutions.... but when the laws undertake to add to these natural and just advantages artificial distinctions, to grant titles, gratuities, and exclusive privileges, to make the rich richer and the potent more powerful, the humble members of society-the farmers, mechanics, and laborers-who have neither the time nor the means of securing like favors to themselves, have a right to complain of the injustice of their Government. There are no necessary evils in government. Its evils exist only in its abuses. If it would confine itself to equal protection, and, as Heaven does its rains, shower its favors alike on the high and the low, the rich and the poor, it would be an unqualified blessing. In the act before me there seems to be a wide and unnecessary departure from these just principles."[2]

Despite the prevailing hostility towards banks and a central banking system, the bankers and their supporters found the matter of setting up a central bank of utmost importance and urgency. As we previously saw, fractional-reserve banking has one big flaw: the seldom yet irrational behavior (in the eyes of bankers) of panicked depositors demanding their money all at once, causing bank runs and market-wide banking crises. One crisis in particular led to the meeting on Jekyll Island and to the US's third central banking initiative.

The crisis, known as the Panic of 1907, threatened to bring Wall Street to its knees. It all began with a benign and seemingly insignificant event unrelated to banking. The story begins with an attempt by a few marginal stock market players at manipulating one copper company's share price.

In the hills of Montana, a gentleman by the name Fritz Heinze had made himself a little fortune from mining copper. In 1907, Heinze felt he could do better and moved to New York with the hope of entering the financial markets. Heinze was smart and charismatic and he quickly opened his company's office, United Copper, not far from Wall Street, where his company's shares were traded. While in New York, Heinze formed a close relationship with a notorious Wall Street businessman and speculator named Charles Morse. Morse owned, controlled, and sat on the board of quite a few banks and insurance companies. These institutions included the National Bank of North America, the New Amsterdam National Bank, and the Mercantile National Bank. At the same time, Heinze's two brothers, Otto and Arthur, established a brokerage firm. Together, they came up with an audacious idea that would unwittingly trigger the massive financial collapse known as the Panic of 1907, and in turn lead to the meeting at Jekyll Island three years later.

The idea was much simpler to understand than to execute. In the stock market, people buy and sell stocks. On top of this, people can also sell stock they don't really have. This action is called a "short" wherein the seller "borrows" the stock he doesn't own but wants to sell from another player in the market who does own such stock. Then, the seller sells the stock at the market's current price. After a certain period of time, the seller needs to "return" the stock he borrowed and thus goes to the market and buys back the stock so he can "cover his short." If the price of the stock goes down between when he sells the (borrowed) stock and when he buys it from the market, then he makes a profit. His profit is the balance between what he sold the "borrowed" stock for (let's say 4 weeks ago at the price of $50/share) and what he buys the stock at now to cover that short (let's say today at a dropped price of $45/share). So, if the price of the stock goes down, he makes a profit (in this example $5/share) and if it goes up he loses, since he would need to buy back the stock at a higher price than he sold it for.

Otto Heinze, the broker, came up with an idea to make some quick money. To start off, he believed that there was a sizable amount of short positions on the market for their United Copper Company. His idea was simple: push the price of the shares up rapidly and thereby force those holding short positions to buy shares frantically in order to cover their shorts, fearful that the rising price will make their short losses even greater. This is known as a *short squeeze*. This rush to buy stocks further drives up the cost of the shares. But because the Heinze family owns the majority of the company stock, the traders in the short positions will be forced to come to the Heinze brothers to purchase shares to cover their shorts. These shares will of course be sold at the new much higher price and the brothers will make a big profit.

In order to finance their plot, the Heinze brothers needed money to create demand and drive up the initial price. So the brothers and Charles Morse met with Charles Barney, one of Morse's old business colleagues. Barney, who had financed some of Morse's previous financial ventures, was the president of one of New York's largest trust companies, the Knickerbocker Trust, which held large individual and corporation deposits.

On Monday, October 14, Otto Heinze started aggressively buying shares of United Copper. As planned, the price shot up 25% from its beginning price of $30 a share. The next day the price moved up an additional 20%, eventually reaching $60 a share at its peak. The ploy, however, wasn't working; apparently there was enough supply in the market for the interested short positions. By Wednesday, only three days later, the share price fell down to $10. This drop triggered a chain reaction: by the end of the week, Otto's brokerage firm went bankrupt and his trading license was revoked. The value of United Copper shares dropped to almost nothing, causing the collapse of the State Savings Bank of Butte, Montana, which used United Copper stock as collateral against large loans to the company. Once the connection between the plotters and Mercantile National Bank came to light, depositors feared that the collapse would spread to this institution as well.

This fear spawned one of those "irrational" moments in a big way. Since every depositor wanted to be first at the bank to access the limited cash on hand at the Mercantile National Bank, a run on the bank was unfolding. The panic spread quickly to other banks associated with Morse such as the National Bank of North America and the New Amsterdam National. By Monday, October 21, just a week after it all began, the board of the Knickerbocker Trust demanded Charles Barney's resignation. The pressure from depositors was mounting from every direction. On the following day, this pressure turned into a flood. At the time, the *New York Times* described it as such: "as fast as a depositor went out of the place ten people and more came asking for their money." One more day passed and the Knickerbocker Trust was forced to suspend its operations. The panic started to spread across the financial market. Before another week could pass, over a dozen of the largest trusts and banks closed. It seemed that nothing could stop the total collapse of Wall Street and of all major US financial institutions.

Just when all seemed lost there was still one last card up history's sleeve. Mr. John Pierpont, "J.P." Morgan. Born in 1837, J. P. Morgan spent all his adult life in banking and business. He specialized in turnarounds and mergers. The biggest of them was the creation of U.S. Steel, the first billion-dollar company in the world. In 1892, he oversaw the merger of Edison General Electric and the Thomson-Houston Electric Company into what would be known as General Electric, or GE. By 1907, Morgan was New York's most prominent banker, and the president of J.P. Morgan. He was also one of the city's wealthiest and most connected individuals. When pressure started to mount at the door steps of the Trust Company of America, he decided to draw a line in the sand. Morgan brought together bankers and industrialists who could assure the Trust Company of America's liquidity in the face of ongoing and mounting pressure from depositors. To his dismay, even the bankers' and industrialists massive deposits did not manage to calm the public.

On October 24th, just 10 days after Otto Heinze initiated his scheme, the panic reached the doorstep of the New York Stock Exchange. There was now a prominent danger threatening the existence of brokerage firms and other financial institutions. The market plummeted by 40%, and two frantic days passed during which J. P. Morgan raised funds to keep the exchange afloat. The money reserves Morgan managed to collect were not bottom-less; so on the critical weekend of October 27, 1907, God was called upon to help. The bankers asked the clergy to calm their communities during the Sunday mass. They also tried to enlist the press to help calm the public. Furthermore, the New York Clearing House issued $100 million in certificates for use in interbank trading that Monday. These certificates created more money to meet depositors' requests at the institutions facing the greatest pressure. With the help of the press, the clergy, and the newly created money, the city started to calm down.

But the crisis was far from over. It also required an all-night conference in J. P. Morgan's home where more than 100 bankers and trust company managers had to be persuaded to contribute funds. The bankers' contributions together with Morgan's con-nections with U.S. Steel allowed for the finalization of a deal that would enable liquidity for the trust companies and save one of the major exchange's brokerage firms from collapsing. The following day barely an hour before the stock market opened, President

Theodore Roosevelt met J. P. Morgan's confidants in the White House and agreed to put aside the Sherman Antitrust Act in order to allow one aspect of the complex deal to go through (U.S. Steel bought the iron and railroad companies, whose shares served as collateral in the major exchange's brokerage firms). With this, things calmed down and calamity was narrowly avoided.

Following the Panic of 1907, Congress formed the National Monetary Commission whose purpose was the investigation of the causes and suggesting prospective solutions for the financial crisis. At the head of this commission sat Senator Nelson Aldrich. The Commission issued more than 30 reports. Its final report was published on January 11, 1911. Considering Senator Aldrich's background, confidants, affiliation, and advisors, it should come as no surprise that the commission never seriously considered a solution to the problem of bank liquidity that would move away from fractional-banking practices. Excessive lending, after all, was the heart and soul of modern banking and the source of most of its revenue.

Keep in mind that although bankers like to claim that fractional banking is a necessary source of liquidity for the market in general, this idea should not be blindly accepted and endorsed. Leaving aside any transition period from the current system, there is no proof that the economy necessarily needs a set amount of money to operate. Of course, if gold is money and there is only one ounce of gold in the entire world, or if paper is money and there is only one bill in the entire world, then it would be practically impossible to operate any money-based system because there would not be enough of it to physically distribute the currency so it could function as a means of exchange. If money is, however, a fixed and unchangeable quantity of papers, then it does not really matter if there are a billion or a trillion of them in circulation. As long as the papers are a simple measure of account with enough units (notes) available, their value will always and only be determined by the amount of goods these papers are representing and not by the actual physical quantity of those papers.

The liquidity claim made by bankers and supporters of fractional-reserve banking assumes that the economy demands constant money creation in the shape of bank loans in order to advance. But this money, borrowed from the future and created by issuing loans for more money than currently exists, has to be returned. Thus the reigning assumption is that the returns earned on such money—the investments—will generally create more wealth than the combination of the loans, the interest, and cost of managing the loaning activities and process, i.e. the cost to the banks. Furthermore, the idea that the economy needs fractional-reserve banking loans also assumes no setbacks that would offset whatever possible value that such borrowing from the future might generate. These two assumptions are questionable when calculating broad long-term averages. Their soundness also comes into question when closely examining the damages resulting from bank runs and the devastation created by boom-and-bust cycles, both of which are direct results of fractional-reserve banking and of its attending demand for the creation of money through loans. Keep in mind that, as we saw in previous chapters, the practice of loaning significantly predates fractional-reserve banking so what is in question here is not the loaning as an institution but the acceleration thereof via fractional-reserve banking.

Given what we have learned, it should also come as no surprise that bankers' conclusion from the Panic of 1907 was that the US needed to create a government-backed bank which could provide funds to private banks when they come under pressure from depositors. The establishment of a permanent government institution legitimated and reified J. P. Morgan's ad hoc solution to the 1907 crisis. Knowing Americans' healthy distrust of elected officials and their long-standing disdain for the banking industry in general and the idea of a central bank in particular, the bankers had to craft a masterful plan to accomplish their goal. It would take more than a very sympathetic political ally, in the form of Senator Aldrich, to get this initiative— which was as much self-serving as it was unwanted by the public—passed. The bankers would have to build support, manipulate information and education, and carefully persuade the members of Congress to vote as desired.

The National Monetary Commission was one platform for such education. This government initiative slowly built the case for a central bank by engaging in studies, events, and public speeches, and recruiting the support of the *Wall Street Journal* to spread the message. The efforts seemed to be successful and the time seemed right to put a bill before Congress. Senator Aldrich, however, wanted the help and assurance of Wall Street before drafting an actual detailed bill and formulating the institution. This desire brings us back to the strange trip to Jekyll Island in the winter of 1910. At the club on Jekyll Island, after nine days of deliberation, the group of top bankers and Senator Aldrich had put together a "reform plan" for the creation of a government-sponsored central bank. The plan was to be entered into the National Monetary Commission's conclusions regarding the Panic of 1907. Years later, Jekyll Island participant Frank Vanderlip, president of the National City Bank at the time, proudly recalled:

Since it would be fatal to Senator Aldrich's plan to have it known that he was calling on anybody from Wall Street to help him [...] precautions were taken. [...] Discovery, we knew, simply must not happen, or else all our time and efforts would be wasted. If it were to be exposed publicly that our particular group had got together and written a banking bill, that bill would have no chance whatever of passage by Congress.[3]

Given the unpopularity of bankers and general public's wariness, the name of the institution would have to avoid the word *bank* altogether. *Federal Reserve System* sounded much more innocent, a system created and funded "by the banks and for the banks." In the words of the National Monetary Commission: "It is not a bank, but a cooperative union of all the banks in the country for definite purposes and with very limited and clearly defined functions." Hence through lies and deception would the most powerful institution in the US economy be born.

However, the proposal's wording was changed over the course of its transition from proposal to law. In the end, in spite of its name or ownership (originally officially owned by the banks), the Federal Reserve was an institution which functioned almost exactly like a central bank, with significant control over the nation's monetary issues and under the pervasive influence of private financial institutions. Furthermore, for the Fed's first fourteen years, the organization's de facto governor was none other than J. P. Morgan's representative at Jekyll Island, Benjamin Strong.

It took three years for the Federal Reserve Act to pass in Congress, but not before one last twist. During the November 1912 elections, the Democratic Party was strongly opposed to the "so-called Aldrich bill for the establishment of a central bank." Once Democrat Woodrow Wilson won the presidency and the party gained majorities in both chambers of Congress, however, it seemed to forget its staunch resistance. The politicians now in power settled for a few changes to the original bill mainly surrounding the position and manner of election to the Federal Reserve Board. Finally, on December 23, 1913, the Federal Reserve Act became law and brought a fourth branch of government into existence, one arguably second in power only to the executive branch.

The new law established a Federal Reserve System and its accompanying 12 regional branches. All large national banks were required to join and deposit a defined amount of money, interest free, at the local reserve branch. This money—the reserve—was intended for transfer and use in case of an emergency run on a member bank. The system was headed by the Federal Reserve Board appointed by the president and confirmed by the Senate. Under section 11 of the law, the Federal Reserve would receive a long list of authorizations including control over the banking system and far-reaching rights over member banks (initially, local small banks were not forced to join). These rights included control over interest rates for transactions between member banks, which translated to de facto control of national interest rates.

Though it was formed as a result of the Panic of 1907 and though its main objective was the prevention of similar crises, the Federal Reserve System failed miserably less than two decades later. Between 1930 and 1933, some 2,359 national banks, some 45% of such banks, all of which were members of the Federal Reserve System—closed their doors. In addition, about 7,000 state banks were forced to close,[4] adding to the agony and escalating the Great Depression.[5] Ben Bernanke, future chairman of the Board of Governors of the Federal Reserve, also acknowledged in late 2002, "Let me end my talk by abusing slightly my status as an official representative of the Federal Reserve. I would like to say to Milton and Anna: Regarding the Great Depression. You're right, we did it. (The two had made the claim that the Federal Reserve's inaction had a significant role in the escalation of the Great Depression). We're very sorry. But thanks to you, we won't do it again."[6] Little did Bernanke know that just six short years later he would be called upon to honor this commitment by pulling multiple trillions of dollars out of thin air.

As the years went on, the power of the Federal Reserve (hereafter referred to as the Fed) shifted away from the hands of the bankers and into the hands of the government. This outcome was, in fact, planned: the banks were free to continue taking huge risks with fractional-reserve banking and other leveraged activities while the government (and, in turn, taxpayers) absorbed more and more of this risk by setting up safety nets for the banks, which made taking even bigger risks even more tempting. In 1933, complementary legislation was put in place. The Banking Act set up the Federal Deposit Insurance Corporation (FDIC), a government-owned-and-run agency which ensures the return of deposits in cases of bank bankruptcy. This government guarantee is capped at a certain amount, one that is periodically updated by the government. As of 2013, this cap is set at $250,000 per account per bank. The creation of the FDIC signaled a significant change in the relationship between banks and the general public, transferring a sizable portion of the risks of and responsibility for fractional-reserve banking from the profiting banks to taxpayers' pockets.

Given the removal of significant barriers to risk-taking behavior with the establishment of the Fed and the FDIC, it should come as no surprise that banks went on to drop the reserve ratio even lower. In 1893, when banks were actually held accountable for their lending risks, the reserve ratio in the US and Canada was typically between 22-25%. In the UK, on the other hand, where a "lender of last resort" was already in place, the Bank of England, the reserve ratio was around 15%. By 1923, after the establishment of the Federal Reserve System, the US reserve ratios had already shrunk to half their size, settling at around 13%. By 1953, this number dropped to around 7% and by 1993 sank down to a mere 5%.[7] On the eve of the 2008 crisis, the reserve ratio of financial institutions in the mortgage market was as low as 1.5% (Freddie Mac), 3% (Brokers/hedge funds) and 4.6% (Fanny Mae).[8] In November 2014, the FDIC set the reserve ratio requirement to be between 4% to 10% depends on the size and type of bank.[9]

The Federal Reserve Act has been amended many times since 1913, granting the Fed even more powers and responsibilities including "maximum employment" and "stable prices."[10] The Fed's control of the money supply functions as its main tool for achieving these goals. Until 2009, the Fed's main instrument for executing monetary policy was its ability to control interest rates.

To understand the money supply mechanism and the process of setting interest rates, we need to dive a little deeper into the Fed's inner workings and its balance sheet. It is much simpler than it may seem. When the Fed was set up in 1913, the US was using the gold standard which meant that dollar notes issued by the Federal Reserve were convertible upon demand into gold. Thus these dollar bills were booked in the Fed's balance sheet as liabilities, because of its commitment to pay holders of the notes in gold. The amount of dollars the Fed could print was limited by the fact that it had to keep a gold reserve equal to 40% of the money in circulation. In 1946, the reserve percentage fell to 25%. At the same time, all banks are required by the law to maintain a certain percentage of their overall assets as cash reserves at the Fed. These reserves deposited at local Fed branches were also booked as Fed liabilities as they belonged to the banks. The combination of dollar bills, banks' reserve deposits, and coins issued to the Treasury constituted the monetary base. When a member bank would request Federal Reserve notes (i.e. dollars) for its customers, the Fed would ship them and debit that institution's Fed account for those dollar notes. The Fed's balance sheet would reflect this transaction: the notes (dollars) were a Fed liability—to the holders of the notes—and the same amount was deducted from the Fed's liabilities as recorded on that institution's Fed account, corresponding to the money in bills the bank received.

When, in 1968, the US abandoned entirely any linkage to gold, the recording of transactions on the Fed's balance sheet did not change, even though the Fed's liabilities became meaningless as there was no longer any conversion commitment to maintain. As strange as it may seem, from then on, the Fed's "liability" would be to pay for dollar bills with other dollar bills. Dollar bills, are recorded as liabilities on the Fed's balance sheet to this day. After the enactment of the *Gold Reserve Requirements Elimination Act* of 1968, there were no limits on the Fed's ability to increase the monetary base, which grew from $69 billion in November 1968 to $873 billion on the eve of the 2008 crisis. Up to then, the notes the Fed issued were the largest liability line on the Fed's balance sheet.[11] This monetary base growth and increased the money supply in the market significantly and also expanded the Fed's balance sheet.

Over time, the Fed started to use the money it received for the dollar notes to buy treasury bonds, i.e. IOUs by the federal government. These too became assets on the Fed's balance sheet.

But unlike any other balance sheet, this one's assets are created at will when the Fed prints bills and "charges" member banks for them, or when it lends money to bank members by crediting their reserve accounts with a simple book entry. On the eve of the 2008 crisis, the Fed's balance sheet comprised: total Assets numbering $869 billion, of which Treasury securities $791 billion; and total liabilities $836 billion of which $775 billion Federal Reserve notes (i.e. dollars in circulation).[12]

Due to the way the Fed's money creation mechanism works, there is no limit to how much this balance sheet can expand and the amount of money the Fed can create practically from thin air. This became very clear in 2009 when the Fed increased its balance sheet from less than $1 trillion to more than $4 trillion by 2014, via its QE—Quantity Easing—programs.

When the Fed wants to lower interest rates by increasing the money supply it "buys" assets, i.e. bonds or other securities, from the Treasury or member banks, or to be more precise, it lends the Treasury or member banks money. When the Fed wants to reduce the money supply, it sells those assets typically to member banks, thus sucking money out of the market. This buying and selling is called an open market operation (OMO) and its goal is to reduce or increase the money supply, thereby impacting short-term interest. The Fed has other tools to impact the money supply and interest rates, mainly increasing or reducing the reserve requirement for member banks; changing the discount rate—the rate it charges for loans it issues to member banks; changing the federal fund rate—the rate at which member banks lend overnight balances. The bottom line is pretty simple: since 1968 the Fed can easily increase the amount of money in the economy. Its balance sheet has little real meaning: its liabilities are not really liabilities and its assets are not really assets, they are just means of increasing or theoretically decreasing the money supply, and a face of such increases. As then Governor Ben Bernanke vividly depicted: "the balance sheet of the central bank should be of marginal relevance at best." (Tokyo, May 31, 2003)

Keep in mind, all money supply increases are created via debt instruments, and all such increases expand via the fractional-reserve banking mechanism and thus constantly increase the economy's debt load. As newly created money comes in the form of debt instruments—generated by the banks and issued to people and organizations taking on debt—the interest rate effectively controls the volume of new money created. When the interest rate is low, more people or organizations find debt attractive which leads to an increase in the money supply. Conversely, when the interest rate is high, people are less willing to take on debt, which leads to a slowdown in money creation.

In its century of existence, the Federal Reserve has become more powerful and significantly more influential than Congress, at least when it comes to the US economy. Keep in mind that no member of the Fed is elected and none of its actions are subject to policy hearings, accountability reviews, or audits. This is the state of affairs despite the fact that in Article 1, Section 8 of the US constitution, all money-related powers are specifically granted to Congress, including: "To coin money, regulate the value thereof." Yet today, so mammoth is the Federal Reserve's clout that even one of the House leaders, Democratic Whip Steny Hoyer, willingly relinquished even the mere idea of Congressional oversight of this branch of government, stating "I agree with Chairman Bernanke that Congressional review of the Fed's monetary policy decisions would be a 'nightmarish' scenario."[13]

In 2008, excessive and reckless lending practices caused the largest financial crisis since the Great Depression. Almost all of the US's large financial institutions were on the verge of collapse. As a result, the Federal Reserve issued over a $1.5 trillion bailout of Wall Street via various assistance programs. The Fed's behavior in the wake of the 2008 crisis effectively forced the public to take on all the risks of fractional-reserve banking yet left the bankers with their notoriously excessive financial compensation. Andrew Huszar—the man responsible for the management of the first Fed's Quantitative Easing program, which ran from 2009 to 2010—shared some reflections on the program:

I can only say: I'm sorry, America. As a former Federal Reserve official, I was responsible for executing the centerpiece program of the Fed's first plunge into the bond-buying experiment known as quantitative easing. The central bank continues to spin QE as a tool for helping Main Street. But I've come to recognize the program for what it really is: the greatest backdoor Wall Street bailout of all time.[14]

Thus, a century later, the gathering in Jekyll Island achieved its ultimate goal: the public holds the risks, and the bankers the bonuses. In 2011, the Government Accountability Office published the first ever review of the Federal Reserve.[15] In a 239-page report that is as hard to follow as it is soft in tone, some facts came to light. One such fact was that the Federal Reserve had been providing billions of dollars in financial assistance to foreign banks and corporations for years. One beneficiary was the Arab Bank Corporation, an entity partly owned by the Libyan Central Bank. Another interesting discovery was that the Federal Reserve had provided conflict of interest waivers to its employees and private contractors so the Federal Reserve could continue making emergency loans to institutions connected to these insiders. For example, the CEO of JP Morgan Chase served on the board of directors of the New York Fed at the same time that his bank received more than $390 billion in financial assistance from the Fed. Furthermore, a press release issued by Vermont Senator Bernie Sanders's office in July 21, 2011 noted:

The Fed outsourced virtually all of the operations of their emergency lending program to private contractors like JP Morgan Chase, Morgan Stanley, and Wells Fargo. These same firms also received billions of dollars in Fed loans at near-zero interest rates. Altogether, some two-thirds of the contracts that the Fed awarded to manage its emergency lending programs were no-bid contracts.

In July 2012, Congressman Ron Paul (R) introduced a bill requiring a full audit of the Board of Governors of the Federal Reserve System and the Federal Reserve banks by the Controller General of the United States before the end of 2012. The bill passed the House of Representatives with bipartisan majority of more than two thirds (327:98). The Senate majority leader Harry Reid (D) vowed that the bill would not be put up to vote in the Senate, and, indeed, it never was.

In the aftermath of the financial crises of 2008 the Fed has presided over the greatest exercise of money creation in history. Through its three QE programs, the Fed has orchestrated the creation of almost $4 trillion. This flood of money was largely the result of two Fed actions: the purchase of treasury securities and of mortgage-backed securities. The purchase of treasury securities entails creating money and "lending" it to the federal government. As of late 2014, the Fed has lent around $2.4 trillion to the government in this way. Buying mortgage-backed securities means basically buying mortgages from banks. As of late 2014, the Fed has purchased around $1.6 trillion worth of such securities.[16]

The Fed's policy of purchasing government debt with money created by the Fed—since, after all, the Fed has no money, only the power to create it—has pushed down interest rates dramatically. (Technically, the Fed "paid" for those securities by crediting member banks' reserve accounts, as explained in detail above when reviewing the Fed's balance sheet). In fact, the interest on government debt (treasury bills and bonds) has sunk to literally zero. As of November 2014, the rate on 12-month treasury bills was 0.1%, and the yield, i.e. interest on 10-year Treasury notes (government bonds of 10 years) had hit a 200-year low.

From 2009 through most of 2014 the Federal Reserve has been committed to the continued creation of billions of dollars every month, fueling some increases in housing prices and significant stock market activity in some segments of the tech market in particular, making 1999's infamous tech bubble pale in comparison. This dramatic increase in stock market prices was not merely an expected consequence but rather one of the goals of the Fed's post-2008 program. In a 2014 speech, Fed Vice Chairman Stanley Fischer said, "While the Fed's asset purchases were composed wholly of Treasury [...] securities, the program also aimed to boost the prices of riskier assets."[17]

Following the Fed's money creation programs other central banks rushed to print money, devaluing their currencies and hoping to ignite some economic activity. Since 2008, the major central banks in the world have created some $10 trillion under the pretense that money creation would reignite their respective economies and prevent unemployment and economic slowdown. As we saw in previous chapters and will examine in detail later, money creation, especially in the form of government spending, has positive economic effects only in the short term while inflicting longer term damages and exacting a social price. So although stock prices have almost tripled since 2009, this growth has overwhelmingly benefited Wall Street and the top 1%. Main Street meanwhile has not experienced the same economic prosperity: high unemployment and a drop in labor participation are ongoing, salary incomes are eroding, and prices are rising. Food prices alone have grown by at least 20% since 2008.[18] It should therefore come as no surprise that as of November 2014 an average of 7 national polls show that a record number of Americans—more than 66%—feel that the country is on the "wrong track."

We will get back to the events of 2008 and to the Federal Reserve's part in its creation and aftermath. For now, we will return to where we left off in chapter 5: the 1800s and the days after the creation of paper money.

Chapter 7:
A Sabre Dance—Gold and Paper

"You have to choose between trusting to the natural stability of gold and the natural stability of the honesty and intelligence of the members of the government. And, with due respect to these gentlemen, I advise you, as long as the capitalist system lasts, to vote for gold."
—George Bernard Shaw[1]

In this chapter we will closely examine how paper money in a period of just a few hundred years came to replace the 5,000 years old metal coins, and became the world's most common means of exchange.

As we saw, from early days coins were made up of gold, silver, and copper. Each of these metals had its strengths and weaknesses when it came to volume, weight, and obtainability. Silver turned out to be the metal of choice: it didn't weigh too much, it was fairly available but not too available, and its volume allowed it to be small enough to pocket. Thus, silver emerged as the most commonly used material for coin making. A pound of silver became one of the first currencies as early as 775 AD. A pound of sterling silver, split up into 240 silver pennies, was the currency of the early Anglo-Saxon Kingdom. Though silver became most common for coin creation, gold was far from obsolete. Gold's rarity and beauty made it perfect for creating precious jewelry. Its condensed volume—a gallon of gold weighs around 160 pounds—made it perfect for large transactions, wealth preservation, and international trade. The debate over which should be used for money, and the tensions related to conversion rates between the two, would persist into the beginning of the 20th century.

117

From kings to presidents, rulers used silver coins for several reasons. Coins served as publicity platforms for regimes, both because they physically portrayed leaders and were engraved with governmental mottoes; they generated revenue for leaders from minting services; and they provided a handsome commission for the "seal of approval" inherently included within the minting process. On occasion, rulers also mined the silver content of the coins, debasing the coins and pocketing the difference. The shortcomings of coins, however, presented challenges that required innovation. Coin variety and the inconvenience of carrying coins and exchanging them, especially for larger trades, led to the invention of exchange banks. The exchange bank, the first of which opened in January 1609 in Amsterdam, was a place where merchants could deposit coins and get unified assessments of their value as well as a note of deposit. This promissory note symbolized the bank's commitment to return the amount of the deposit to the depositor when the latter should wish to retrieve it. Later this note started being called a banknote. Many times, the note was addressed to the depositor or the "bearer," a designation that allowed the notes—as well as the money they represented—to exchange hands without requiring the transfer of the physical money they represented. These notes were in fact the first form of paper money in Europe.

Given the growth in popularity of fractional-reserve banking in the 1700s, the quantity of banknotes grew significantly. The notes were denominated in the currency that represented the redeemable value of such a note: 10 pound sterling was redeemable for 10 pounds of silver. Obviously, the value of the notes fluctuated in terms of their purchasing power, just like the value of the metal they represented did. If the amount of gold or silver in circulation grew, due to the mining of new deposits, for example, then the price of silver or gold went down in terms of the product they could purchase. The greater the quantity of metal available the greater the quantity necessary for the purchase of products. Such was the case in the late 1500s when Spain found and mined huge amount of silver from Cerro de Potosí—also referred to as the Cerro Rico (Rich Mountain)—in what is now Bolivia. So much silver was mined that silver deposits in Europe increased by as much as 50% over the course of 150 years. This flood drove down the value of silver. This drop in turn drove up the prices of products. Conversely, if the amount of silver in circulation were to decline, typically due to hoarding or supply interruptions, the value/price of silver money would go up and thus the prices of goods would decline (when the price of money goes up less of it is needed to buy goods—this effect is known as deflation). Such a scenario arose in the mid-1700s when the Seven Years' War, which involved all the great European powers of the time, caused a severe shortage of gold, and hence a price decline. This shortage led the Bank of England to print the first 10-pound denominated note.[2]

After the execution of Charles I in 1649, England was de facto a republic. However, in 1660, after the death of Oliver Cromwell, the monarchy was restored but with much less power, control, and influence over Parliament. The restored king, Charles II, was no longer allowed to freely levy and collect taxes, but rather was granted by Parliament an annual budget to run his government. This condition led to constant deficits financed by loans mainly from individual goldsmiths. The constant deficits eventually led to the bankruptcy of the monarch in 1672, an event dubbed the Stop of the Exchequer.

A better solution for financing government deficits had to be found. Twenty years later, in 1694, William III urgently needed money to finance his wars in Europe. As a result, the crown was granted a loan of 1.2 million pounds by a group of wealthy individuals. In return, the parliament and crown granted the group a charter to set up the Company of the Bank of England. The company was allowed to operate as a limited-liability organization held by its shareholders. The charter and mission of the company, at this stage, were mainly to raise money to finance the wars in Europe. Shortly after its establishment, the bank started to take deposits and issue notes in return, making commitments to pay the bearers of the notes their value in gold on demand.

This promise made these notes a popular means of exchange. The notes of deposit were written by hand on the bank's paper for the sum of the precise deposit and signed by one of the bank's clerks. Over time and to simplify redemption, the notes were made for a set sum, initially of 50 pounds, a very large amount of money in those days. In 1725, the bank started to partially print the notes, reducing the work for the cashier accepting the deposit. It was not until 1853 that a fully preprinted note came into use. Though the bank's notes became legal tender—money legally accepted for payment of taxes and debts—in 1833, it was only in 1844 that the bank became the semi-exclusive issuer of banknotes in Britain. Still, private banknotes lasted until 1921.[3]

The Bank of England continued to operate as a privately owned entity as late as 1946, when it was nationalized. Its influence extended far beyond the country's borders: by the 1800s, more and more sovereigns were following England's lead and granting single organizations the exclusive right to print notes and accept these notes as legal tender. As time went on, the quantity of notes exceeded the actual amount of gold and silver they presumably represented, making it impossible to fully convert all notes at the same time into gold or silver as promised and stated on the notes. Still complete *simultaneous* convertibility was never put to the test, and thus the Bank of England and other European national banks flourished. As a result, the notes issued by these central banks, which represented a conversion commitment on the part of these national financial institutions, became the most commonly used form of money.

The trend spread to England's colony in North America. In 1690, the Massachusetts Bay Colony issued the first paper money note in America. The paper notes were declared acceptable for paying taxes and other public payments. Other colonies soon began issuing their own paper currency, usually referred to as Spanish milled dollars.[4]

In June 1775, the Continental Congress approved the issue of $3 million in notes, nicknamed *continentals*, to pay for the expenses of the Revolutionary War. More money was issued later, totaling more than $200 million. The massive inflow of printed continentals caused their value to plummet. Between 1777 and 1779, the continentals lost almost 99% of their value and in turn eradicated the wealth of those in possession thereof. Benjamin Franklin observed "this currency as we manage it, is a wonderful machine. [...] It pays and clothes the troops, and provides victuals and ammunition, and [...] it pays itself off by depreciation." Franklin labeled this money depreciation a "gradual tax."[5] This miserable experience with paper money no doubt contributed to the inclusion of article 1, section 10, clause 1 of the US Constitution, which states: "No State shall [...] coin Money; emit Bills of Credit; make any Thing but gold and silver Coin a Tender in Payment of Debts."

In 1792, Congress passed the Coinage Act, establishing an official mint. In the lead-up to the passage of this act, Congress also affirmed the dollar as the country's legal tender and defined the exact amount of silver in a dollar and the conversion rate between gold and silver. With this act, the dollar became a dual—silver and gold-based—currency.

The 1700s witnessed another revolution, second only to the Neolithic Revolution, ten thousand years prior. This revolution would change the world in unimaginable ways: the Industrial Revolution, a period that entirely changed how we interact with the world around us.

The Industrial Revolution, like the Neolithic Revolution, changed everything. The steam-powered engine and subsequent inventions based around steam technology increased productivity and food production dramatically and in turn considerably improved standards of living. This advancement, like that ensured by the Neolithic Revolution, also created the conditions for huge population growth all over the world. From 1700 to 1900, the world's population almost tripled, going from around 662 million to 1.65 billion. This growth easily eclipses the 33% population growth of the 200 years prior to the Industrial Revolution. In Europe, the heart of the Industrial Revolution, the population rose even more significantly. In Great Britain, the population multiplied more than four-fold, from around 8 million to around 38. This growing population was also better fed and lived longer; between 1700 and 1890, life expectancy in Britain went from around 35 to around 48 years old. The average Briton's height also rose: from 1.61 to 1.68 meters.[6] This huge spike in production output, population, and efficiency of transportation brought about an unprecedented increase in trade and economic activity.

This newfound economic prosperity was far more pronounced in Europe and North America than in the rest of the world. As a result, the two continents leaped forward economically, thereby opening a huge gap between them and the rest of the world. While the GDP per capita ratio between the UK and China stood at 2:1 in 1700 (the UK's to China's was $1250 to $600, respectfully, in 1900 international dollars), by 1900 this ratio grew to 8:1 ($4492 vs. $545). Note also that the GDP per capita in China declined by 10% while Britain's grew 350%. Other European counties experienced similar changes as well. Germany's per capita GDP grew 3.2-fold and France's 3.1, to around $2900 per capita. The rest of the world, however, saw much slower growth in much lower absolute numbers. Brazil's GDP per capita in 1900 was $678, representing a growth of only 150% since 1700. Japan's GDP per capita grew two-fold to $1180, resting at about 40% of France and Germany's per capita GDP and only 28% of that of the USA. The US, which was able and willing to exploit its significant natural resources, had the highest per capita GDP growth rate in this period. Over the course of two centuries it multiplied almost 8 times, going from $527 in 1700 to $4091 by 1900.[7] This gap between Europe and the US and the rest of the world came to be known as the Great Divergence.

These jumps in both population and per capita GDP made Europe the center of the global economy. Britain was at its helm as the financial and military powerhouse of the world.

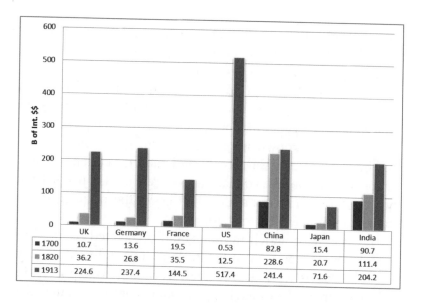

	UK	Germany	France	US	China	Japan	India
■ 1700	10.7	13.6	19.5	0.53	82.8	15.4	90.7
■ 1820	36.2	26.8	35.5	12.5	228.6	20.7	111.4
■ 1913	224.6	237.4	144.5	517.4	241.4	71.6	204.2

The Great Divergence.
1820-1913 while the UK GDP grew 6.2 fold, Germany's 8.8 and the USA by a factor of 41. China's GDP remained unchanged; India's grew by a factor of 1.8 and Japan's by 4.6.
Source: Angus Maddison, *Contours of the World Economy, 1–2030 AD.*

Over the course of this Great Divergence, gold and silver were the base of money, and paper money wherever used would be fully convertible to the gold or silver upon demand.

As we briefly mentioned, in 1792, US Congress formally affirmed the dollar as the legal tender and defined the amount of gold and silver to be minted into each of the coins. Thus, both gold and silver were used as the bases of the currency. The ratio of silver to gold was set at 1:15. During the War of 1812, the treasury issued notes for the first time. These paper notes represented a promise of convertibility to gold or silver. Though the notes were not declared by Congress to be legal tender, they were quite popular for transactions. Due to changes in the price of silver in the world markets, as well as some adjustments by Congress, silver coins began disappearing. This phenomenon was only furthered by the discovery of gold in California. The Gold

123

Rush brought the price of gold even lower relative to silver. By the 1850s, silver coins had nearly disappeared from circulation, making gold a more popular means of exchange.

During the Civil War and the resulting financial pressure, the Union government abandoned gold and silver and issued non-convertible paper money, which was declared legal tender. This money was known as a greenback due to its color. Due to the large quantities of the greenbacks issued, the currency's value against the gold-backed dollars, which were used in parallel, fell by up to 50%. To no one's surprise, the significant quantitative increase in money led to inflation.

The ease with which money could be created resulted in one of the strangest episodes in American political history. Greenbacks, as well as the steel, iron, and transportation industries that blossomed over the course of the war, fueled a boom in railroad construction in the years following the war. As railroads tracks were laid all across America, more money rushed in, fostering further the railroad boom. By 1873, banks, businesses, and individuals were heavily invested in this new expansion. Leading the boom was Philadelphia's Jay Cooke. From the Civil War until 1873, Jay Cooke and his investment house aided in the construction of more than 35,000 miles of new railroad tracks. Jay Cooke was also a leading figure in the fledgling national banking system and the exclusive underwriter of US government bonds. Cooke's first project was the transcontinental Union Pacific. Thereafter he was involved with the Northern Pacific Railroad, a project that received tens of millions of acres in federal government land grants. As a result of his dealings, Cooke also became one of the largest employers in the nation. These large rail development projects required large amounts of capital obtained from individual banks and other financial institutions. Ongoing cash inflow was key to maintaining this boom. But after the Civil War, Congress was firm in abandoning paper money and returning to a gold- and silver-based monetary system. This decision made money flow tricky. In 1869, Cooke wrote,

"Why should this Grand and Glorious country be stunted and dwarfed—its activities chilled and its very life blood curdled by these miserable 'hard coin' theories—the musty theories of bygone age."[8]

Financial booms and credit money pouring into an industry result in malinvestment, over construction, and the misallocation of resources. Such was also the case with the US railroad boom. Countless unnecessary miles of railroad tracks were built. The tracks' freight capacity eclipsed actual demand, which caused prices of freight, and thereafter the financial returns on these investments, to rapidly drop. In September 1873, the boom came crashing down. On September 8, the New York Security and Warehouse Company became the first financial institution to suspend its operations because its customers (among them large railroad companies) were unable to pay their debts. The effects of this shutdown quickly spread, and by September 18, Jay Cooke and Company, America's best-known financier, collapsed. The events lead to a panic. A *New York Times* report from Sep 19, 1873, describes the scene:

> The first intimation which came into the Stock Exchange of any change in the programme was contained in a brief notice which said authoritatively that Jay Cooke & Co has suspended payment. To say that the street became excited would only give a feeble view of the expressions of feeling. The brokers stood perfectly thunderstruck of a moment, and then there was a general run to notify the different houses in Wall Street of the failure.
>
> The brokers surged out of the Exchange, tumbling pell-mell over each other in general confusion, and reached their respective offices in race-horse time. The members of firms who were surprised by this announcement had to time to deliberate. The bear clique was already selling the market down in the Exchange and prices were declining frightfully. [...]

The news of the panic spread in every direction downtown, and hundreds of people who had been carrying stock in expectation of a rise, rushed into the offices of their brokers and left orders that their holdings should be immediately sold out. In this way prices fell off so rapidly that even Vanderbilt could not have stemmed the tide.[9]

In the following days, other reputable banks and trusts followed suit and the market was shut down for 10 days. This closure sparked a sell-off in London as the crisis spread to Europe.

In response, the US government announced it would buy $10 million of bank bonds, and President Grant traveled to New York. Grant was greeted by crowds of bankers pleading to increase liquidity in any way possible, declaring that unless the government came to the rescue, the entire country was headed towards bankruptcy and ruin.[10] When the stock exchange was reopened the panic subsided. It still took another month and the failure of dozens of banks and NYSE member companies before calm returned to Wall Street. The repercussions of the malinvestments and excessive rail building continued in the guise of ongoing defaults on railroad debt, a 75% drop in rail building, and an overall recession which carried on for three more years.[11] The sharp drop in railroad building also caused a collapse in farmland prices where most of that railroad expansion activity took place.

In 1874, as a result of the panic and its aftermath, a third political party—the Greenback Party—was formed. This populist movement consisted mainly of farmers— a sizable part of the US population in those days—who demanded the issuance of more greenbacks. The party's main goal was the expansion of the money supply. One of the party's goals was to reduce the debt burden taken out at the time of high farmland prices. In 1878, the party managed to elect 14 members to Congress, and in the 1880 presidential election the Greenback candidate received 3.3% of the vote. At the core of the party's platform was the growing difference between the value of the metal-backed dollar and the greenback paper money. At the end of the Civil War, more than

$400 million greenbacks were in circulation. The greenbacks were not convertible to gold and thus their value at that time was about 20% lower than that of the gold-backed dollar even though both were legal tender and both were denominated equally. In 1875, Congress passed the Resumption Act which called for the restoration of the metal-backed dollar at pre-war parity and the gradual elimination of greenbacks from circulation. This act was intended not only to reduce the overall amount of money in circulation, but also to force the exchange of greenbacks for silver- or gold- backed dollars at a lower rate for the greenbacks. This exchange would increase the farmer's debt burdens since their debts were kept in the more expensive metal-backed dollars but their assets were in the lower-valued greenbacks.

From the 1877 to 1881, at the height of the Greenback Party's popularity, Ohio Congressman Thomas Ewing, a retired Union Army General, was a key Greenback Party speaker. In a series of public debates he explained the Greenback Party's demand for greater money creation:

That cry of 'more greenbacks' was a cry that came from the wrung hearts of those poor men. More greenbacks meant: 'Let industry revive!' More greenbacks meant: 'Take off this terrible dread of the reduction of the currency which paralyzes the industries in which our labor is employed.' It meant: 'Tell the business men of this country that [hundreds of millions] of their money shall not be destroyed… 'More greenbacks' means simply that the business of this country shall live and not perish.
[…]
Getting the greenbacks on par with gold involves this contraction of the currency, and the contraction of the currency involves a fall in all the values of labor and property… and all the means by which debt can alone be paid will be shrunk, and, practically, every man that is at all considerably in debt…may prepare for banckruptcy if this devilish scheme…is executed.[12]

The Greenback Party didn't manage to gain real traction. The "hard money" majority continued to rule. With the restoration of full commodity backing for the dollar came the end of loose money creation. This policy curbed war inflation, which had reached highs of 23% in 1863 and 27% in 1864. By 1879, the stock market index was on the rise again, and the country had fully recovered from the recession. By 1884, the Greenback Party had faded into history. Still, if we compare those days of serious debates about money, its creation, quantity, and impacts, to our current world of 30-second sound bites, catchy slogans, bumper sticker-sized political platforms, and candidates whose election rests on a few minutes of television performance, you cannot avoid wondering which is the more advanced society.

One greenback dollar note (back side)

The hard money majority prevailed and the Resumption Act of 1875 returned the US to a commodity-metal currency. By 1879, greenbacks were back on par with the gold-backed dollar. This act also meant that the government was again willing to exchange greenbacks for gold upon demand though holders of the greenbacks were not forced to convert them to metal-backed dollars. As a result, about two-thirds of the greenbacks issues during the Civil War stayed in circulation for many decades. The successful introduction of the greenback spelled the return of paper money as legal tender in the US after the Revolutionary War continentals fiasco. As part of the return to a metallic currency system, the legislation also put an end to the bimetallic system. Even though silver continued to have some limited uses, the US was now using a de facto gold standard.

At about the same time gold also became the only money base in Europe. The international gold standard emerged after millennia of bimetallism. Britain adopted the gold standard in 1717 after accidentally driving silver coins out of circulation. Throughout the 19th century, more and more European nations followed suit. The move to gold was not a result of any international treaty, but rather a voluntary choice made by individual nations. Most nations also simultaneously adopted a note paper–based monetary system that would replace most gold and silver coins in circulation. Still, gold was the base for the monetary system. All other means of payments (paper notes or silver coins) were pegged and convertible to gold at the fixed price and on demand. This marked the beginning of the Classical Gold Standard period (1870-1914) when gold was the exclusive currency base of the world's major economies.

Under the gold standard, the amount of money in circulation was limited, and central banks (or the issuing authority where central banks did not exist) were allowed to issue money only if it was backed by gold reserves. In some countries, an extra, albeit limited, amount of money could be issued, backed by government bonds. This extra money, known as fiduciary currency, allowed the government to influence the money supply without acquiring or selling gold.

A 1907 ten dollar bill from the Classical Gold Standard
period, it reads: "This certifies that there has been deposited
in the treasury of the United States of America Ten dollars
in gold coin payable to the bearer on demand."

It was not only the government that issued notes, but banks
as well. After the Civil War, national banks were also allowed
to issue notes. Although these notes were not legal tender, they
were quite popular as they could be converted into gold upon
demand. To ensure the notes' convertibility, the issuing banks
had to make deposits in government bonds which served as
collateral. These banknotes were unified, simple, convertible to
gold, and reliable because they were backed by collateral. As a
result, the notes served also as the basis for a widespread paper
money system.

In 1900, Congress passed the Gold Standard Act. The act
was silver's death knell. Gold was declared the standard unit
of account. All government-issued money was tied to it and
all government-issued money had to be redeemable for it. The
government established a gold reserve carrying $150 million to
back paper money and the convertibility commitment. Furthermore, the Gold Standard Act restricted the issuance of notes
in section 2 thereof: "the gold coin and bullion in the reserve
fund, together with the redeemed notes held for use as provided
in this section, shall at no time exceed the maximum sum of
$150 million."The establishment of the Federal Reserve in 1913
made the creation of money the Fed's exclusive purview. The

gold standard, however, remained. By law the Federal Reserve was required to hold enough gold to back 35% of the reserve deposits of its member banks and 40% of its Federal Reserve notes (i.e. dollar bills).

Currencies based on gold or silver were international by nature and encompassed a built-in solution for keeping balances of trade between countries in equilibrium. When a certain country runs a deficit trade balance, meaning its imports are greater than its exports, the money therein starts flowing out to the countries whose products it is importing. This money-supply shrinkage causes prices and salaries in the country to drop since there is now less money chasing the same quantity of products and services. On the other hand, in a country running a trade surplus—exporting more than it is importing—the process is reversed. Silver and gold money coming in from other countries causes an increase in money supply, which, in turn, raises prices and salaries, as more money is chasing the same quantity of products and services. As a result, both the exporting country and its products are more expensive and thus less competitive, and vice versa for a country running a trade deficit. This inverse relationship between prices and balance of trade slowly reverses the flow of trade and thus of money and restores balance, a mechanism known as the price–specie flow mechanism.

This mechanism was first recognized in the 1700s by one of the most important and influential figures in the European Enlightenment and Western philosophy, a Scotsman named David Hume (1711-1776). Hume also pointed out that an ongoing imbalance in trade cannot continue indefinitely because money must somehow flow back into the importing/deficit territory, which otherwise would just run out of money. Under the gold standard and with all currency convertible to gold, the price–specie flow mechanism would operate automatically and inherently. This is because at the core of the gold standard was a total commitment by the governments involved to the convertibility of their currencies to gold, making gold the real underpinning medium of exchange, and its absence unacceptable.

131

To achieve this convertibility, central banks had to hold and defend their gold reserves. A key tool for doing so was interest rates. In the 1800s, prices, and more importantly wages, were flexible and fluctuated easily. If a country suffered a drop in balance of payment and its gold reserves were falling, its central bank wouldn't just wait for the impact of the price–specie flow mechanism, but rather actively increase interest rates to encourage inflow of investors' money from overseas, which was equal to an inflow of gold. This full commitment to convertibility and the willingness to raise interest rates to encourage incoming gold flow when needed, regardless of the domestic consequences for prices and wages, was known as the "rules of the game." The fact that wages were flexible meant that they could go down as the balance of payment required, rather than create unemployment, the latter an inevitable result when there is no demand for overly expensive/uncompetitive products. The combination of the two—the "rules of the game" and the flexible pricing of labor and products—enabled a relatively stable period marked by small ongoing balancing.

The gold standard system was a framework within which economies made small adjustments rather than avoiding corrections and postponing the pain of such just to eventually experience much bigger shocks later. In essence, the gold standard was a system built on bending rather than breaking. It wasn't a perfect system, as no human system is, and its foundation was deeply rooted in the pre–World War I social structures and conventions. Still it fared quite well in comparison with the systems conceived to replace it later on. This comparison is especially salient when considering what was to come in Germany, Russia and Eastern Europe.

The height of the gold standard was the period between 1870 and 1914, also known as the classical gold standard period. This was a period of European domination and colonialism and also of great worldwide stability and peace. It was an era of international cooperation, and globalization, a time of free flow of capital and people. It was a period of great optimism and of many new inventions. It was the time of Louis Pasteur, Thomas Edison, Alfred Nobel, the Wright brothers, and of a young scientist named Albert Einstein working on his theory of relativity. It was during this time that many progressive ideas, advances in human rights and political movements came about. It was the golden age of European civilization, full of excitement and development, as well as of hypocrisy, romanticism and social conflict. The people of that time would stream in tens of millions to the World Fair in Paris and Chicago to see new wonders and their imagination captured by writers like Jules Verne and his stories about voyages around the world and under the sea. They would live with more passion and optimism than their ancestors or offspring, believing the world would always be moving forward, while confining their definition of world to "white Christian Western Europe." This sentimental Old World would soon forever vanish in the bloody and muddy trenches of the Somme and the horrendous killing fields of Verdun.

Chapter 8:
A World Off Balance: Between Two Wars

In Flanders fields the poppies blow
Between the crosses, row on row,
That mark our place; and in the sky
The larks, still bravely singing, fly
Scarce heard amid the guns below.
We are the Dead. Short days ago
We lived, felt dawn, saw sunset glow,
Loved and were loved, and now we lie
In Flanders fields.

—*John McCrae*

The 30 years between 1914 and 1945 were incredibly brutal, tumultuous, and exacting. The last time Europe had experienced any serious internal military conflict was a century prior during the Napoleonic Wars. Save a few skirmishes in Crimea and the short Franco–Prussian War of 1870, Europe had been experiencing a sustained period of peace. The continent had also moved forward dramatically socially, technologically, and financially. The benefits of the Industrial Revolution and the improvement in the standard of living the revolution enabled were felt across Europe. In June 1914, Europe was undoubtedly the economic, financial, military, political, and intellectual center of the world. Despite some local, national and social tensions, there was no outstanding sign indicating that anything would change dramatically anytime soon. Yet the peace was not to last.

On June 28, 1914 Archduke Franz Ferdinand of Austria, heir to the Austro-Hungarian throne, and his wife were shot dead in Sarajevo. Though this was a shocking event, few expected this incident to escalate into anything global, let alone a European war on an unprecedented scale. In the days after the shooting the financial markets held steady with no signs of panic as politics were playing out across the European capitals. Yet by the end of July, when armed conflict seemed inevitable, savers and banks in London started liquidating their holdings in stocks and asking to convert them to gold. Given that the gold standard era was one of globalized financial markets, the panic in the London stock market—the world's financial capital trading more stock than New York and Paris combined—quickly spread. In just a few days stock market crashes and bank runs were plaguing more than two dozen countries. In New York, European banks, institutions, and individuals in possession of large amounts of securities were liquidating and requesting to exchange their securities for gold. The number of liquidations grew so rapidly that on July 31, 1914, the New York Stock Exchange shut down. The stock exchange would not open for the next four months, well after the initial stages of the war. In London, banks and individuals frantically tried to liquidate securities and savings accounts in exchange for gold.

The crisis was further exacerbated by the fact that many stock trades were financed by margin loans—loans issued to finance security purchases. As stock prices dropped, margin calls (i.e. requests to cover such loans) forced even more sales, as traders rushed to cover their loans. To avoid a total collapse, the Bank of England flooded the English banks and financial institutions with newly printed money, enabling banks to fulfill their financial commitments to depositors. Consequently, the Bank could no longer honor the convertibility of money to gold as there was just not enough gold in the Bank's vaults to convert so much money at the set rates. Thus, the Bank abandoned the gold standard and convertibility altogether, and by doing so, ushered in the death of the classical gold standard era. The demise of the gold standard period was the first casualty of what would soon be known as the Great War.

In the last days of July 1914, the anachronistic Austro-Hungarian Empire declared war on Serbia. Russia, as Serbian protector, mobilized its armies. Germany, locked between its foes, Russia on the east and France on the west, sprang into action. If the German government had known that the war would not be over by Christmas, as it imagined, but rather would last four years and cost millions of lives, it would have perhaps given more consideration to diplomacy and to London's de-escalation proposals. Instead, the powerful German military machine was eager to put its daring Schlieffen Plan, named after its strategic planner and chief of staff Alfred von Schlieffen, into action. The plan called for a deep maneuver of the French front through its northern neighbor, neutral Belgium, which would presumably be forced to allow the German army to pass through. The army would then surprise the French by encircling Paris and the French army from the northwest. It has been said that on his deathbed, von Schlieffen reminded his listeners to "let the last man on the right brush the Channel with his sleeve," so deep was the maneuver supposed to be.

It was amidst cheering crowds that the German army mobilized and attacked neutral Belgium on the morning of August 4, 1914. The military operation was, however, poorly executed and the Germans were halted before they could reach Paris in a battle forever to be known as the Miracle of the Marne. So from September 1914, along 450 miles of trenches, the armies of the western front were locked in bloody stalemate for four years. This war, and its grave repercussions, would forever change the course of history and the face of Europe.

In the face of mounting financial pressure, all European nations abandoned the gold standard and reverted to printing money to finance the war. Inflation soon followed: whereas the average annual inflation rate in Britain in the 10 years prior to the war was around 0.5%, it jumped to 12.5% in 1915, 18% in 1916, 25% in 1917, and 22% in 1918.[1]

The US, however, was in a different position altogether. Although its financial markets were put under significant pressure by European sellers, the US was initially not involved in the war and had no fighting military to finance. A few bold measures undertaken by Secretary of the Treasury William McAdoo—such as shutting down the stock exchange for four months—lessened the pressure on the dollar, US gold reserves and on New York financial markets. This relief enabled the US to stay on the gold standard and thus made the dollar a unique and promising currency. McAdoo's decision not to follow Europeans by suspending the gold standard was critical for America's future economic development. In the words of Alexander Noyes, the business editor of the *New York Times* from 1920 to 1945, staying on the gold standard "almost immediately made New York the banking center of the world."[2] In only a few years, major clients of London's capital markets like Argentina and Canada turned to New York for fund-raising. The dollar was, naturally, the currency for these endeavors.[3]

Two and a half years later, in April 1917, the US joined the war. However, since it had no army to deploy, it wasn't until late spring of 1918 that the first American troops started arriving in weary Europe. The fresh US troops played a critical role in the final acts of the war in the summer and fall of 1918. The transference of military power complemented the transference of financial power, ushering in the beginning of the American Century.

The Great War was the first mechanized total war, involving all parts of society. Such a scale demanded not only millions of young bodies, but also resources like never before. As the war progressed, food shortages became common, which led to food rationing. Fixed quantities of sugar, meat, butter, and tea were allocated per person. In April 1916, the shortage reached a point that Britain had only six weeks of wheat on hand, and with the depletion of other edibles, bread became a major part of people's diet.[4]

The cost of the war dramatically increased government spending. In the 5 years prior to the war, the British government's average spending was around 340 million pounds sterling a year. This number jumped to 1.75 billion in 1916, to 2.381 billion in 1917 and 2.893 billion in 1918. This huge growth in expenses was financed by increased taxes, debt, and money creation. In 1900, the UK's national debt stood at around 30% of GDP. By 1919, the debt reached 135%. Most of it was owed to the US government and American bondholders. Most of this debt would never be paid back. In 1931, the US declared a one year moratorium on war debt repayments. In 1934, the outstanding debt to the US was $4.4 billion (about $76 billion in 2014 CPI adjusted dollars). It would remain unpaid.[5]

The situation in Germany was much worse. Germany also abandoned the gold standard when the war broke out, and used money printing as the main means of financing the war. In the coming years, the amount of money in circulation would grow fivefold.[6] As a result, inflation took off and wages dropped in value by 22-42% in only two years.[7] Food rationing was instituted as early as 1914, and in the winter of 1916-1917 the shortage was so desperate that turnip was the country's main food item. That winter was later nicknamed the Turnip Winter. By 1918, food was so scarce that sawdust became a flour substitute in bread. Coal, too, was scarce, and hunger and disease were common in large urban centers. By 1916, the economy became fully government planned and controlled. At school, children were called on to help the war effort by collecting things like kitchen waste, fruit seeds, pinecones, green leaves, paper waste, rubber waste, rags, and women's hair.[8] The war would end up costing Germany 80-85 billion 1913 gold marks, the equivalent of about $1.25 trillion in 2014 gold prices. Germany also lost three-quarters of its gold reserves.[9]

The country's capital resources were significantly depleted by the war: cow and pig inventories, for example, fell by 30% and 45% respectively.

On the eve of war, Germany was the most populous country in Europe, with around 65 million citizens, followed by Britain, which had a population of 45 million. The US, in comparison, had 97 million residents. The German economy was the second largest economy in the world, with a GDP of $237 billion (all following numbers are in 1990 International Geary-Khamis dollars). The UK was close behind with $224 billion, whereas the US had a GDP of $517 billion. By 1919, much of Germany's great wealth and might had disappeared. Out of Germany's 11 million mobilized troops, almost 65% were dead, wounded, or missing.[10] And Germany's GDP dropped by more than a third, to $156 billion.[11]

On November 11, 1918, at 11 AM, the guns were silenced on the western front and the war ceased. In its wake were 16 million dead, 21 million wounded, and multiple shattered nations with devastated economies. It also led to the demise of long-standing political powers like the Austro-Hungarian, Russian and Ottoman Empires, which had dominated Eastern Europe, the Balkans and the Middle East for hundreds of years. The wealth, glory, and most social structures of the classical gold standard period were gone, and with it, European supremacy. A completely new era in the world's history was ready to unfold.

Enraged by the war's devastation and bent on revenge, the winners were determined to make Germany pay. Although a shortly negotiated armistice agreement ended the military conflict on November 11, 1918, it would be another 7 months before Germany and the Allied Powers signed the Treaty of Versailles on June 28, 1919, five years to the day of the assassination of Archduke Franz Ferdinand. The Treaty of Versailles formally ended World War I and would set the stage for a new world order. As part of the treaty, Germany was forced to give up the coal mine–rich territories of Alsace-Lorraine—which they had taken from France during the Franco-Prussian War—as well as the Saar and Upper Silesia. Germany was also forced to pay heavy reparations—what amounts to almost $1 trillion in today's money—for the devastation caused by war. This sum, though shortly after cut by half, poured salt on Germany's wounds. Germany was already bankrupt due to the war, and these reparations would do nothing but guarantee further instability. The few objecting voices to the heavy reparations—like that of John Maynard Keynes, a consultant to the British delegation to the talks—were brushed aside. The war was bitter, and so was the peace. Keynes, who at the time was a professor of economics at King's College in Cambridge, had spent the war years at the British Treasury department. He published his observations in *The Economic Consequences of the Peace* (1919), an extremely popular book that was translated into 12 languages. In the book, Keynes stated that the Treaty of Versailles effectively "skins Germany alive year by year" and that it embodies the "most outrageous acts of cruel victory," which he claimed would ultimately result in catastrophic consequences and an even more extreme and aggressive Germany.

In the meantime, in Germany, an unpopular newly installed government was trying to establish a republic to replace the prewar monarchy. This new regime was battling a strong Marxist opposition on the one hand and right-wing paramilitary groups on the other. On the economic front, inflation was rampant. By war's end, prices had more than doubled in Germany and the mark had lost 60% of its prewar purchasing power. Under the social and political pressures of the post-war years, which included a few revolution attempts, the German central bank continued printing money as it had done to finance the war. Consequently, the money supply grew dramatically, and so did its velocity, or speed of usage. The government's attempts to address the nation's real and perceived threats led it to run huge deficits. During the war, taxes were able to cover less and less government expenses; by the end of it, taxes only paid for 15% of the government's expenditures. This number would continue to fall: by October 1923, taxes covered less than 1% of the government's expenses. Germany's central bank, the Reichsbank, was printing money and lending it out freely to the government and to businesses at next to zero percent interest rates. The private sector, on the other hand, stopped lending money as it would lose all of its value by the time it was paid back. This unwillingness to lend exacerbated the cycle further since it forced the central bank to take on an ever larger lending role and print even more money.

By November 1923, the Reichsbank had issued 92.8 quintillion marks (that's 92 with 18 zeros), and the value of the mark had dropped to essentially zero. The yearly hyperinflation of 1923 reached 5,000,000%.[12] In October *1923,* prices rose at a rate of 41% *per day.* With hyperinflation real economic activity came to a standstill. Retailers and farmers were not willing to exchange their real products for worthless paper. Unemployment, which had been remarkably low due to the rush of activity created at the early stages of money creation, started to soar. By the end of 1923, unemployment was around 30%, and many of the employed only worked part time. This central bank–induced inflation could no longer continue. Although the Jews were about 0.7% of the Germany's population, the valueless marks became known as *Judefetzen,* or Jew confetti.

All inflation, big and small, follows the same pattern. In *The Economics of Inflation* (1931), Constantino Bresciani-Turroni outlines the process:

At first inflation stimulated production…but later it exercised an increasingly disadvantageous influence, disorganizing and limiting production.… It destroyed incalculable moral and intellectual values, […] A few people accumulated wealth …whilst millions of individuals were thrown into poverty. It was a distressing preoccupation and constant torment of innumerable families; it poisoned the German people by spreading among all classes the spirit of speculation and by diverting them from proper and regular work, and it was the cause of incessant political and moral disturbance. It is indeed easy enough to understand why the record of the sad years 1919-23 always weighs like a nightmare on the German people.[13]

To resolve the issue, the mark was replaced by a new currency, the Rentenmark in November 1923. The ratio of mark to Rentenmark was one trillion to one. In parallel, the government and the central bank jerked the emergency brake on the money creation machine. Rentenmark were limited, and the central bank stopped the practice of credit disbursal to businesses. The public longed for stability and for a real means of exchange, which had become impossible under the hyperinflated mark. The new currency quickly met these demands and inflation subsided.

In August 1924, a new currency, the Reichsmark, replaced the Rentenmark. Shortly thereafter, the government introduced new taxes and the budget deficit fell sharply. By 1925, the government was already running a surplus. As inflation subsided, resources started to be reallocated away from inflation-related or inflation-created services to new ones, and the number of corporate bankruptcies jumped more than twenty-fold. And although 1924 interest rates were above 70%,[14] economic stability was slowly returning. This stabilization reopened the door to foreign loans and investments, which were mainly coming from the USA. This increase in foreign currency inflow helped the recovery further. In 1926, Germany was admitted to the League of Nations as a permanent member. The *Goldene Zwanziger* ("Golden Twenties") had arrived. In May 1928, elections were held and a little over 31 million Germens cast their vote. A relatively new party, the National Socialist German Workers' Party, aka the Nazi Party, got some 810,000 votes, a mere 2.6% of the electorate, becoming the 9th in size holding 12 out of 491 seats in the German legislature.

The years after the war were a struggle to return to normality. Yet all attempts to forget the horrendous years of 1914–1918 were futile. Return to prewar life was impossible. In Russia, a new type of regime had arisen. Following the Russian Revolution and the ensuing civil war, Russia's new government was devoted to Karl Marx's ideology, one that was diametrically opposed to capitalism. Controlling a vast territory, it was aggressively enforcing the abolishment of private property and the transfer of all economic decisions to a centrally planned and state-controlled bureaucracy. Social turmoil and instability, however, were not exclusive to Russia. The fragile Weimar Republic government also faced its share of attempted right wing and Marxist rebellions. In the UK, a severe postwar recession increased unemployment to more than 11% by 1921. Economic hardship combined with political turmoil led to four different governments between 1922 and 1924.

The Allies, and above all Britain, were eager to return to the prewar gold standard, despite their wartime abandonment thereof led by the belief that this would restore order to the markets and stabilize currency exchange rates. Stable exchange rates would lead to the resumption of international trade, a key factor in economic recovery. However, the Allies faced a dilemma similar to the one the US faced with the greenbacks after the Civil War. Over the course of the war, the amount of money in circulation had increased substantially, and consequently, declined in its value and increased overall price levels. While in prewar days, the gold standard included an exchange rate mechanism, it was now difficult to determine what the right "price" for gold would be for each currency. Representatives of 34 governments gathered at an international conference in Genoa in 1922 to address the return to the gold standard. Returning to the old gold standard was, however, nearly impossible. First, Europe's ongoing need for US capital and materials during the war years had caused most of the world's gold to come into US possession. Indeed, by 1923, three-quarters of the world's gold belonged to the US.[15]

In an attempt to circumvent this problem, the participants put in place a new system known as the gold exchange standard. According to the gold exchange standard, central banks were allowed to keep gold reserves not only in the shape of actual gold, but also in US dollars and British pounds. Dollars and pounds were convertible to gold and thus considered by the participants in the exchange standard as equivalent to gold when held by the central banks. Under the new gold exchange standard, individuals were no longer able to exchange their bills into

144

gold coins or bullion as they had in the classical gold standard years. Gold was now for use exclusively in large international transactions, and gold convertibility could basically only occur between central banks and large institutions.

Given the general rise in price levels, it would have made sense to also raise the price of gold. After all, why should the price of gold stay at its prewar level when the prices of all other products had increased significantly due to inflation? But such a change in gold price was more complicated that it seemed. During the war, loans were made to the Allied government in their respective currencies. Should the price of gold be increased above its prewar rates, these loans would be worth less in terms of gold. Thus, a return to the gold standard at higher parities—i.e., exchange rates that would reflect money's decrease in value—would translate to a partial default on wartime debt since lenders would be getting paid back less value (in gold) than what they had disbursed.

A de facto default of this nature was seen by many, including Chancellor of the Exchequer Winston Churchill, as dishonorable and unacceptable. Churchill also feared that it would prevent London from once again becoming the financial center of the world. Thus, in mid-1925, Britain returned to the gold exchange standard at prewar parity, meaning that the exchange rate between the gold and the pound remained at prewar levels and did not reflect the pound's actual devaluation relative to gold as a result of the flurry of wartime money creation.

This move to ignore the sterling's drop in value as a result of the past decade's inflation had several implications. For one, the artificially high price of the sterling made British exports far too expensive to compete in world markets. With the unchanged gold parity the only way to make British products more competitive would have been to reduce their prices, a move that would require production cost reduction through lowered wages and material costs. In a political climate in which socialism was growing in popularity both politically and socially, lowering wages was not practically possible. In fact, the tension between labor and government was so high that in May of 1926, for the first time in Britain's history, trade unions went on a 10-day general strike. So with an expensive sterling and no path to cost reduction, Britain endured a slow economy and high unemployment that rarely dipped below 8%. These conditions would have a significant impact on the world's economic thinking and policies for years to come.

Like the mark and the pound, the French franc had also lost value during the war. It had declined in value by almost 80% between 1918 and 1926. Unlike the British, who chose to return to prewar parity, however, the French returned to the gold standard at a new, much lower postwar rate. This choice gave France an immense trade and financial advantage. Gold and foreign exchange reserves quickly began accumulating in France and exports flourished. There were only two ways to resolve this growing imbalance between the two countries. France could revalue its currency and thus slow this flow, or the Bank of England could increase its interest rates to encourage the flow of investors' money back to England, a standard procedure during the classical gold standard period. But neither of the countries would agree to budge. The Bank of England refused to raise interest rates as the British economy was already severely stressed due to the decision to return to prewar parity. Furthermore, the governor of the Bank of England felt that the French advantage was purely the result of the manipulation (i.e. sharp devaluation) of the franc. The French, on the other hand, had a flourishing economy and dreams of making Paris the new financial capital of the world. The payoffs were just too good, so while they promised to revalue their currency, they never did.

The gold exchange standard was faulty from the outset. In reality it was an attempt to circumvent the huge destruction of the war and social pressures of the postwar years instead of addressing them. As it was based on currencies (the dollar and pound sterling) rather than on gold, this new quasi-gold standard enjoyed neither the built-in strengths and global cooperation, nor the clout and favorable political climate of the classic gold standard days. Under the exchange standard, gold no longer functioned as the monetary system's neutral base. It also did not force its members to adhere to the rules of the game as in the classical gold standard years.

The war also created a massive power vacuum across southern and eastern Europe. In its aftermath, weak governments tried to manipulate exchange rates to shift the economic burdens of the postwar years elsewhere. The social and political pressures exerted on governments by their changing societies combined with the monumental destruction brought about by the war allowed little space for those governments to maneuver. Thus, in a few short years, the exchange standard disintegrated.

War can be thought of as the culmination of malinvestment and misallocation; the mother of all bubbles. From a purely economic perspective, war has little value. Even in the days of the Roman Empire, the ROI (return on investment) on wars was mostly negative. Modern wars are even worse, as they are so much more costly and the "plunder" is minimal. In the past 200 years, wars were mostly financed by newly created money printed or loaned by governments. The expenditure of this newly created money generates a rush of activity in the war-related sector. Most of its products however have very little value beyond the war, and many of them end up burning in a field or sinking to the bottom of the ocean anyway. This is the malinvestment of the war bubble. Once the war is over, these resources must be reallocated to more productive domains that create products and services people actually need, want, and are willing to pay for with real money. Machinery previously devoted to the war effort becomes obsolete and people employed during and for the war face unemployment. In short, national economies are forced to reorganize and reallocate at war's end.

While Europe struggled with the aftermath of the Great War, future US President Warren Harding, who served from 1921 to 1923, was promising "a return to normalcy." Although the US did not suffer the horrendous casualties the European nations did[II], the US economy had fully shifted to accommodate the war.

II Roughly 116,000 Americans died during American engagement in World War I—50,000 died in battle and 67,000 died from disease.

Prior to the war, federal spending accounted for about 2.4% of GDP; by 1918, after the US joined the war, this number had grown sevenfold and reached 17%. This growth in federal spending was mandated by the rapid expansion of the military and of other branches of government dedicated to war needs. Between 1914 and 1918, the US government and military increased their number of employees by 3.5 million. About the same number of employees was added to the weapons manufacturing sectors. This sharp demand reduced unemployment dramatically; it fell from about 8% in 1914 to about 1.5% by 1918.

The government turned to three sources to finance this great expansion. The first was taxes, which covered around 22% of this expansion. Income tax rates alone climbed around tenfold and the government also introduced indirect taxes—on cigarettes, alcohol and other consumer goods—for the first time. The second source was borrowing from the public, which covered around 58% of the burden. The third source was new money creation, which covered around 20% of the expenses. This huge increase in spending increased money supply dramatically and inflation followed. Between 1914 and 1919, US prices climbed 78%.[16] When the war ended and as America returned "to normalcy," adjustments had to be made. As millions of military-related personnel were let go, unemployment increased significantly. The closure of many war-related factories led to a chain reaction that spread to other economic sectors. By 1921, unemployment had jumped to more than 12%.[17] The elimination of war related activities caused the GDP to drop by almost 7%. The US economy fell into a depression known as the 1920–21 Depression.

With no need for the large-scale war expenditures, President Harding and Congress slashed the defense budget aggressively: it fell by more than 80% between 1919 and 1921. By 1923, the defense budget stood at a mere 10% of its size at the war's peak. The downsizing thereof also caused the overall federal budget to shrink. First it fell to 30% of its wartime peak (to, not by) and then, by 1922, to 20% of its peak. The drop went from

$18.9 billion to $3.7 billion.[18] This drastic drop in government spending was followed by a similarly dramatic one in income tax rates: by 1924 income tax rates were about one-third what they had been in 1918. Someone making $3,724 annually in 1924 ($50,000 in 2012 dollars) would have had an effective tax rate of 2%, and someone making $7,448 in 1924 ($100,000 in 2012 dollars) would have had to pay an effective federal income tax rate of 2.9%.[19]

The recovery from the recession was rapid. Within a mere eighteen months, and with no stimulus or Federal Reserve intervention, the economy was back on track. Unemployment fell to 2.5%, and the government was once again operating at a surplus. The Roaring Twenties were just beginning.

The massive wartime spending accelerated the development of certain technologies invented prior to the war. Only 15 years elapsed between the Wright brothers' pioneering 800-foot flight in 1903 in a remote field near Kitty Hawk, North Carolina, and the first transatlantic flight. Regular air services between once far apart destinations soon followed. Aviation was of course not the only field to benefit from the war. Food processing and preservation technology was also advanced during that period, making canned and frozen foods part of Americans' diet. The war also enabled the popularization of electricity and of the telephone. During the 1920s almost two-thirds of American households were attached to the nascent electrical grid and set up for new inventions like refrigerators and radios. Assembly line production laid the ground for new mass-produced and packaged consumer products like ready-made clothing, cigarettes, and many others. These developments facilitated a big jump in the standard of living and consumption habits of the average American. In effect, it was during this period that America became a consumer society.

No inventions were bigger and more influential than the radio and the automobile. In 1922, radio sales were $60 million; by 1929 they had reached $426 million. Programming followed suit: before 1919 there were no commercial radio stations, but by the mid-1920s dozens of stations were creating endless hours of content. With the advent of radio, Americans became a unified audience for advertisements and sales messages. Modern marketing was born.

The automobile was quickly becoming the center of the new consumer society and a major pillar of the economy. The popularity of the car was possible for two reasons. Ford's assembly line allowed for a steep drop in car prices. By 1925, a car was affordable for the average America family. The average family was furthered aided in its car purchase by the invention of financing, originally offered by General Motors via its new GMAC car financing company. Of the 4.5 million cars purchased in 1929, 65% were bought on credit.[20] That year, the total number of cars in the US grew to around 26.7 million as compared to the 500,000 cars on the roads just 20 years prior.[21]

But the new idea of "buy now, pay later" didn't stop with cars. It caught like wildfire and quickly spread to many other products. Manufacturers, banks and other financial institutions offered loans and installment plans (also a form of credit) to meet and fund the growing consumer demand for items like furniture and home appliances. Indeed, by the late 1920s, 75% of radios and 60% of furniture were bought on some form of credit.[22]

Banks and other financial institutions subsequently became increasingly involved in financing home purchases through mortgages. In 1920 only about 16% of residential units were mortgaged, and in 1910 total outstanding real estate loans stood at roughly $1 billion. By 1930, this number had multiplied six times to around 6.5 billion dollars.[23] This big growth in credit for housing caused a boom in residential construction. In 1921, there were 250,000 units in construction; by 1929 that number had reached a million.[24] Just as it would 80 years later in 2006, Florida took center stage in attracting real-estate investors. In 1922, the *Miami Herald* was the heaviest newspaper in the nation because of its real estate section advertising. Two-thirds of the real estate for sale in Florida in those boom years was sold by mail to people who had never even visited Florida. The large supply of money available for real estate purchases caused prices to rise. Nationwide, prices rose about 20% between 1921 and 1926. Some places, like Washington D.C., Seattle and Florida, saw prices grow 35% to 50% in that time span, elsewhere they rose even more.[25]

The proliferation of various new types of consumer credit was reflected in the stunning growth in household debt, which tripled from $9 to $30 billion between 1921 and 1929. This was the highest growth rate of such debt in any decade of the 20th century.[26] The expansion of consumer credit contributed very significantly to the era's boom and dazzle.[27]

Goods and real estate were not the only booming domains. The stock market was blossoming as well. The Dow Jones Industrial Average stock index stood at 64 in mid-1921, at 160 in 1926, and peaked at 381 in September 1929. These numbers translate to a 600% growth in eight short years. This growth was mostly fueled by the explosion of credit available for stock trading. This credit was managed by brokerage houses, which would borrow the money they lent their customers from banks, corporations, and other financial institutions. A 1929 New York Stock Exchange survey found that margins (stocks bought on credit) composed 40% of customers' accounts.[28] Many times, up to as much as 90% of a stock's value was purchased on credit. Brokers borrowed money not only to give their customers the means to buy stock on credit, but also to purchase securities (stocks, bonds, etc.) themselves, which they would typically hold and sell later to investors. The total amount of such loans taken on by brokers grew 600% from 1920 to late 1929. In 1920, that credit was worth $1.4 billion, by October 1929 it had risen to $8.5 billion.[29] Most of the financial press was cheering the double bubble in the real estate and stock markets, especially the latter. Wall Street and many in America started to believe that they lived in a new era where old rules didn't apply and that "old-fashioned precaution [was] out of date."[30]

Still a few voiced their skepticism, among them Alexander Noyes, the *New York Times'* financial editor. In November 1925 he warned:

"...a movement of the kind...with speculation rising to huge proportions, would be interrupted by violent downward reaction."

He would continue to caution Americans in the coming years, but his calls remained unheeded, as were those of other people not singing the praises of the bull market. "Playing the stock market has become a major American pastime," noted *Times* article published on March 24, 1929. It went on: "it is quite true that the people who know the least about the stock market have made the most money out of it in the last few months. Fools who rushed in where wise men feared to tread ran up high gains."[31] As the 1920s neared an end, the future seemed bright. President Herbert Hoover, secretary of commerce under Warren Coolidge, won in a historic landslide in 1928 with 444 electoral votes and 60% of the popular vote.

Under the surface, trouble was brewing, however. It was none other than the Federal Reserve that delivered the first blow. The real estate boom had started slowing down in late 1926 and continued its decline into 1927.[32] To ease the pain, the Fed reduced interest rates in 1927. However the stock market's dramatic 39% rise in 1928 worried the Fed. Concerned with an overheated stock bubble, the Fed raised its discount rate (the rate at which banks borrow money) from 3.5% to 5% between January and July 1928 and simultaneously sold government securities (government bonds) to drain banking system reserves. Although by mid-1929 economic activity in the US and abroad was slowing down, the Fed nevertheless raised the discount rate once again to 6% in August 1929.[33]

It was September 3, 1929, just another day on Wall Street. The Dow Jones Industrial Average reached a peak of 381.17 points. Little did anybody on Wall Street know that this number wouldn't be reached again for another 25 years. From early September onward, the stock market entered a period of slow decline.

On Thursday, October 24, 1929, the Dow opened at 305.85, a 20% drop from the September 3 peak. That day, soon to be known as Black Thursday, the Dow dropped another 11%, though by day's end it had recovered and ultimately lost only 2% of the previous days' worth. The next day, leading financial institutions worked hard and bought shares to instill confidence. The market remained stable. Investors, however, were not convinced. The next week opened with a bang. On Monday, the Dow lost 40 points. The following day, October 29, 1929, also known as Black Tuesday, the market fell to 212 points, although it closed at 230. Black Thursday and the following Tuesday put in motion a selling surge, exacerbated by margin calls pushing investors to sell stocks to cover their debts. The market would continue to fall until November 13, 1929, when it hit 198.69 points, an almost 50% decline from its September peak. Although the stock market entered a period of recovery thereafter and although it would regain half of its worth—reaching 294 points in mid-April 1930—the recovery was short-lived.

The Wall Street collapse marked the beginning of the Great Depression. This was a turbulent period during which fortunes were wiped out and millions dislocated. Outside the US, the global economic collapse set the stage for the rise of the Nazi party in Germany, which would eventually lead to an even more deadly and destructive world war. During the Great Depression, production in America fell by half, income by close to a third, and stock prices by 91%. Unemployment in the US would jump from around 1.6% in 1929 to 25% of the workforce, or 13 million people, by 1933.

The Great Depression would also forever change the role, size and power of the federal government. In the 1920s around 550,000 civilians were employed by the federal government. This number would jump to around 1,050,000 by 1940. Incidentally, today, the government employs around 2.75 million people.[34] The Great Depression would also create lasting institutions like Social Security, the FDIC (Federal Deposit Insurance Corporation) and Fannie Mae (a government-sponsored mortgage enterprise). We will meet these three players as we enter the chapters of the book dealing with current events. Arguably the era's most lasting and noteworthy outcome was the change in the economic thinking of mainstream economists and politicians. This shift would lay the foundations for the present and the future, as we will see in the final chapters of this book.

From this distance, it is easy to see the Great Depression as a single event. Its importance in American and global history has unsurprisingly inspired countless books, articles, and opinions regarding its causes, duration, and resolution. The three major schools of economics—Austrian, Keynesian, and Monetarist—identify three different causes of the Great Depression. This attitude is reminiscent of the story of the six blind men who all touch an elephant and come to different conclusions about the elephant's identity based on their senses.

Austrians, also called Liquidationists back in those days, saw the excess of easy money and the credit bubbles of the 1920s as the main root of the Great Depression. This credit bubble had a profound impact on Wall Street, because it increased stock prices, and on Main Street, because it enabled consumption on credit. Thus when the credit bubble burst, be it through the Fed's interest rate increase, households' inability to take on more credit, the inability of the bubble to continue expanding, or other reasons, both parts of the economy started to sharply decline. This eventually dragged down the banking sector, the initiator of much of the credit. Once the bust cycle began it decreased manufacturing dramatically due to a lack of demand for consumer products. In 1929, the US manufactured a little over 4 million cars. This number dropped to around 2.5 million in 1930, to 1.8 million in 1931 and to 928,000 by 1932, a drop of more than 75%(!!).[35] This drop in demand obviously had an impact on employment and created a downward spiral: less demand led to less production which meant less employment, which led to even lower demand and less production and so on. According to Liquidationists, the situation allowed no simple fix. Rather, the economy had to purge itself of the misallocations and malinvestments created by the credit boom. Once done, the market would be ready for a new beginning. This was a popular view in the years soon after the meltdown.

In the early 1930s, brilliant British economist John Maynard Keynes developed a new and revolutionary concept that would eventually dominate economic thinking for the next four, if not eight, decades. Keynes dismissed all this money talk. He claimed that the cause of the Great Depression was the drop in aggregate demand due to the drop in business investment and household consumption. The solution was therefore for the government to step in and increase the economy's aggregate demand, even at the cost of large deficit spending. Such a tactic would restore confidence. Consumer and business demand would pick up again. The government would then be able to decrease its spending and step down from its dominant economic role.

In a series of books and publications, the pinnacle being the renowned *General Theory of Employment, Interest and Money* (1936), Keynes challenged the idea that market forces alone can ensure full employment. He claimed instead that an economy can actually reach equilibrium even with considerable unemployment. In such cases only government- stimulated demand can bring about a new level of higher employment. He reasoned that governments should take on deficit spending and debt to protect their nations in times of peace as done in times of war. In practice, his ideas translated to government-financed large-scale projects. He laid out his proposal in an open letter addressed to President Roosevelt, published in the *Times* on December 31, 1933. "I lay overwhelming emphasis on the increase of national purchasing power resulting from governmental expenditure which is financed by loans," he wrote. Although he acknowledged the difficulty and time required for the creation of useful large-scale public work programs, he dismissed the notion that the enlargement of the money supply would be enough. He equated that approach with "trying to get fat by buying a large belt." Keynes counseled swift public spending: "preference should be given to those (public works projects) which can be made quickly on large scale."[36] For the most part, however, Keynes avoided addressing the root cause of the downturn. He preferred addressing the more pressing problem of the difficulty of life for millions of people across western countries.

Keynes and his followers dominated the economic thinking after the Great Depression. It was only in 1963 that an opponent arose. In 1963, Milton Friedman, monetarism's founding father, and Anna J. Schwartz published their groundbreaking book, *A Monetary History of the United States, 1867-1960, which closely* studied the trends and impacts of changes in money supply. In the book, they claimed that it was ultimately monetary forces and mainly the failure of the Federal Reserve, the creator of monetary policy, that was responsible for the Great Depression. According to them, it was the Fed that permitted a mild recession to become a catastrophic depression.[37] In their work they name a few decisions and policy mistakes, both active and inactive, that led to a sharp decline in the money supply, which in turn significantly exacerbated the situation.

Although the sharp decline in the money supply cannot be disputed since the US money supply dropped by one-third between 1929 and 1933,[38] whether or not this fall was a cause or an effect is a matter of debate. If the Liquidationists are right and the origin of the depression was overspending and malinvestment during the 1920s, then the drop in money supply was merely a reflection of the reduction in economic activity once the credit bubbles burst. In other words, was the reduction of the money supply the cause of diminished economic activities or did lower economic activity reduce money supply since people needed less money to meet their needs once activity dropped?

This debate reflects a broader disagreement concerning the true nature of money. Is money a type of product by itself or is it only a mean of exchange, a mere reflection of real products in the marketplace? Monetarists assert the former. Money and its supply are the main ingredients: if there is enough money in the marketplace, the economy will do just fine. If the central bank takes its eye off the ball and money supply escalates, the result will be inflation. If money supply falls, the result will be deflation and contraction. Ultimately, for monetarists, money supply creates demand. An appropriate money supply ensures demand and achieves growth. While Keynesians focus on the government creating demand via deficit spending, monetarists believe in creating or ensuring adequate demand and price stability via monetary tools, i.e. by controlling the amount of money. At the core of the difference between these two schools lies an argument about velocity (the speed and frequency with which money is used). If velocity is more or less stable, meaning people use money at a constant rate, then more money will always result in more activity, while less money will lead to contraction. But if velocity can fluctuate significantly then only government spending can create new demand and stimulate the economy.

Meanwhile, Austrians see money as no more than a means of exchange and reflection of the products in the market. Therefore arbitrary and sizable money supply increases result in the misuse of this new and unneeded money—the boom—which will inevitably be followed by the bust. Money supply increases distort the relationship between goods and their value, i.e. the pricing mechanism. The artificial creation of money via printing or credit always and inevitably leads to a sharp correction once the short-term impact of the money creation has run its course.

Fundamentally, this is an argument about short term vs. long term outlooks on the economy and society, and about Puritanism and morality vs. practicality and the lesser of evils. So while Austrians view new money creation to be the "father of all sin" that always creates more long- term damage than short-term value, John Keynes preached that short-term unemployment is a much more acute and immediate problem. After all, said Keynes, "this long run is a misleading guide to current affairs. In the long run we are all dead." Keynes's revolutionary ideas of the 1930s made a lot of sense. The delay of immediate pain creates space for major, paradigm-changing events, like technological breakthroughs capable of preventing the future originally envisioned.

Furthermore, I would argue, Keynesian economics is much more in line with the human psyche and group mentality which often unfortunately lacks the ability to think or act in the long-term interest. Maybe the knowledge that "in the long run we are all dead" actually subconsciously impacts the way we behave, as opposed to what we say. Clearly Keynesian economics are fully in line with politicians' psyches and codes of conduct, as they always seek to address the most visible, politically impactful and popular issues as opposed to vague future threats, even if they could be avoided.

Still Keynes's ideas provided the intellectual foundation and economic justification for what people wanted to do naturally, which is to spend today what they did not have, in the hopes of finding the means of payment in the future. Though Keynes did not preach continuous government deficit spending, he laid the intellectual groundwork for such behavior, which has been warmly embraced and executed by most Western economies in good and bad years alike.

At its base, Keynesian economics' core weakness is that one day the future becomes the present, and unlike individuals, societies do not die. And when the delayed future arrives, one generation has to pay a very high price. Eventually an ever-growing debt society reaches a point of no return.

As 1930 went on, the situation became more and more dire. The credit that had been so abundant in the 1920s was drying up. In the words of Federal Reserve Chairman Marriner S. Eccles, "The time came when there were no more poker chips to be loaned on credit."[39] Not only were stressed banks retreating, but so were consumers who were increasingly avoiding new credit that they could not afford. As even one missed payment led to repossession, consumers focused their resources on paying for what they already owned and owed. They also cut down on consumption to serve their outstanding debt. The sharp fall in demand pushed prices downwards and unemployment upwards, further decreasing demand which further increased unemployment and pushed prices down even further. This cycle didn't end until a quarter of the work force was unemployed.

Meanwhile, the Federal Reserve and President Hoover were trying to come up with some type of response that would stem the tide. In mid-1930, Congress passed the Smoot-Hawley Tariff Act, an extremely protectionist piece of legislation. The act raised import tariffs to an average of 52%. This shortsighted legislation did very little but provoke retaliation tariffs. Now that America couldn't efficiently export products it was excelling in, Americans had to pay extra for local versions of products the country did not produce efficiently.

In the immediate aftermath of the crash, the Federal Reserve eased monetary conditions by extending almost unlimited lines of credit to banks and by dropping the discount rate sharply. This slowed down the spread of the crash, but the new policies were short–lived. By mid-1930, the crisis seemed contained so the Fed resumed stricter monetary policies by increasing interest and lowering credit for banks. Government revenue was also declining, and the budget was running large deficits. So, in an attempt to balance the budget, the president asked and Congress passed a sizable tax hike. The additional tax further reduced the families' already shrunken disposable incomes. Hoover's efforts were for naught as a series of other ill-considered policies imposed growing and production quotas. As 1930 drew to a close, a new crisis loomed on the horizon.

For almost a year the banking system stood firm, but the decline in demand for credit caused pressure to mount. In 1929, there were over 24,000 banks in the US; most of them small local banks that were unaffiliated with the Federal Reserve System. During the 1920s, about 600 or so of these banks would fail yearly. But towards the end of 1930, the number of failures grew at an alarming rate: 761 banks failed between November 1930 and January 1931. This wave of bank failures in late 1930 was concentrated in the St. Louis area and was sparked by a large local bank that had heavily invested in real estate. Although this panic remained local, overall confidence in the banking system started to erode. A few months thereafter, in April-August 1931, a second wave began. This time it was concentrated in the Chicago and Cleveland areas, where again banks that had heavily invested in the real estate boom led the way.[40] All in all, some 1,350 banks folded in the early-1931 wave of banking crises.[41] Britain's abandonment of the gold exchange standard in

September 1931 exerted fresh pressure on US banks as concerned US depositors clamored to withdraw their money and convert it to gold. This wave's outcome was some 2,293 new bank failures.

In early 1932, Congress passed the Reconstruction Finance Corporation Act which signaled the government's commitment to ensuring bank liquidity. The act was a success, depositor pressure subsided and failures and depositor losses dropped by almost half in 1932.

The saying "better be lucky than smart" is quite apt when it comes to presidents. The president typically does not shape the environment he operates in. Although his personality and experience shape his reactions to events, the events themselves however are largely cards dealt by history and are out of his control. President Herbert Hoover was clearly one of the presidents that were dealt a horrible hand. Despite the fact that he was not responsible for the credit bubble or for the Fed's pre-1929 policies, he nonetheless became the symbol of the nascent depression. His rational character and unemotional facade did not help. Congress didn't either. "Why is it," he once asked, "that when a man is on this job as I am day and night, doing the best he can, that certain men...seek to oppose everything he does, just to oppose him?" With the help of his political opponents he quickly became the face of the depression. The tin camps where displaced crowds camped were named Hoovervilles, and newspapers covering the homeless became Hoover blankets. It came as no surprise when he was defeated in a landslide by New York Governor Franklin Delano Roosevelt in 1932.

At the time, the presidential inauguration took place in the beginning of March. But in February 1933, rumors circulated that the new president would devalue the dollar against gold, which was still the standard for US currency. Wary depositors were piling on banks asking for their money and converting it to physical gold. The rumor took bank failures to a whole new level. Seeking to relieve the pressure, Hoover tried convincing Roosevelt to issue a statement reassuring investors, but he refused. Consequently, by March 3, the last day of Hoover's presidency,

4,000 banks closed their doors and dozens of states suspended banking activity all declaring a bank holiday. The news reached the president on his last evening in office. "We are at the end of our string" he uttered angry and depressed.

On March 6, two days after taking office, the new president declared a four-day national bank holiday, which would later be extended another three. On March 9, Congress passed the Emergency Banking Relief Act. This far-reaching law—the first of many to come in the following months—essentially empowered the executive branch to take over all banks' business: "To give the comptroller of the currency the power to restrict the operations of a bank...and to appoint a conservator, who shall take possession of the books, records, and assets of every description of such bank." It also endowed the Federal Reserve with the power to issue banks cash against their long-term assets, or loans, thus solving any liquidity gap and helping banks meet their obligations to depositors. On March 12, Roosevelt took to the airwaves with his first of many Fireside Chats and informed the public that sound banks would soon be licensed to reopen: "We shall be engaged not merely in reopening sound banks but in the creation of sound banks through reorganization.... Confidence and courage are the essentials of success in carrying out our plan....We have provided the machinery to restore our financial system; it is up to you to support and make it work."

The president's radio address was effective. When banks reopened on March 13, people stood in line to deposit the cash they had withdrawn. The Emergency Banking Act of 1933 also created a framework for deposit insurance. It was complemented later, on January 1934, by the Federal Deposit Insurance Act. This law created the Federal Deposit Insurance Corporation, a government organization that guarantees bank deposits up to a certain sum.

After the bank holiday, 4,215 banks never reopened their doors.[42] Overall, roughly 10,000 banks, or 40% of the banking system, went out of business in the early years of the Great Depression.[43]

As the Great Depression wore on, the gold exchange standard came under growing pressure. As noted above, Britain paid dearly for its decision to enter the gold exchange standard at the prewar parity rate. So in 1931 a government commission devoted to examining the issue recommended a 10% devaluation of the sterling against gold. This counsel further increased the pressure on the sterling as investors tried to sell pounds and convert them to gold before the devaluation could occur. The Bank of England was reluctant to raise interest rates because of the effect they would have on an already depressed economy. As such, it was left with no other option but to abandon the convertibility commitment all together. Thus, in September 1931, Britain left the gold exchange standard and allowed the sterling to float freely. Because of Britain's international importance, its decision had global repercussions and threw an already unstable international financial system into turmoil.

By early 1932, it was everyone for himself. Although the gold exchange standard was collapsing and nations were devaluing their currencies in an attempt to export their economic problems, the US remained committed to its convertibility at the historic rate of $20.67 per ounce. But this commitment came at a price: not only was the US unable to devalue its currency like many others were, but it was also forced to raise interest rates to protect its gold reserves and thus further tighten the money supply, stressing even more its already struggling economy.

All this came to an abrupt end once Roosevelt was sworn in. On April 5, 1933, just a few weeks after taking office, the president signed Executive Order 6102. Calling on a questionable executive power that had been enacted in 1917 during and for the war named The Trading with the Enemy Act, Roosevelt ordered: "All persons are hereby required to deliver on or before May 1, 1933, to a Federal Reserve Bank or a branch or agency thereof...all gold coin, gold bullion and gold certificates now owned by them."

POSTMASTER: PLEASE POST IN A CONSPICUOUS PLACE.—JAMES A. FARLEY, Postmaster General

UNDER EXECUTIVE ORDER OF THE PRESIDENT

Issued April 5, 1933

all persons are required to deliver

ON OR BEFORE MAY 1, 1933

all GOLD COIN, GOLD BULLION, AND GOLD CERTIFICATES now owned by them to a Federal Reserve Bank, branch or agency, or to any member bank of the Federal Reserve System.

Executive Order

FORBIDDING THE HOARDING OF GOLD COIN, GOLD BULLION AND GOLD CERTIFICATES.

Executive Order 6102 as posted in public places. It is worth noting that a similar confiscation of gold did not take place in Britain when it abandoned the gold exchange standard.

The Federal Reserve would exchange the gold for cash at a rate of $20.67 to the ounce. Failing to abide by this mandatory transfer would result in high fines or a 10-year prison sentence. This bold action was unprecedented, and a profound infringement of commonly held ideas of personal freedom, private property, and government powers.

A few months later, in January 1934, Congress passed the Gold Reserve Act which transferred all the gold from the Federal Reserve to the US Treasury. It also essentially reiterated Executive Order 6102 and outlawed all private possession of gold or even gold certificates. The government subsequently significantly devalued the dollar, raising the price of gold from $20.67 dollars to $35 per ounce, thereby reducing by 40% the payment the government had just made for the confiscated gold, and transferring purchasing power from the gold's previous owners, the public, to the new obligatory owner, the Treasury.

The value of the gold in the hands of the Treasury increased by $2.81 billion overnight,[44] which represented about 80% of the 1931 Federal budget. Some of these profits were used to fund a slush fund still in existence, belonging to and managed by the Secretary of the Treasury. This Exchange Stability Fund, containing above $102 billion in assets as of June 2014,[45] has no Congressional oversight. The fund's mandate is to "buy and sell foreign currency to promote exchange rate stability and counter disorderly conditions in the foreign exchange market."[46]

The new policy also canceled all gold clauses in public and private contracts. Gold clauses gave parties to such contracts the right to obtain payment linked to the value of gold. Such contracts accounted for an estimated $100 billion of federal, state, municipal, railroad and industrial debts and obligations.[47] Today that number is equivalent to some $2-3 trillion. The cancelation of all gold clauses, narrowly upheld by the Supreme Court, reduced by 40% all such debt.

With Executive Order 6102, the US rejoined the prevailing order in Western economies. The classical gold standard era was now officially and finally dead. Nonetheless, under the new Gold Reserve Act gold was still the base of money as the US continued to define the dollar in terms of gold, and hold gold reserves to back up its currency. Transactions in gold however were limited to dealings mainly between central banks.

The arbitrary confiscation of one asset class, gold-no similar tax was set on any other property- and the deliberate creation of panic and bankruptcy were not the only new ideas of the day. Probably the strangest of all was the Agricultural Adjustment Act (AAA). Enacted on May 1933, it restricted agriculture production and established subsidies for farmers to abstain from cultivation. These subsidies and the new agency set up to manage them are still in effect 80 years later. It also paid for the slaughter of millions of pigs and other livestock. The goal of the bill was to fight "overproduction," this at a time when many Americans were unable to afford food. Presumably, this overproduction had driven down crop prices.

The bill also included the Thomas Amendment, which empowered the president to issue up to $3 billion of new dollar notes, and in addition to force the Federal Reserve to buy $3 billion of government debt, which was about the size of the 1931 federal budget. The act and the amendment had one mission: price inflation. Deflation and price drops—especially in the case of crops—were viewed as a cause, not as a result, of the depression, so a big part of the solution was trying to push these prices back up.

Roughly a quarter of the workforce was unemployed in 1932.[48] To manage this problem, Congress enacted the Federal Emergency Relief Act in 1933. It established a new agency, one originally set up by President Hoover called the Federal Emergency Relief Administration, or FERA. FERA was involved in many relief projects aimed at boosting employment. Over time more agencies and projects of its ilk were set up. They employed millions in public works projects like road, school, and bridge construction. In March 1933, a program for young adults was initiated. Across the nation, in 1,300 camps, two million young men were employed in planting trees, digging reservoirs, building dams, and other similar occupations.

Roosevelt's goal wasn't simply to fight the Great Depression. It was to change America. Between 1933 and 1938, dozens of new programs and new federal agencies were created. Among them: the FHA (Federal Housing Administration), the Home Owners' Loan Corporation, the Social Security Administration, the Glass-Steagall Act, and the FDIC. For better or for worse, the American we live in today is Roosevelt's America.

All these programs and federal agencies were financed by government debt. By 1929, having some of WWI debt, the federal government debt had reached $17 billion, roughly equivalent to $250 billion today. Government debt would never be so low again. By 1939, the eve of WWII in Europe, it had more than doubled to $40.5 billion.[49] This debt would never be paid back. With the addition of compound interest, it reached around $4 trillion—or about 40% of the national debt—on the eve of the 2008 crisis.[50]

In 1936, the international community made one last attempt to regain stability in international currency markets. In 1936,

Britain, the US, and France joined a Tripartite Monetary Agreement, in which the parties agreed to stop the currency devaluation wars and maintain currency values at their existing levels. Later, a few other nations joined as well. But it was too late. The repercussions of the global financial crisis and depression helped topple the weak democratically elected government in Germany. The new Nazi totalitarian regime had very different plans. Pegged or floating currencies were the least of its concerns. And though European leaders preferred to turn a blind eye, Europe and the rest of the world were just three years away from the most devastating war in history.

Chapter 9:
The Golden Dollar: the Bretton Woods System

"In considering the requirements for the rehabilitation of Europe, the physical loss of life, the visible destruction of cities, factories, mines and railroads was correctly estimated, but it has become obvious during recent months that this visible destruction was probably less serious than the dislocation of the entire fabric of European economy."
—George Marshall, General, Chief of Staff, Secretary of State

Some 160 miles north of Boston lies a small hilly village of less than a thousand people. It is surrounded by New Hampshire's White Mountains which paint beautiful and peaceful views of green and white on a canvas of open skies. Nothing could have been more distant from the bloody scenes of destruction all across Europe and the Pacific in the summer of 1944. Here, in an old classy hotel called the Mount Washington Hotel, in an area known as Bretton Woods, delegates from 44 Allied nations gathered and put together a framework for a new international economic and monetary system for the days after the world war. This was July 1944, and the war's end was still a year and millions of casualties away, but a new system was already in the making.

The conference, known as the Bretton Woods Conference, was heavily influenced, if not dictated, by the new world superpower, the United States of America. The accord, signed on the last day, created the Bretton Woods system. This system, known in short as Bretton Woods, would become the international monetary framework for the coming 26 years.

The main goal of the new monetary order was to maintain peace and stability. The experiences of the preceding fifteen years were horrific and its scars fresh. The governments of the winning nations believed that monetary policy mistakes had paved the path for global economic misery, the collapse of the young and fragile German democracy, and the Nazi rise to power.

The goal of the new monetary system, therefore, was to develop a scheme based on stable exchange rates that would streamline trade and, above all, ensure full employment.

The system was developed by the UK and the US in the years prior to the meeting at Bretton Woods. Britain's John Maynard Keynes proposed one plan, the US's Harry White another. Keynes's plan included some radical ideas, among them the establishment of a supranational central bank that would issue an international currency called Bancor. The US plan was less ambitious and rested on the establishment of an international monetary stabilization fund.

Despite their differences, the two plans shared some ideas. Both advocated setting fixed exchange rates for all currencies in the system, pegging each of them to the dollar at a set rate and then pegging the dollar to gold. Both also favored capital control, meaning harsh limitations on the movement of capital in the international financial markets. The idea behind avoiding international big capital movements was the prevention of scenarios in which hot investor money moved in and out of different currencies when the economic realities did not support their preset exchange rate. The concern was that these types of money movements would further destabilize exchange rates.

The final plan was adopted on July 22, 1944, and named the Bretton Woods system. All currencies were pegged to the US dollar at an individually fixed rate. Member nations made commitments to intervene to maintain currency parity with the dollar—within a spread of 1%—when necessary. The dollar remained pegged to gold at its prewar price of $35 per ounce. To ensure this rate, the US Treasury committed to selling gold to central banks exclusively at this price. As in the days of the

168

classical gold standard, all currencies would again be anchored, though indirectly, to gold. The system set up the International Monetary Fund (IMF). This fund had the task of bridging temporary payment imbalances between member states.

By the end of the war all major world economies were totally devastated with the exception of the US. In Europe, cities, factories, and indeed, national infrastructures were destroyed. Most the nations were also in an extreme state of debt. Their gold reserves were largely depleted. By the end of the war, two-thirds of the world's gold reserve was in the US's possession. These ruined economies lacked the means to jump-start themselves. Reconstruction and importation—mostly from the US—were the only solutions to moving forward. These twin objectives were particularly difficult for Germany, the UK, and Japan as these countries lacked the resources to finance them.

The famed Marshall Plan was a response to this impasse. It funneled some $13 billion in aid to Europe in materials, grants, and loans and extended similar assistance to Japan. This crucial financial assistance, coupled with hard work, set Europe's main economies mainly Germany, France and the UK, on the path to recovery: by 1952, their industrial production had increased by 40%.

Although the Bretton Woods system contributed to the global economy's recovery, it failed to address some crucial issues. Currencies are windows into the state of the economy at large. They are focal points where larger issues come to light. Given that no economy can afford to be entirely self-sufficient since no country has sufficient materials, know-how or natural resources to meet its citizens' needs and desires, countries must inevitably trade with foreign partners. On the other hand, countries cannot run with continuing trade and budget deficits. In both cases the missing balances have to come from somewhere. If these imbalances are not resolved, they transform into currency problems.

An ongoing trade deficit inevitably leads to exchange rate devaluation.

The exporting country exchanges its goods for the importing country's currency, increasing the supply of such currency in its local market and thus driving up the value of its own currency and down the value of importing county's currency. A permanent budget deficit also brings down the currency value as it results in an increase in the money supply which is required to finance such a deficit.

Unlike the gold standard system, with the price–specie flow mechanism, and the rules of the game, the Bretton Woods system fundamentally did not address the issues of ongoing imbalance in trade or budget, as if it did not anticipate their existence. Another built-in problem with the Bretton Woods system was the pegging of the dollar to gold at a fixed rate of $35 an ounce, and the US Treasury's commitment to unlimited gold convertibility at this price. When the Bretton Woods system was instated, the US was practically the world's only functioning economy. Unlike other major economies, the US was running sizable trade surpluses and was a credit nation that lent money to others. The American architects of the Bretton Woods system couldn't imagine a change in the country's fortune, nor did they envision any problems maintaining the exchange rates or the gold convertibility commitment. As a result, they did not make space for any flexibility.

Over time, things started to change. First, the European economies rebuilt quickly, especially Germany's. Indeed, Germany's rapid recovery was even called *Wirtschaftswunder*, the economic miracle. In 1960, Germany's per capita GDP has tripled 1945's. Japan's experience was similar. The dramatic improvements in productivity in these countries drove the value of their currencies up, though an adjustment to their official value was impossible under the Bretton Woods system. The US economy, on the other hand, was losing steam by the 1960s. Growing expenses incurred by the Vietnam War and Johnson's Great Society led to sizable budget deficits. These resulted in money creation, which, as usual, raised prices throughout the US. The dollar's value was deteriorating—inflation means that

170

the money is worth less—even as its price relative to gold and other currencies remained fixed. The dollar would have to be devalued for its price to reflect its value, but this was impossible under the system. The Bretton Woods system was at odds with growing government deficits. In addition, the fixed exchange rate system set in 1944 ignored completely the huge changes in the German and Japanese economies. Simply, the Bretton Woods system had no pressure valves.

As the dollar's value declined, the conversion commitment of dollars to gold became very attractive for other nations, while the US's commitment to convertibility became increasingly burdensome for it. The US sought to resolve the problem by adjusting the exchange rate to devalue the dollar. Many system members, however, did not agree to such devaluation. They saw this solution as an attempt on the part of the US to export its deficits and currency problems to other countries, engendering a repeat of the period between the two world wars. They thought the US should handle its economic problems internally. This solution, however, required a policy that would translate into a slowdown of the US economy.

Meanwhile, the US refused to consider a unilateral step to increase the price of gold for its convertibility commitment mostly for reasons of prestige and politics. Increasing this price would have likely saved the system for at least some time. At the same time, Germany and Japan which were running big trade surpluses rejected any plan that would lead to a real evaluation of their currencies. The Bretton Woods system was thus locked between two contradictory forces.

As the value of the dollar continued to fall, it became obvious that the established gold conversion rate was much too low. National banks started sending devalued dollars to Washington and demanding gold shipments at $35 per ounce in return. French President Charles de Gaulle memorably offered to send the French navy to escort the gold back to France. After France's miserable mid-century, which involved not only WWII but costly colonial wars in North Africa and Asia, its leader sprang at the chance to publicly humiliate and profit off the USA. Even the support of countries with large gold reserves didn't help. As gold flowed out of Fort Knox, the dollar's devaluation eroded the very foundations of Bretton Woods.

In response to growing conversion demands, President Johnson asked Congress to "free our gold reserves so that they can unequivocally fulfill their true purpose—to insure the international convertibility of the dollar into gold at $35 per ounce."

The President continued:

The gold reserve requirement against Federal Reserve notes is not needed to tell us what prudent monetary policy should be— that myth was destroyed long ago.

It is not needed to give value to the dollar—that value derives from our productive economy.

The reserve requirement does make some foreigners question whether all of our gold is really available to guarantee our commitment to sell gold at the $35 price. Removing the requirement will prove to them that we mean what we say.

In adherence with President Johnson's request, Congress passed the Gold Reserve Requirements Elimination Act in August 1968. As its name indicates, it eliminated the requirement, as adjusted in June 1945, that the Federal Reserve hold 25% of US currency in gold. And thus, the connection between US currency and gold, first established in 1792, was severed.

This change helped increase gold availability for a limited time, but the convertibility requests kept pouring in. Help from close allies like Germany and Britain, willing to contribute their gold reserves, did not manage to alleviate the situation. At the rate things were going, the US Treasury's gold reserves would soon be emptied.

The Johnson administration had a few options:

› Devaluate the dollar against gold so the convertibility rate would reflect the dollar's real value. Such a choice would have been embarrassing for the US as it would signal that the US was unable to fulfill its obligations under Bretton Woods. This solution would also require some type of sign-off from key members of the Bretton Woods system.

› Devaluate the dollar and convince Germany and Japan to revalue their currencies. Germany had already agreed to this by this point, but Japan had not.

› Impose import tariffs, which would increase the value of imported currencies, but such tariffs would risk retaliatory steps, which would harm US exports.

› Force the US economy back to equilibrium by balancing the budget. Balancing the budget would require increased taxes and a reduction in deficit spending.

By the end of 1968, President Johnson was exhausted, depressed and war weary, so the administration was unable to reach a solution. The problem would therefore be passed to the next president, Richard Nixon. Nixon's administration was looking for a quick fix, one that would be painless, save face, and maintain the US's reputation. The stage was set for the next big move.

Pressures on the dollar and on American gold reserves were coming to a head in early August 1971. The Treasury attempted to mitigate the situation by buying dollars, a move mimicked by other central banks also hoping to prevent the dollar's devaluation against their currencies. The administration felt that a final run on gold was a matter of days. The president and his top advisors rushed to Camp David. It was Friday, August 13, 1971.

Getting rid of Bretton Woods completely was tempting. It would enable the US to devalue the dollar and thus address its continuing deficits and growing trade problems. Eliminating

Bretton Woods would also end its commitment to gold conversion. It was also very much in line with the way Nixon and his Secretary of the Treasury, John Connally, saw the world. As Connally memorably put it: "Foreigners are out to screw us. Our job is to screw them first." Connally, a colorful and aggressive character and the former Democratic governor of Texas, conceived a plan, which amounted to a unilateral cancelation of Bretton Woods. It ended the commitment to gold conversion, imposed wage and price control, and slapped a duty tax on all US imports. The latter was seen as a means of forcing concessions on the dollar devaluation front from trading-exporting countries.

William Safire, President Nixon's speechwriter from 1968 to 1973, gave an insider's glimpse of the unfolding events. The gathering opened with a meeting on Friday afternoon, he recalled in his memoir, *Before the Fall*. President Nixon was first to speak. He stressed the importance of secrecy. After Nixon, Secretary Connally presented the new policy. The meeting itself was short: it ended in less than two hours.[1]

On the evening of August 15, 1971, the president took to the airwaves live on national TV to deliver what would later be known as the Nixon Shock. In this defining address, Nixon told the American people and the world that:

> In the past 7 years, there has been an average of one international monetary crisis every year. Now who gains from these crises? Not the workingman; not the investor; not the real producers of wealth. The gainers are the international money speculators. Because they thrive on crises, they help to create them.
>
> In recent weeks, the speculators have been waging an all-out war on the American dollar. The strength of a nation's currency is based on the strength of that nation's economy—and the American economy is by far the strongest in the world. Accordingly, I have directed the Secretary of the Treasury to take the action necessary to defend the dollar against the speculators.

I have directed Secretary Connally to suspend temporarily the convertibility of the dollar into gold or other
reserve assets, except in amounts and conditions determined to be in the interest of monetary stability and in
the best interests of the United States.[2]

Thank god that the US president found the source of all of
its economic miseries: the "international money speculators!"

In the following months the leading economies, the G-10,
scrambled to put together a new global monetary system. They
reached an agreement that would be known as the Smithsonian Agreement, named after the venue where it was created.
In accordance with it, the dollar was devalued against major
currencies, resulting in a 10% adjustment. The participating
parties agreed to keep these new exchange rates within a 4.5%
spread, meaning that exchange rates could move 2.25% up or
down. In exchange, the US agreed to end the import tax it had
imposed. The pegging and convertibility of the dollar to gold
were not reinstated, making the dollar and all other previously
pegged currencies fully and exclusively fiat money, totally and
completely detached from commodity money, gold or silver.
Fiat is a Latin word meaning *it shall be* or *let it be done*, or in
a larger sense, an order or decree of the ruler. From then on,
money became exclusively a state matter.

The Smithsonian Agreement, however, was short-lived since
it simply failed to deliver a new balanced system. After 18
months, in February 1973, it was canceled, and all currencies
were free to float as they found fit. The pegging of the currencies
to the dollar and of the dollar to gold were part of a fading past.
The post WWII Bretton Woods monetary system was now
finally and officially dead.

Since the end of the Bretton Woods system in 1973, members of the IMF have been free to choose any form of exchange
arrangement. A country's currency can freely float or can be
pegged to another currency as each member sees fit. Pegging
currency to gold, however, is forbidden. Gold, the base of money

for the past 6,000 years has been retired, making it now a collectible item, taxed by the IRS at almost twice the capital gain rate that stocks and other assets are.

It was the dawn of a new era, a time of worldwide fiat money. Nixon's 1971 announcement was largely unprecedented in human history and was most undeniably unconstitutional (Article 1 section 8). Starting from the very dawn of trade some 6,500 years ago, gold and silver had always been money. Even when paper currencies were used, they were backed, drew their value, or linked in some way to these precious metals. Only for very limited periods and in very confined territories was this rule abandoned, and typically with devastating consequences. But with a mere stroke of a pen on Executive Order 11615, the president of the United States caused *the entire world* to abandon its gold-based money system. As a result, there were now no more restrictions on paper money creation or printing. Previously, gold quantity restricted these activities. From now on, money could be created at will, at almost no cost and in unlimited quantities.

You would think that such a dramatic move was taken after consultation with, if not approval from, Congress. After all, Article 1, Section 8 of the US Constitution gave Congress the power to coin money and regulate its value. Barring consultation with Congress, perhaps it would have been worthwhile to consult with the US's key international allies, all joint members of Bretton Woods, the very system Nixon's declaration was rendering obsolete. You might at least hope for a deep analysis and meaningful review by the president, considering the historic weight of such a move and of its potential impacts. Well, think again! Not a single one of these actions were taken in the days leading up to the weekend of August 13, 1971, when the President and his financial team met in Camp David. No approval from Congress, no respect of the Constitution, no consideration of allies, no profound evaluation, and of course, no inclusion of the American people, not even after the fact.

Paul Volcker, the Under Secretary of the Treasury at the time, and the man who would later become the Chairman of the Federal Reserve, acknowledged "there was no real debate about the new policy."[3] William Safire, Nixon's speechwriter and a Camp David attendee, added in his memoir, "Nixon made it clear 'About closing the gold window—we cannot know fully what effect it will have.'"[4] And this is the most troubling point. At the most basic level, neither Nixon nor his advisors fully understood the repercussions, namely, that by fundamentally changing the nature of money they were changing the course of history. With this short Friday afternoon meeting, the 37th US president, with help from President Johnson, delivered a significant blow to core tenets of capitalism and free markets. The consequences would still take many decades to manifest and to be fully understood, but on that weekend in August 1971 the global economy and world history had been set on particular new path; just as they were when Nero first began debasing the denarius in the 1st century AD. Time and human nature would now play their part. Nonetheless, the die was cast, and would eventually lead us to the 2008 financial collapse and to the impending end of the fiat money era that awaits us.

Gold may be a "barbaric relic" as stated by Keynes and many before him. Gold truly has no intrinsic value. As Milton Friedman noted, it also makes very little sense to risk lives and spend fortunes digging gold out of the ground just to bury it back in Fort Knox. Nevertheless, gold does possess one critical quality that undercuts all of the statements above: gold's scarcity. No matter how much people want to spend it, how much bankers what to create more of it, and politicians are tempted to use it for their political goals, gold simply cannot be created in unlimited amounts out of thin air. This is gold's most basic and critical quality that even fractional-reserve banking bent but could not break. This rarity was exactly one of the key qualities that attracted people to gold and led them to adopt it as money in the first place.

In the days of limited money supply, money was nothing more than a mirror, reflecting the ratio between a means of exchange and goods in the market place. When production improved, be it through technological advances or weather impacting harvests, prices would go down. Prices would go up on the rare occasions when new gold and silver deposits were discovered increasing significantly their volume. Products were created by people, their labor, capital, innovation, drive, and luck; money was just a way to exchange and store the worth of these products. Fractional-reserve banking added another dimension: money became a type of product that could be created, sold, and generate economic activity. Though often, fractional-reserve banking had a harmful effect on markets. Still money was limited, finite in quantity, and with limited independence from the products it represented.

Everything changed with Executive Order 11615 and the preceding Gold Reserve Requirements Elimination Act. Suddenly money became something totally different. Money had become a magic wand that would move the economy. Money no longer reflected products but was creating them and generating demand for them through its own new creation.

Previously, as a means of exchange money was the "mother of all market signals" in that it reflected the value people assigned to products. People "voted" their priorities via the pricing mechanism. This free "vote" is the essence of capitalism and of free people. Capital is something people own and use and which moves freely, addressing and reflecting the free tastes and priorities of hundreds of millions of people, households and businesses that comprise the market. This movement of capital creates the investments, products, services, and industries people actually want and to which they are ready to allocate their limited resources.

Now money suddenly ceased to serve only as a voting mechanism and as a reflection of goods and services in the marketplace. Now the government and the Federal Reserve (or any central bank or government for that matter) could create $100 million, or $100 billion, or $4 trillion new dollars at practically no cost and buy products and services worth those billions or trillions. Money was now a product, created on a whim, with the capacity to move and ignite sizable parts of the market, shifting labor and investment allocations, creating booms and busts, and redistributing purchasing power from the masses to the lucky or connected few. With this haphazard move, Nixon and his advisers enabled the distortion of all the critical mechanisms and balances that had acted as the foundations for all economic activity, foreign currency values and international trade since the first usage of silver and gold for trade in Mesopotamia and Egypt 6,000 years prior. And though it will take 40 or 50 more years for things to fully play out, the course of history was set and there would be no turning back.

Not only did the price mechanism and the role of money change, but language itself started to change, and not in a coherent and rational manner. For example, rising housing prices are widely considered good. They are promoted by the government and the Federal Reserve who tout the "housing recovery." At the same time, an increase in healthcare costs is bad that needs to be curtailed, as repeatedly stated by President Obama when selling his healthcare plan to the American public. What can possibly be the logic behind liking one price rise and hating the other? Do family budgets for healthcare come from a different place than their resources for housing? Why is it that housing prices going up and enriching real estate builders and previous owners—typically the more affluent and older generation— is good, while healthcare cost increases that enrich insurance company executives is "bad"? You could argue to the contrary that people live in houses every day and go to a doctor much less frequently only when they are sick or old. Doesn't it make more sense to strive for prices to fall all over so that people can afford more rather than less, exactly as the prices of consumer electronics did in the past 20 years?

Executive Order 11615 and Johnson's Gold Reserve Requirements Elimination Act unleashed a powerful beast—the power of unlimited money creation. It is this same money-debt creation machine (new money is mostly created in the form of debt) that would bring America to its knees less than 50 years later, and on its way cause significant damage economically, socially, and morally. It is this wild force that would make the few, the happy few, rich to an unimaginable degree while forcing the vast majority of American families to take on two and sometimes three full-time jobs to support their families, families that are smaller than those of the previous generation. It is this self-destructing mechanism that would lift China to superpower status and enable its government and many of its citizens to own growing parts of America and of the rest of the world. It would give birth to an anti-democratic and corrupt-by-nature lobbying industry whose underlying function is buying elected officials. It would create a political class of politicians addicted to money. The contrast hits hardest when you consider how far removed we are from the days of Thomas Jefferson, who, after a life of public service still left behind a debt that forced his heirs to sell his beloved estate, Monticello. It appears timing is everything: if only Jefferson had lived today when former presidents earn hundreds of thousands of dollars for brief speaking engagements and 67% of Senators are millionaires!

This money-debt machine would drag Congressional approval ratings down and lift Wall Street bonuses and salaries to their dizzying levels of greed. It would make Washington, D.C. suburbs the richest in the nation and a model of income inequality. It would widen the gap between the haves and have-nots and put tens of millions of American kids into crushing debt just in order to attend school. It will also open an unbridgeable gap between millennials and baby boomers.

Its time therefore to take a close look at this new and unique era, a time of worldwide unlimited money creation possibilities, a time of endless debt, a unique and new time in world history, the fiat money era.

Chapter 10:
Bye-Bye, Gold; Hello, Fiat Money

"The study of money, above all other fields in economics, is one in which complexity is used to disguise truth or to evade truth, not to reveal it. The process by which banks create money is so simple the mind is repelled. With something so important, a deeper mystery seems only decent."
—John Kenneth Galbraith

The entire story of the era that followed the cancelation of Bretton Woods, i.e. the fiat money era, can be told in a few graphs. You can find them below. The rest of the chapter will be devoted to explaining them, their intricacies, and their interplay. Later, we will explore why these graphs and the phenomena they represent arose and the social impact behind these graphs. Once these are fully understood, the world we live in will become much clearer and illusionless.

And these are the telling graphs:

> Change in total debt, all sectors of the US economy, 1960-2014
> Change in purchasing power of the dollar, 1971-2014
> Changes in US GDP, Median household income, and Stock prices, 1970-2014
> US Balance of Trade 1960–2014
> China's Foreign Exchange Reserves, 1977-2014
> Financial sector liabilities, 1970-2014
> The S&P 500 Stock Market Index, 1970-2014
> The US economy, Debt-to-GDP ratio, 1960-2014

Graph 1: Total debt of all sectors

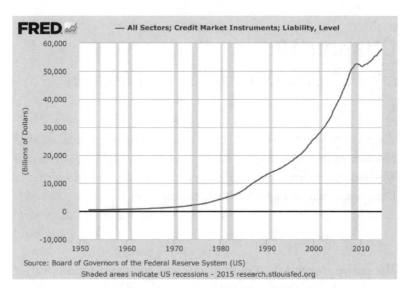

USA - Total debt of all sectors of the US economy:
government, business, and consumers as of late 2014.
Source: Federal Reserve Economic Data (FRED)

Interpreting Graph 1

As of mid-2014, the combined debt of all sectors of the US
economy is almost $58 trillion; up from around 700 billion in
1960. This means that the US debt has multiplied 81 times in
50 years. The debt is 3.6 times the US GDP, which means it
is the equivalent of 3.6 years' worth of the total output of the
US economy.[1]

This number does not include unfunded liabilities, like
government pensions, which technically are not monies borrowed and thus are not accounted for as actual debt. These
obligations are estimated at least another $4–10 trillion,
depending on various factors like calculation method and
time span.

Detail of the total economy's debt and growth by key sectors and decade (not all sectors included):

Decade	Total all sectors Billions of $$ From – to	Of Financial Sector Billions of $$ From - to	Of Federal Government Billions of $$ From - to	Of Households Billions of $$ From - to
1964-1973	970-2,200	45-205	300-470	290-630
1974-1983	2,000 -6,600	205-900	470-1,400	630-1,700
1984- 1993	6,600-16,300	900-3,300	1,400-4,500	1,700-4,200
1994-2003	16,300 –34,400	3t,300-11,000	4,500-7,000	4,200-9,500
2004-mid-2014	34,400- 57,500	11,000-14,000	7,000-17,600	9,500-13,400
		Peak of 17,000 in 2008		

Graph 2: Change in purchusing power 1971-2013

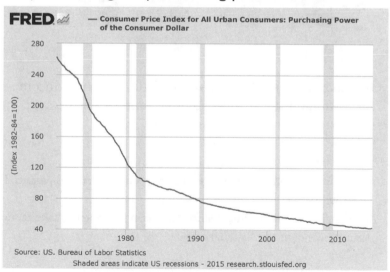

Source: US. Bureau of Labor Statistics
Shaded areas indicate US recessions - 2015 research.stlouisfed.org

Interpreting Graph 2

The US dollar has lost almost 85% of its consumer purchasing power since 1970. This means that today you will need $660 to buy what $100 bought you in 1970. This graph is based on official CPI measurements, with all their limitations as we will see them later.

Graph 3: Growth in US GDP, Income and Stock prices

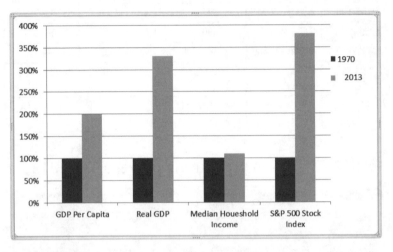

Growth in total US GDP*, Median* US household income, and stock prices adjusted to inflation.

*Gross domestic product: the total value of goods and services produced in a country in a year.

*Median household income: half of American households make more than this amount and half make less.

Year	1970	2011/2013	1970 to 2013 (Inflation adjusted)
GDP Per capita In 2011 dollars (inflation adjusted)	$24,000	$48,300	200% GDP per capita doubled.
Real GDP (adjusted to 2013 dollars)	$4.8 T	$16 T	330%
Median household income 2011 dollars (inflation adjusted)	$46,000	$51,000	110% median household income almost no change
S&P 500 stock index (2013 inflation adjusted)	484	2050 (Nov 2014)	420% (Nov. 2014)

Sources: Federal Reserve Economic Data (FRED) and Census Bureau.

Interpreting Graph 3

Whereas the GDP, the "pie" has tripled in real terms since 1970, the real, inflation adjusted, income of the median household in America has remained practically unchanged. Meanwhile, the S&P 500, the stock index that represents most large publicly traded companies, has in real terms, quadrupled.

Graph 4: US Balance of Trade (1963-2013)

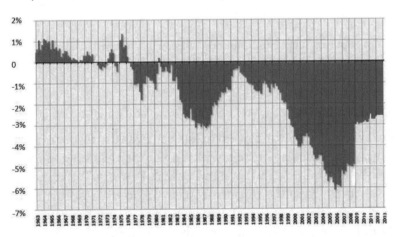

US balance of trade from 1960 to 2013 as percentage of GDP
Source: US Census Bureau, Foreign Trade Division

185

Interpreting Graph 4

Since 1976, the US has run constant and growing trade deficits. These deficits were around $400 billion a year at the beginning the 2000s. They peaked at around $700 billion a year between 2005 and 2008, and settled at an average of 525 billion a year from 2010 to 2013.[2] The US's cumulative trade deficit since 1975, the last time the US had a positive trade balance, is more than 9 trillion dollars as of mid-2013.[3]

Graph 5: China's Foreign Exchange Reserves (B/$)

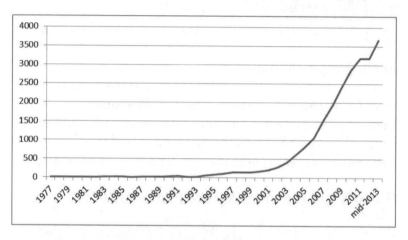

Source: State Administration of Foreign Exchange, People's Republic of China and the People's Bank of China

Interpreting Graph 5:

In 1977, China's foreign exchange reserve (the balance in foreign non-Chinese currency in China's possession) was $2.3 billion. By mid-2013 this number had grown 422 times, with adjustment for inflation, and reached $3.66 trillion. This figure is closely related to the trade deficit the US and the European Union have accumulated over this time span.

Graph 6: The financial sector

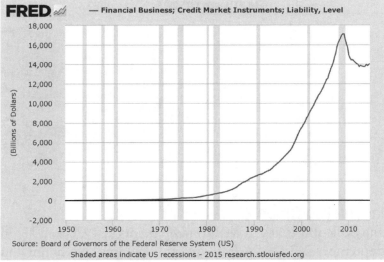

Source: Federal Reserve Economic Data (FRED)

Interpreting Graph 6:

Between 1970 and today, financial sector liabilities (debt), have grown from around $120 billion dollars to around $14 trillion, a 116-fold growth. This figure is representative of the financial sector's current state. In terms of percentage of GDP, the financial sector occupied around 2% of GDP in the 1950s and today accounts for 8% of the GDP.[4]

Graph 7: US Stock market

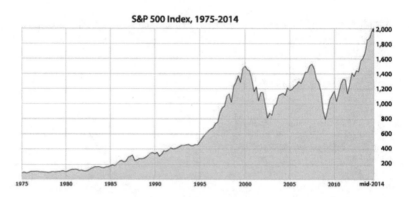

S&P 500 Index, 1975-2014

Interpreting Graph 7:

The S&P 500 Index moved from 83 points in 1970 to 2000 in September 2014, a 24-fold growth including two boom and bust cycles in 2000 and in 2008.

Graph 8: Debt-to-GDP ratio

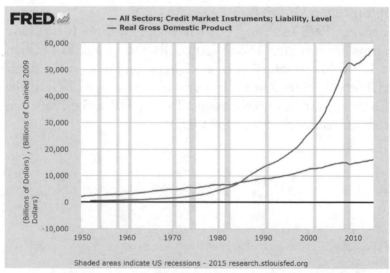

Source: Federal Reserve Economic Data (FRED) - the GDP- is the Bottom line in the above graph, the debt is the top one.

Interpreting Graph 8

Debt growth has significantly surpassed GDP growth. This gap is increasing continually.

This final graph is the most telling of them all. It acts as an X-ray of the nation's economy and demonstrates very simply that America will never manage to outgrow its debt problems. Quite to the contrary, the gap between the country's debt and its GDP is constantly getting larger. There is no chance, then, that GDP growth could resolve the debt problem by serving as a debt payment source.

The situation is similar to that of a family that takes out a loan and, after the end of the first year, needs to make interest and some principal payments. The family has four options:

> › Option one: If its income increased (perhaps due to successful loan investment), they can make the payment from their newly increased income.
> › Option two: If its income didn't increase, it can make the payment by cutting down on other expenses, which would mean lowering its standard of living.
> › Option three: The family takes on an extra loan to pay the interest on the first loan which will result in them being in even greater debt.
> › Option four: Try to declare bankruptcy and hopefully avoid paying its debts altogether.

The graph above shows that time and time again, the US selected option three. This family's income—the GDP—did not increase enough to pay the loan, and making payments by cutting the standard of living was too painful. Thus, the US family opted to take on more and more debt to cover the past debt. It also took out new loans to spend more on new "stuff." By now, this family has accumulated debt equivalent to almost 4 times its annual income *and* its yearly budget also operates at a deficit. The family is not only unable to pay its past debt, but it needs new debt to pay its ongoing bills.

189

But where did all this debt come from? Who owns all this debt? And what will happen if it's not repaid? As we know, the vehicle for the creation of new money is debt. As we saw in previous chapters, fractional-reserve banking is the mechanism by which money multiplies itself based on the cash reserve requirement of the financial system. Even when the Federal Reserve creates money outright, it appears as either a loan given to banks, a financial asset purchased from banks, or as bonds purchased from the Treasury. In every case, the money is debt. From there, it starts multiplying itself again and again via the fractional-reserve mechanism.

After 1971, it was no longer only the Fed that could create money. Since money creation really means the creation of any means of payment, money and debt became synonymous, and thus any organization with the capacity to circulate credit became, de facto, a money creator. And as the reserve ratio continued to drop, finally reaching a low of 1.5%, the amount of debt created grew exponentially.

Within the fractional reserve framework, one person's debt is another one's asset and almost every asset is also a debt. The government's debt, for example, is partially people's social security funds. These funds are retirement assets for Americans. On the other hand, the government owns a trillion dollars in student loans—an asset—but this number represents millions of students' debts. This back-to-back debt-asset-debt-asset is a house of cards: the collapse of one card triggers the collapse of the counter instrument. Simply put, if a debt is forgiven, somebody else's asset will vanish. So the $58 trillion in liabilities of the US economy are also for the most $58 trillion of financial assets belonging to foreign governments, US companies, American households and investors, pension funds, and dozens of other entities.

The above rule has one practical, though not theoretical, exception. The money the Treasury "owes" the Federal Reserve is entirely meaningless, just a line on the Fed's balance sheet. Though for political and standing reasons they act as if it's a real "debt" which should eventually "wind down." All of these asset holders expect and plan on receiving their financial assets back. They depend on them to cover their own liabilities and expenses or to maintain their standard of living. If, as in 2008, one link in the chain fails to fulfill its obligations, the scheme ends and the results are catastrophic.

Graph 8 also demonstrates that the concept of stimulus, i.e. debt spending which grows the economy is extremely limited. To be sure, the debt money changes hands and on its way generates economic activity, but ultimately, the fact is that only a small percentage of the debt money translates into GDP growth or long-term activity. If we take into account the huge ascent in productivity and GDP growth brought on by the Digital Revolution between the 1970s and today, it becomes even more obvious how little real and sustainable growth can be attributed to debt.

So why didn't the national debt grow the economy in any meaningful and ongoing way? Doesn't the constant flow of credit improve the economy and grow it as modern *Keynesians* taught us? Was the Fed wrong to preach and exercise money and debt creation from 2008 to 2014?

There are a few reasons why the ongoing growth in debt had such a small impact on per capita GDP growth. The first reason was what von Mises called malinvestment. "The essence of a credit-expansion boom is not overinvestment, but investment in wrong lines, i.e. malinvestment." In short, creating and investing in unneeded activities—like building 3.6 million empty houses in 2008, or worthless companies going public so that Wall Street bankers could sell their stock to overeager investors— does not result in lasting economic growth. Because, as von Mises said, "there is no means of avoiding a final collapse of a boom brought about by credit expansion," such malinvestments' contributions to the GDP are short-lived. Meanwhile the debt they create is lasting and will continue to generate compound interest until it's paid off. Essentially, the debt money was wasted but the debt obligation remains until repaid.

The second reason this debt had little impact on GDP growth is that taking debt for consumption creates no lasting returns, as opposed to debt invested in creating new and lasting revenue streams. Thus, even if spent locally, the money has a limited dwindling effect on GDP while the debt lingers. Such behavior is akin to that of a family that takes on credit card debt and uses it to go on a vacation. After the vacation is over, it has to find means of loan and interest repayment. Otherwise, the debt remains and continues growing. If the debt is applied toward the purchase of cheap imports, then even the limited benefit to the GDP will be negligible because most of the debt was spent abroad in the first place.

As seen in Chapter 3, credit was given for yield-bearing project as early as 4,000 years ago. Consumer credit, on the other hand, is only some 90 years old. It relies on a belief in ongoing growing productivity, increasing wages and government budgets from which this credit can be repaid. This behavior has exploded during the fiat money era on the private and public level alike. In reality, however, productivity growth has fallen short of debt growth.

All of this translates into one simple concept: debt taken out and used mostly for malinvestment, social-complexity or consumption (within the country, or even worse, abroad), cannot create any lasting growth in GDP or any lasting positive returns. With no positive returns, the only way to pay the interest on the debt, as well as the principle, is from current expenditures i.e. reducing standard of living. Since this option is unacceptable the debt continues to mount. This constant growth in the debt is also an ongoing unethical practice by which the current generation passes on its debts to the next generation.. Forty years of debt creation placed America in a vicious cycle with only two options for the future: stopping the debt cycle, which would have a significant negative impact on debt owners and on living standards; or accumulating compound debt to maintain existing debt and finance new activities. As time went on, the price tag attached to each of these options grew exponentially but for one big difference: the price for stopping the debt cycle is always immediate, while the price for continued debt accumulation is always sometime in the future. The public, and politicians, always prefer a vague pain in the future over a sharp pain today.

Just as in a Ponzi scheme, the American economy chooses to continue the debt cycle until it exhausts itself, regardless of the immediate short-term consequences and the devastating long-term ones. At this point in the game, rewinding the debt cycle is hardly realistic. The consequences would be so harsh that no politician would be able or willing to try and sell this medicine to the American people, nor would the public be willing to listen. Thus, the debt money–creation train continues full steam ahead increasing the debt to above $58 trillion by late-2014.

Before we move on to chronicle how this $58 trillion mass of debt traveled through the economy, and how it changed the world, we have to address one small issue that repeatedly comes up; namely, the claim that the debt isn't a problem because there are many assets against it. This notion was echoed by one blogger who claimed, after the release of some official statistics in mid-2013: "US Household Assets: $78.2 Trillion, Liabilities: $13.5 Trillion; Net Worth: $64.8 Trillion". This simple math demonstrates a fundamental lack of understanding of how debt and asset ratios work and how these are calculated. While all of those assets prices can quickly change in value the debt is set and doesn't change downwards unless there is a default. The "value" of the US household assets, in the example above, is extrapolated from the value of the latest transactions, which of course does not mean you can actually sell all the assets in the market at this price. Consider the way a company's market value is calculated. As of the beginning of March 2014, the Facebook's market value was estimated at $180 billion. This value was based on some 5 million shares that had last been bought and sold. These shares had been purchased at $71 a share. Given that Facebook has some 2.45 billion shares, these 5 million shares account for less than a quarter of one percent of the outstanding shares. So can we really extrapolate the entire company's worth from such a small sample size? Can we really consider these 5 million shares representative if we were trying to sell 500 million or a billion shares? Between March 2014 and May 2014 these shares went down around 20% to around $58 a share and the value of the company dropped to $148 billion. Though only a fraction of the total shares changed hands, more than $32 billion in on-paper assets disappeared. But if an investor took out a loan and bought shares at $71/share, his debt wouldn't fall in tandem with the company's market value.

The same logic applies to every asset whose value is based upon most recent transactions of similar assets. When you are looking at an individual debt and the value of its collateral asset, calculating the value of the asset based upon the last known transaction of a similar asset makes sense. Trying to apply the rule to an aggregate large-scale calculation, however, just doesn't work. This miscalculation was fundamental to the 2008 housing market meltdown. The valuations of the houses covered by the mortgages was based on the last deals, but when many rushed to suddenly sell the value dropped sharply leaving the lenders' collateral worthless.

So now let's go back and try to examine how did it all come to this point with a debt four times our GDP?

Once the 25% gold backing requirement was eliminated in 1968, so was the last brake on fractional-reserve banking. Low interest rates also made borrowing money attractive: the average interest rates between 1969 and 1978 were around 6.5%, which, after subtracting for inflation, came out to around zero percent.[5] Between 1972 and 1976, households increased their borrowing by about $60 billion per year, totaling $200 billion. This was an increase of about 0.5% of GDP, not at all an insignificant number. Household loans played an important role in increasing national money supply, but they were not alone. The increase in money supply combined with the infamous increase in energy costs due to the 1973 energy crisis instigated by OPEC, led to a surge in inflation. Inflation went from an annual average of around 1.3% in the early 1960s to an average of around 7% in the early 1970s and then to over 10% between 1979 and 1981.

Although there are different theories regarding the cause of the Great Inflation, all the theories share, according to a research paper by the St. Louis Federal Reserve, an "important common ground: monetary policy was, in retrospect, too expansionary [i.e. driven by new money creation] [...] a tighter monetary policy would have been required to produce lower inflation"[6] but this would require a price politicians were not willing to pay. This inflation was not brought under control until the Federal Reserve, led by Paul Volcker, raised interest rates sharply to a peak of 21% in 1981. This drastic action helped temporarily curb the expansion of the money supply and pushed the economy into a recession lasting more than two years.

Still between 1964 and 1983, the federal government's debt grew almost 4.5-fold. The blossoming financial sector took on twenty times more debt in those 20 years. Household debt, largely in the form of mortgages, ratcheted up almost six-fold. This trend continued with little deceleration in the next three decades, bringing the total debt to $58 trillion as of late-2014. Among other projects, this debt financed an expanding government; a large military-industrial complex; a huge increase in consumption, of which a significant part was done abroad; and largely unnecessary financial engineering and malinvestments. It has also financed the cost of an ever growing complex society, its increasing inefficiencies, and corruption. Of course, it has also paid for the interest on the compounded and unpaid debt. But what is so bad about it? Didn't this money-debt creation just improve life all over? To answer these questions we need to take a close look at what this money accomplished, where it went, and how it changed America. With so many new dollars, the value of each drastically declined: 95% decline against gold and 85% compared to the official price index. This index, known as Consumer Price Index, or CPI, is measured by the Bureau of Labor and Statistics. In fact, the Bureau of Labor and Statistics publishes many hundreds of CPI indices. Its most watched CPI is the core CPI which measures all urban consumers products yet excludes changes in cost of energy and food from its calculations.

(Legislation like social security benefit calculations does not exclude those two, food and energy).[7] Core CPI also does not track changes in special taxes imposed on products, like on gas or alcohol, even though they clearly impact the real cost of living. Furthermore, it swaps out products in the measured basket with cheaper products if the prices of the original products climb too high. Thus, the CPI is not a real indicator of price changes in the basket of goods. In fact, the Bureau of Labor and Statistics itself states that "the CPI's objective is to calculate the change in the amount consumers need to spend to maintain a constant level of satisfaction."[8] This is a startling admission considering the price index should measure changes in prices, not an elusive and completely subjective "level of satisfaction." Regardless, even the Bureau of Labor's method yields an 85% growth in price index since the beginning of the fiat money era. Other methods of calculation suggest that the true increase in living cost is sizably greater.[III]

If all of this inflation calculation sounds a bit confusing that is because one of the more sinister goals of constant money devaluation is, in fact, sowing confusion. After all, it was John Maynard Keynes, the founding father of "positive inflation," that pointed out that it is easier to raise prices than to reduce wages, though the impact is the same.[9] He rightly pointed out that labor will typically vigorously resist wage reduction but remain unaware—and thus reluctant to fight—the practically covert and ongoing erosion of its purchasing power through inflation.

By its very nature, the money created through debt is never evenly injected into the marketplace. Typically debt is exclusively available to specific segments of the population: mortgages for real estate buyers or student loans for college students. The domain into which the debt money is infused experiences significant price increases. The effects of this new money diminishes as the money travels through the economy.

III To find out more about how the CPI is calculated, go to www.shadowstats.com/article/no-438-public-comment-on-inflation-measurement.pdf

Though the student loan system was set up in 1965 under the Higher Education Act it was only around the early 1990s that it started to take off. In the past three decades, more than $1.2 trillion of student loan money was created and injected into this market. The impact on the level of college tuition and fees was swift: between 1983 and 2013 college tuition multiplied by a factor of three in real terms. Contrary to the conventional wisdom and politicians' demagoguery, student loans do not make college more accessible to those who cannot afford it. More money for student loans also do not create significantly more spots in college; they just increase the cost of each available spot, since there is more money chasing the same amount of seats. What *does* make college more accessible is increasing colleges' student capacity. Increasing capacity, however, requires planning, teachers, staff, buildings, infrastructure, disciplines and even a reputation that will attract qualified teachers and students. All of these factors can only grow in a limited way in existing institutions, whereas new institutions take decades to come into being. In the long run, increasing budgets can create more college seats, but this is a lengthy process that takes many decades.

In 1988, the University of California decided to create a new campus in Merced called UC Merced. It finally opened in 2005. Nine years after its inception, this campus is hardly successful. UC Merced has 15% of the enrollment of the average major UC campus, which were set up some 70 years ago, and has no impressive national ranking or prestige to attract top students and faculty. So all this student loan-money creation we saw above had one noticeable impact: it sharply increased tuition, and with it lavish university spending.[10] Ironically, all the loans taken out to make college education accessible to all had the inverse effect as prices have skyrocketed, making universities even more unaffordable than before.

Real Growth in College Tuition 1983-2013

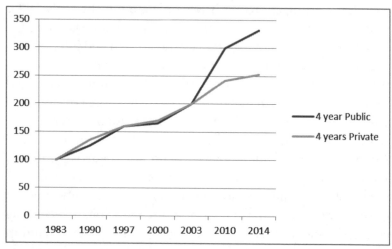

Source: The College Board, Annual Survey 2013-2014

It comes as no surprise, therefore, that in the aggregate, more than 60% of college graduates in 2012 graduated with an average of $29,400 in debt.[11] It is also unsurprising that total student loan debt has passed the $1.2 trillion mark as of early 2014, of which some 80% is held by the federal government.[12] This debt is owed by some 37 million Americans, mostly young. Among the under-30 set, more than 60% of college graduates have outstanding student loans. Even more disconcerting is that, as of 2011, about 27% of college loans are in varying stages of delinquency.[13]

Young people are not the only ones engulfed by this debt. About 1.7 million retiree households are still paying student loans. Their total debt has grown six-fold, from $2.8 billion dollars to $18.2 billion, in the past decade. Of these retirees' households, 32% are defaulting on their student loans;[14] and social security payments are garnished to pay for these loans.

The country's total college debt is higher than the annual economic output of Mexico or South Korea, and it has been growing at a rate of over $100 billion a year since 2007. This influx of money has affected universities, which have started building lavish buildings, increasing their administrative staff— the past 30 years the number of administrative staff more than doubled: significantly beyond the growth in number of students[15]—and bettering employment conditions. University employee income has grown 15–18% in real terms between 1998 and 2011 alone.[16] Thus, one of the biggest losers in the fiat money era are millennials, so many of whom are overwhelmed by debt, crushed by the high cost of housing, struggling to find employment, and above all, heirs to the mountain of debt created by their predecessors.

Now that we have visited one of the losers of this debt-money creation machine, let us review one of the fiat money era's biggest winners— if not the biggest—the financial industry. The entire river of debt and money was channeled through the financial industry, and a significant part thereof was created by it. The financial industry was the junction, the initiator, and the controller of most of the tools that created or utilized this debt. The financial sector also influenced where the debt and money were funneled to. This position of immense power combined with the new types of businesses created after the collapse of Bretton Woods, the easing of capital controls, and the relaxation of laws governing foreign exchange transactions made this industry the biggest winner of the debt-money creation era.

In the 1970s, there were no glories or riches in Wall Street. The 1970s were a decade when brokerage firms closed down and some 90% of trained brokers would leave Wall Street in less than a decade. With no fat salaries and year-end bonuses, the ones that stayed would supplement their income with occupations like writing books and being chauffeurs. Eventually the survivors of the 1970s would be handsomely rewarded. As one veteran recalled, "if you had invested in 1975 and held until 1985, you had some very fine returns."[17] And what fine returns they were. In fact only in 1985 did Wall Street year-end bonuses pass the one billion dollar mark; in 26 years they would grow more than 34-fold and reach almost $35 billion at the eve of the 2008 collapse. Salaries saw similar growth, below you can see a graph comparing the change in salaries between New York private sector employees and Wall Street employees, the difference is staggering.

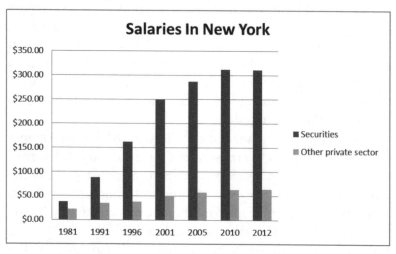

Average Salaries in New York City, Securities Industry vs. All Other Private Sector Industries, 1981-2012.
Source: New York State Comptroller October 2013.

The ongoing influx of new money generated new activities and new financial products and dramatically scaled up existing activities. For four decades, the financial sector grew faster than the economy, rising from less than 4% of GDP in 1971 to more than 8% today. The business of money accounts for about a third of total corporate profits in America.[18]

Large financial firms' assets, in the form of loans and liabilities, in the form of deposits, both grew significantly for conventional and investment banks alike. In 1986, Goldman Sachs had $38 billion in assets.[19] By 2007, on the eve of the housing collapse, Goldman's assets were valued at $1.1 trillion. The investment bank's assets had grown nearly 3000%. As financial institutions grew, they engaged in more and more leveraged and risky activities, increasing their risk and debt. At the end of 2007, Fannie

May and Freddie Mac owned or guaranteed $5.3 trillion in mortgage-related assets against just $70.7 billion of capital, a 75:1 ratio. Many other institutions were operating at similarly ratios of 1:18 to 1:25. Between 1974 and 2007, the financial sector's liabilities grew 82-fold from $205 billion to $17 trillion.[20]

This huge expansion in size, assets, and liabilities, was of course followed by similar expansions in staff and compensations. For decades following the 1929 collapse, compensation in the financial industry was equal to compensation in the general economy. With the growth of the financial sector, all of this changed. By 2008, compensation in the financial sector was almost double that in the economy at large.[21]

No compensation is more egregious than executive pay. By 2005, the average annual salary of an executive in the financial sector was $3.4 million. In some subsections this number climbed to an average of $7 million a year.[22] In the 1980s, the highest paid executive on Wall Street was the CEO of Salomon Brothers. In 1986 his compensation was $3.2 million ($6.8 million in 2013 dollars). To see how much the situation has changed, look to the salary of the CEO of Merrill Lynch in 2006. He received an annual compensation of $91 million ($105 million in 2013 dollars). This pay is 15 times higher, inflation adjusted, than that of his 1986 equal. Without a doubt, the CEO that led Merrill Lynch to de facto bankruptcy was paid exorbitantly, but other Wall Street executives weren't exactly starving either. The CEO at Goldman Sachs received $68.5 million; the CEOs of Lehman Brothers and of JPMorgan Chase received around $30 million.[23]

But at the top of this food chain were the biggest winners of the money-created glut, hedge fund managers. Hedge funds are private investment pools for institutions and wealthy individuals. Hedge fund manager earnings were not even on the same scale as those of bankers. In 2006, four hedge fund managers made $1 *billion* or more in annual compensation, each. Twenty-one more managers made more than $240 million. Combined, the top 25 hedge fund managers grossed $14 billion total.[24] This sum is more than the annual income of 260,000 middle-earning households in America. A last fun fact is that many of these earners paid reduced taxes, capital gains rates, on these incomes, while regular earning households paid a higher rate on their employment compensation.

Wall Street claims that these compensation packages occur naturally in the free market and that they are payment for "delivering value." Nothing could be further from the truth. Capitalism is about free people using their capital freely to "vote" their priorities and choices through purchasing decisions, and businesses reacting to those votes and priorities. It is not about creating huge amounts of capital out of thin air. In the past 35 years, capitalism has been distorted by the massive money-debt creation and government-sponsored cronyism. A market that is financed by debt, a government (federal, state and local) that accounts for 40% of the economy and in which the financial sector is engaged in massive money creation and financial engineering which is sponsored and guaranteed by the state, is hard to describe as free market or capitalist. Our system is as much capitalism as Bernie Madoff's Ponzi scheme was an investment firm, though for 20 years it looked like one. The true face of our system became very clear in the summer of 2008, when Wall Street's "delivering value" machine brought America to the verge of total financial collapse. If not for the bailout-rescue packages and increased money printing by the Federal Reserve, all those institutions and executives claiming to "deliver value" would have gone bankrupt. Wall Street's growth and exploding compensation is nothing more than a version of the Cantillon Effect: Wall Street is rewarded with the highest premiums merely because of its proximity to the entry point of gushing fiat money.

The 2008 financial collapse was hardly the first meltdown caused by Wall Street's consistent increase in leverage and risk taking. Nor was it the first time the tax payer came to the rescue. In 1984, Continental Illinois, the nation's 7th-largest bank, was rescued by the Fed. In 1988, it was First Republic (14th largest), in 1989, it was MCorp (36th), and in 1991 the Bank of New

England (33rd).[25] The case of Continental Illinois Bank brought into being a new term and a new official policy. The bank's rescue cost the government a then-significant billion dollars. Congress held hearings to assess the decision. During these hearings, an official from the Department of the Treasury stated that "federal regulators would not allow the 11 largest 'money center banks' to fail." Congressman McKinney (R-CT) immediately replied: "Mr. Chairman, [...] we have a new kind of bank. It is called too big to fail. TBTF, and it is a wonderful bank."[26]

The Wall Street gravy train didn't only favor Wall Street executives and hedge fund managers. The top executives of publicly traded companies got nice slices of the pie as well. These top executives are an integral part of the Wall Street ecosystem. After all, Wall Street needs products to trade. In the fiat money era, the popularity of compensation for top executives in the form of shares and stock options grew in tandem with the stock market. This practice increased executive pay significantly: from 1978 to 2011, compensation of CEO's of public companies increased on average by more than 700%.[27] A *USA Today* review of 174 S&P 500 companies' filings found that CEO pay is made up of a salary-to-stock option ratio of about 1:5 to 1:10 salary to stock compensation. For example, the CEO of AT&T had a salary of about $1.5 million in 2010 while his stock and option package was valued at $13 million, with another $5 million in bonuses. Colgate's CEO received a salary of $1.15 million and a stock and options package of $9.3 million (and also around $3.3 million in bonuses).[28] In addition, as we will soon see, this custom also offered a substantial incentive for executives to make decisions based largely on their impact on stock prices.

The consistent growth in stock prices brought on by the money creation machine widened the gap between CEOs and their employees. Indeed, when considering CEO pay, which includes shares and options, the CEO to employee compensation ratio grew more than ten times, from around 1:18 in 1965 to around 1:210 in 2011. These multimillion dollar executive compensations in public companies are not limited only to CEOs, but include a handful of top executives. Yahoo, for example, had around ten executives with compensations between $4-39 million in 2012. This payment structure is by no means an outlier. One of Yahoo's executives just wasn't cutting it for the company's CEO, so he was fired less than a year and a half after being hired. His compensation for one and a half years on the job? $109 million.[29]

The overgrown, overly powerful Wall Street does not create any real product; Wall Street simply trades securities—stocks, bonds—and derivatives—options, future contracts—as well as invests and lends money. Thus, Wall Street needs something to trade that customers will want, or better yet, that they will borrow for. Nothing trades better than dreams, and no dreams are more exciting and limitless than the cutting edge world of high-tech. A natural next stop for the money glut was, therefore, the Silicon Valley. Without taking anything away from Silicon Valley's ingenuity and innovation, it is no coincidence that Silicon Valley was the center of one of the three major bubbles in the history of Wall Street and twentieth century America.

If you are looking for the date of birth of the dot-com bubble, you can probably mark it on August 9, 1995. On that day, a young and small company from Mountain View, California, went public. The name of the company was Netscape and its main product was a strange software tool called a browser. This browser enabled people to connect to "the web," whatever that was. The company was hardly a year old when it filed the pre IPO statement with the Securities and Exchange Commission. (IPO or Initial Public Offering is a process by which a company raises money by selling some of its shares to the public. Afterward, its shares are listed for trade on stock markets). With a product that had barely been on the market 6 months at the time, the company could show only one quarter's financial results. Their financials showed only revenues of almost $5 million and losses of $2.7 million. Furthermore, the company's main product was Netscape Navigator, a free web browser, so the source of ongoing revenues wasn't completely clear. These small details didn't bother Morgan Stanley too much, which handled the public offering and thus marketing the shares to investors.

Four months before the public offering, Netscape sold 11% of the company to a group of media companies for around $17 million, giving Netscape a respectable value of approximately $170 million.[30] On the end of the first day of trading, however, Netscape's shares closed out at $58 dollars a share, giving the company a value of, wait for it, almost $3 billion, about 18 times its value four months prior. This explosion in value made many of Netscape's early employees millionaires overnight and sent one of the founders on his way to becoming the first Internet billionaire. The overnight success of a company that was hardly 16 months old and practically revenueless caught the eyes of Wall Street, investors and entrepreneurs alike. Netscape managed to galvanize a new gold rush. Billions in investment money rushed in to fund the thousands of Internet startups springing up, all with the goal of going public as soon as possible.

Let's not forget that, after all, Wall Street was running this show. The ecosystem was simple: companies were set up quickly, with large investments mainly from VCs.[IV] If a new company had a good story, some kind of track record, and, most importantly, good connections with Wall Street investors, the company would offer its shares to the public and list them for trading on NASDAQ. From there, investors, individuals and institutions took over, typically continuing to push up the share prices. The listing on the NASDAQ public market helped the original VC investors, the founders, and the employees sell shares and hit the jackpot.

Before the Netscape phenomenon, companies almost never went public until they were profitable for at least a few quarters. By 1999, companies were primarily offering their shares on the strength of their hopes and dreams. While experts and pundits were all giving rationales and educated explanations, buyers were pushing share prices higher and higher. An online toy company

---

IV VC refers to venture capital firm, an early-stage investment company whose source of money are typically pension funds and other institutional money.

called eToys.com was soon valued at almost twice that of the established retailer ToysRUs , though it had less than 0.5% of its annual sales.[31] Between 1986 and 1990, some 90 companies in the extended Silicon Valley, the San Francisco Bay area, went public. A decade later between, 1996 and 2000, almost 400 did.

Money was not only being funneled into IPOs. Early-stage companies attracted both billions of dollars in investments and many high-powered executives who left established jobs and careers at large corporations in exchange for a crack at the fortunes start-ups promised. One of these early-stage companies was Webvan. Webvan is perhaps one of the best examples of malinvestment and of resource misallocation during a credit bubble. Webvan had a noble idea: why bother going to your local supermarket if you can order groceries online? Founded in early 1997 by Louis Borders (the founder of the Borders bookstore), the company raised around $120 million from top Silicon Valley VCs, a sizable sum in those days. Soon thereafter, Webvan hired top executives from companies like FedEx and Andersen Consulting and launched its service in 1999. The company invested heavily in warehouses, technology, and automation, and continued to raise money in successive rounds of financing. In the first six months of operation, sales reached $13 million and losses $144.5 million. By November 1999, the company offered its shares to the public. It raised $375 million dollars in its IPO. At its peak a few weeks later, the company was valued at $11 billion. This is an $11 billion value on the basis of $13 million in sales, and more than $140 million in losses! In 2000, the company was stocking and delivering tens of thousands of items, many of them perishable. Webvan was flying high, receiving the highest accolades from many pundits and experts.

This acclaim, however, was short-lived. By July 2001, less than two years after its IPO, the company filed for chapter 11 bankruptcy. Over the course of its operation, the company had lost around $830 million in investor money. This number does not take into account the losses of investors who had bought shares from previous investors on the public market. At its height, Webvan had 2,000 employees, many of whom put their hearts and souls into the company. All of the employees were sent home. 1,700 hourly employees lost their job they received a $900 gift from an anonymous donor.

In early March 1997, the NASDAQ Composite (an index of the thousands of companies, heavily technology tilted, listed on the NASDAQ stock exchange) stood at around 1,300 points. By the end of 1999, it hovered around 4,000 points. It had tripled, quadrupled or more the value of new and older companies alike.

As time went on, the market heated up rapidly. In 1996, first-day returns[V] on IPOs averaged about 17%, whereas the median was a 10% increase. In 1999, first-day returns averaged 69% when the median was 35%. In 1999 and 2000, dot-com IPOs averaged a first day pop of 88% with a median of 56%. In 1999, the dot-com bubble reached its peak. They represented 55% of all IPOs, or a total of 289 companies that had raised some $25 billion. This number was up from $2 billion raised for 45 deals in 1998. The average Internet company ended the year around 260% above its offering price.[32] The rush to go public and cash out, shared by bankers, investors, and entrepreneurs, brought about a sharp drop in share quality. Median company revenue dropped from $22.8 million in 1996 to $10.6 million in 2000.[33]

As the third millennium approached, everybody was confident and joyful, especially on Wall Street where the hot IPO market yielded record bonuses, up 49% from previous year. The average Wall Street bonus for all finance employees now stood at $75,000 (more than $100,000 adjusted to 2013 dollars).[34] Most experts were sure this party would keep going and going. *Business Week*'s online year-end headline read: "The IPO Market Should Keep Rolling in 2000: S&P analyst expects the tech issues to keep leading the market."[35] By March 10, 2000, the NASDAQ Composite index had reached 5,048 points, an almost four-fold growth from 1996.

V First-day returns indicate the jump in a new stock's value on the first day of trading. The first day of trading is the first time retail investors have access to these new shares.

Then suddenly, the public's seemingly insatiable appetite for tech stock, which had seemed so natural just a month prior, started to abate. With no advance sign or specific reason, on March 15, the index found itself at 4,582 points. This was a modest 10% drop after an extended bull market so nobody really cared. By March 27, the index was almost back at 5,000 points. This fall seemed like just as a small correction. But by April 15, the NASDAQ index had slipped to around 3,300 points. This drop was more than a technical correction, but it still slowly recovered back to around 4,200 points by the end of August. On Sep 1, 2000, the index had climbed to 4,234 points. This was a short relief. A year later on September 7, 2001, the NASDAQ index stood on 1,687. It had returned to 1996 territory. The dot-com bubble was officially and finally over.

A painful adjustment, the typical aftermath of a finance-driven boom, was taking place across the tech industry. Over the course of the next two to three years, as they ran out of money, thousands of companies would close their doors and fire hundreds of thousands of employees. Dozens of the new publicly traded dot-com companies filed for bankruptcy or sought a fire sale. Other companies trimmed down operations. All surviving publicly traded companies lost three-quarters or more of their market value. Even a year before the September 2001 low, in November 2000, 79 of the 280 stocks in the Bloomberg US Internet index were down 90% or more from their 52-week high. Another 72 were down 80 to 89%. Only five of the once high-flying companies were down less than 5%.

In the aftermath of the bubble, the fate of the more established technology companies was no different. They also shed more than 80% of their boom value. Cisco Systems, for example, a prominent technology company, was trading at $10.5 a share at the beginning of 1998. Its stock price shot up to $77 a share in February 2000. By September 2, 2001, it was back to $12 a share.

Overall, investors lost $1.755 trillion in real money and paper profits.[36] Tens of billions of dollars in pension fund money went down the drain. A portion of these lost fortunes ended up in the pockets of thousands of high-tech industry venture capitalists, entrepreneurs and employees, along with the attendant tech-supporting industries, changing their lives forever. Thus, Silicon Valley, too, joined the ranks of winners of the fiat money era.

By 2001, the economy was officially in a recession. Its state was further exacerbated by the horrific events of September 11th. The unemployment rate reached a peak of 6.3% in June 2003. In only 7 years the classic boom and bust cycle had come and gone. Newly created money via credit expansion was funneled into this tech promised land, bringing a sharp rise in asset prices all across the industry. This rise in asset prices subsequently drew in more money which drove prices even higher. All of this together created lots of unneeded activities, excitement and buzz, all of which "surprisingly" and with little prior warning collapsed one day. Once again, von Mises's prediction that "there is no means of avoiding the final collapse of a boom brought about by credit expansion" had come true.

The parade of winners in the debt-money creation era would not be complete without taking a close look at the federal government, its employees, and its satellites. Almost a third of the debt created—some $18 trillion—was the work of the federal government. Household debt is composed of tens of millions of different mortgages, student loans, and credit cards. But when the federal government spends trillions of dollars, it is up to a mere 536 individuals (Congress and the President) to appropriate money through legislation for what they see as the "greater good." The government's practice of spending money it doesn't have permanently contaminated the American political system.

The elimination of serious and real budgetary constraints also changed the dynamics between the elected officials and their constituencies. The assumption that the government actually had the resources it was spending translated into a belief that getting politicians to spend these resources was just a matter of demanding, pressing, or lobbying. The country that was founded on the idea of "liberty and the pursuit of happiness" was turning into a place where free government cell phones were a given right (An FCC-mandated, government-sponsored program which includes a free government cell phone) and where self-reliance morphed into reliance on hundreds of billions of dollars in government subsidies and bailouts for the most powerful and affluent.

This culture, of course, is not confined to the federal government alone. Between 1971 and 2013, the state and local governments ratcheted up some $3 trillion in debt, not including unfunded liabilities, obligations to employee retirement programs, which are not part of the recorded debt.[37] One of the clearest symptoms of the impact of our mammoth government is the wealth of its employees, present and past. Initial skepticism of this notion is warranted. We are indeed not talking about those government employees stationed in Afghanistan or Ft. Bragg, but rather of those stationed in D.C. and its surroundings. These employees, together with the satellite operations feeding from them, have found a goldmine in government money. According to the Census Bureau data in 2012, four out of the top five wealthiest counties in America were in the Washington, D.C., area. With a medium household income ranging from $137,000 in Arlington County to $125,000 in Fairfax County, this area has a median household income 2.3 times the American average in 2012. Washington, D.C. is also ranked first in the Census Bureau's Household Income Inequality.[38]

Washington riches come in many ways. The "revolving doors" are in full bloom: politicians initially working as legislators and regulators rotate positions and become lobbyists and lawyers for the industries they not only previously regulated, but are likely to regulate once again in the future. A notable example at the top of an endless list is Timothy Geithner, the former Secretary of the Treasury who oversaw the Obama administration's financial policy during the financial crisis. Shortly after Geithner left the administration, he joined private equity firm Warburg Pincus. Geithner was not the first to go from regulating Wall Street to profiting within it. Former Treasury heads Robert Rubin and John Snow also moved back and forth between Capitol Hill and Wall Street, a place where the experience and connections of top former government officials are rewarded with top dollars. Interesting how an official treats his future employers when they come asking for bailout money?

A good overview of the grip Wall Street has on D.C. and the nature of the revolving doors was given by Senator Elizabeth Warren (D-Mass.) in a speech she gave December 12, 14 on the Senate floor opposing legislation supported by President Obama and leaders of the Republican and Democratic parties alike:[39]

Mr. President, in recent years, many Wall Street institutions have exerted extraordinary influence in Washington's corridors of power, but Citigroup has risen above the others. Its grip over economic policymaking in the executive branch is unprecedented. Consider a few examples:

> Three of the last four Treasury Secretaries under Democratic presidents have had close Citigroup ties. The fourth was offered the CEO position at Citigroup, but turned it down.
> The Vice Chair of the Federal Reserve system is a Citigroup alum.
> The Undersecretary for International Affairs at Treasury is a Citigroup alum.
> The U.S. Trade Representative and the person nominated to be his deputy – who is currently an assistant secretary at Treasury – are Citigroup alums.
> A recent chairman of the National Economic Council at the White House was a Citigroup alum.
> Another recent Chairman of the Office of Management and Budget went to Citigroup immediately after leaving the White House.
> Another recent Chairman of the Office of Management of Budget and Management is also a Citi alum — but I'm double counting here because now he's the Secretary of the Treasury.

[…] During Dodd-Frank, there was an amendment introduced by my colleague Senator Brown and Senator

Kaufman that would have broken up Citigroup and the nation's other largest banks. That amendment had bipartisan support, and it might have passed, but it ran into powerful opposition from an alliance between Wall Streeters on Wall Street and Wall Streeters who held powerful government jobs. They teamed up and blocked the move to break up the banks—and now Citi is bigger than ever.

The role that senior officials working in the Treasury department played in killing the amendment was not subtle: A senior Treasury official acknowledged it at the time in a background interview with New York Magazine. The official from Treasury said, and I'm quoting here, "If we'd been for it, it probably would have happened. But we weren't, so it didn't."

In the Obama administration alone, more than 200 people from the Executive Office of the President took the ultra-lucrative dip into the lobbying industry. One of the highest ranking White House revolvers was Anita Dunn, a top aide to President Obama who served as the White House Communications Director from April through November 2009. After leaving the White House, Dunn rejoined the SKDKnickerbocker lobbying firm as a partner. One of the firm's most prized clients was TransCanada, the company in charge of the Keystone XL pipeline. Dunn's drastic change of heart about her environmental viewpoints enraged the progressive organization CREDO Action, which publicly exclaimed:

Anita Dunn gained enormous influence and access to the Obama White House as a top strategist who helped get the president elected in 2008, partially on his commitment to action on climate. Now she's cashing in on that close relationship by working on behalf of TransCanada to push for approval of the "game over for the climate" Keystone XL tar sands pipeline. [...]But the truth is that Dunn maintains close ties with the president—she's visited the

White House over 110 times since leaving her job there, including at least a dozen times already this year. With insider access like that, you can bet TransCanada isn't just paying SKDK and Dunn for ad production.[40]

The Center for Responsive Action tracks the employment history of 7,000 such revolvers from all branches of government. One of the companies to which these White insiders head is called Patton & Boggs, a law firm. Its company website clearly states:

We go beyond the obvious. By combining legal expertise with lobbying know-how and business savvy, we offer insights and perspectives that others can't. Over the past fifty years, we have established ourselves as a trusted partner and have formed strategic alliances with government and industry leaders. [...] We can represent our clients' best interests through legal, legislative, and executive action. As a result, we are consistently ranked among the top law and advocacy firms.

To achieve these "strategic alliances with government... leaders," they have employed over 177 Washington revolvers. Their names can also be found on the website mentioned above.[VI]

In 2012, there were 12,433 registered lobbyists in Washington DC. In total, these lobbyists spent $3.31 billion on their lobbying efforts. This amount was more than double the amount spent in 1998 and infinitely more than the amount spent on lobbying in 1971, before the money floodgates were opened. In D.C., *going downtown* means becoming a lobbyist in D.C. terminology. Going downtown became the natural next step for more than 200 elected officials and for countless staffers of elected officials. Such blatant disregard of conflicts of interest was rarely the case in American history prior to the 1980s. The number of Washington insiders involved in lobbying is actually higher than the officially quoted number of 12,433 since not all lobbies are registered. The Honest Leadership and Open Government Act of 2007 does not require those spending less than

VI http://www.opensecrets.org/revolving/search_result.php?priv=Patton+Boggs+LLP

20% of their time *actively* lobbying to register as lobbyists. This 20% threshold obviously leaves some space for interpretation. Former US Senate majority leader and President Obama's nominee to serve as the Secretary of Health and Human Services Tom Daschle (D-SD) became a policy advisor to a leading lobbying law firm. In the first year of Daschle's service, the firm significantly increased its lobbying income. Still, Daschle is yet to register as a lobbyist. Daschle's case is no anomaly. The consulting firm belonging to Speaker of the House Newt Gingrich (R) got paid more than a million dollars by Freddie Mac. Gingrich is also conveniently not registered as a lobbyist. He explained his involvement with Freddie Mac by saying, "I offered advice…my advice as a historian."[41] But it is not only ex-staffers, ex-legislators and ex-top administrators that qualify for such lucrative lobbying positions. Family ties to the political class also go a long way in the questionable world of lobbying.

The billions of dollars spent on lobbying come from every sector of the US economy. In 2012, unions spent around $45 million on lobbying while the agriculture industry spent around $125 million. The health industry considers it important enough to spend almost half a billion dollars on lobbying efforts, while security and investment firms spent almost $280 million. And these are just a few examples. Lobbying money wears different disguises. One of these forms is the political action committee, or PAC. These are organizations that pool campaign contributions to fund campaigns, fight or support candidates, ballot initiatives, or legislation. PACs are more flexible in the ways they spend money. PACs can also conveniently be set up and controlled by members of Congress. In 2013, PACs raised almost $1.3 billion. In 2012, the poultry and egg business donated a total of $600,000 via PACs, most of which went to Republican candidates. In the 2010 cycle, the sum was almost $700,000, though this time the Democrats were poultry's favorites. The computer industry donated almost $7 million, and, as engineers, their choices proved much more calculated: they split their funds almost equally between Democrats and Republicans.

Google's PAC, for example, contributed $885,500 to different government candidates. Of this sum, $430,000 went to Democratic candidates and $445,000 to Republicans. The list of PAC contributions is endless, and likely contains every meaningful business, labor union, or organization in America.

The ubiquity of this practice begs the question of why this happens. Why do all these businesses and organizations spend so much money and effort on Washington, D.C.? The common answer, many times propagated by politicians themselves, is that the lobbyists are "evil" manipulators who want to help "special interests" buy favors and influence, ensconcing themselves in D.C.'s political class. President Obama was especially vocal in pushing this populist narrative.

Reality, however, is more complex. Really, the two parties are in a symbiotic relationship in which both sides have a role to play. The *New York Times* provided a glimpse into this relationship in an October 27, 2011, piece that detailed how President Obama raised millions of dollars from supportive lobbyists, registered and not. These included lobbyists for communications, pharmaceutical and other companies which not only were part of the $500,000 bundling club (Due to legal limitations on individual donations, lobbyists organize—or bundle—groups of people to donate large sums, $500,000 in this case.) but also organized dinner fundraisers for the President.[42]

The November 2013 appointment of the chairman of the Federal Communications Commission (FCC) is the epitome of this web of private interests and of the real D.C. The FCC is a powerful agency that regulates all aspects of telecommunications in the US, including radio, television, wire, satellite, and cable. As you can imagine, this means the FCC has enormous control over entities like cable TV companies, cellular phone providers, and the Internet. This fact makes Obama's chosen appointee, Tom Wheeler, a key lobbyist for the cable and cell phone industries, even more ludicrous. Wheeler's appointment is not exactly the realization of Obama's embellished promises. In a November 2007 speech, he said, "I am in this race to tell the corporate lobbyists that their days of setting the agenda in Washington are over." The man who spent 27 years of his life and made his living by advancing the special interests of cable and telecommunication companies is not exactly "the voice of the American people" hailed by Obama in the November 2007 speech. Having this same former lobbyist run the FCC, the agency that is by far the most important for his former clients and friends could not be any further from a policy of "taking on lobbyists." It seems it pays to have friends in high places, no matter what they may be saying to the public.[43]

Some answers to the question of why all these organizations spend billions on lobbying can be found in a series of fascinating *Washington Post* blog posts by Robert G. Kaiser called "Citizen K Street: How lobbying became Washington's biggest business."[44] In the series, Kaiser goes into long and colorful detail about the history the lobbying industry, how it arose, and what it has become. Kaiser shows how 1975's $100 million lobbying industry became a $3.5 billion industry by 2010. He discusses how rare it was in 1975 to see a former member of Congress become a lobbyist while nowadays some 200 former members of the House and Senate are registered lobbyists.

The series focuses on Gerald (Gerry) Cassidy, founder and owner of Cassidy & Associates, one of D.C.'s most successful lobbying firms. Cassidy's first customer in the 1970s hired him to get the Speaker of the House to help with some funds. Two years later, Congress appropriated $27 million for this client. This was just the beginning. In the coming three decades, hundreds of millions of dollars were directed toward his clients. After all, the river of money has to flow somewhere, and the money collected as taxes and borrowed as loans and appropriated by Congress for the "greater good" has to end in somebody's pockets.

Over time, the lobbying business delivered even more than just billions of dollars in federal money to its customers. The financial goodies took other forms, such as government guarantees on loans taken out by corporations. When the federal government guarantees a loan, financial institutions are quite eager to lend out the money. This guarantee is an especially sweet deal for both the banks and the corporation as it rewards the company in case of success and forces the taxpayer to shoulder the failure, should it occur. Such was the case with Solyndra, which received $535 million loan guarantee in 2009. Just two years later, in September 2011, Solyndra filed for chapter 11 bankruptcy. In the two intervening years, the company planned its IPO and even filed the initial paperwork, the registration statement, with the SEC. This IPO, planned at a $4-6 billion valuation, would have made the shareholders' investment extremely profitable. The government, which was guaranteeing the loan, however, would have gotten nothing out of the IPO. Ultimately, the IPO, did not succeed, and so the taxpayers were called on to front the bill on the loan guarantee. Solyndra's creditors were off the hook and the banks were as happy as can be. Only the government, or rather the taxpayers, suffered from a too-good-to-be-true situation gone wrong. But Solyndra was just one company out of some 40 receiving funds under the Department of Energy's (DOE) loan program. Started in 2007, this program guaranteed around $35 billion in loans. In 2012, the House of Representatives Committee on Oversight and Government Reform shed some more light on who exactly gets these guarantees, while reviewing this loan program:

> As this report reveals, it appears that taxpayer losses associated with Solyndra are just the tip of the iceberg... Nancy Ann DeParle, the current Deputy Chief of Staff for Policy in the White House, had a financial stake in the success of Granite Reliable, which received $168.9 million loan from DOE. Prior to joining the White House, DeParle was a Managing Director of multi-billion dollar private equity firm CCMP and she both had a financial interest in and sat on the Board of Directors for Noble Environmental Power, Noble owned Granite Reliable, a wind energy project.... DeParle misrepresented her relationship with Noble Energy, claiming on disclosure forms that her

interest had been divested, when in fact it had merely been transferred to her 10-year-old son...

Michael Froman currently serves as the Deputy Assistant to the President and Deputy National Security Advisor for International Economic Affairs. Prior to his arrival at the White House, Froman was the Managing Director of Alternative Investments at Citigroup, where he managed infrastructure and sustainable development investments. Citigroup became a major investor in Solar-Reserve which ultimately received a $737 million loan guarantee on September 18, 2011.

Steve Westly co-founded the Westly Group, a clean energy venture capital firm that, according to DOE records, has reaped over $600 million in DOE loans for its portfolio of investments. One recipient company was Tesla Motors, a premium electric vehicle manufacturer to which DOE awarded a $465 million loan guarantee in January 2010. Westly also sat on Tesla's Board of Directors in the company's early days. Westly is a personal friend of President Obama and bundled over $500,000 for his 2008 campaign. Since the election, Westly has visited the White House multiple times for both business and pleasure, and has privately dined with the President in small group fundraising. After President Obama's election, Westly was rumored to have been a primary candidate for Energy Secretary. When Secretary Chu received the appointment, Westly was given the opportunity to serve on an advisory board to the DOE, "a pivotal [sic] advisory committee that made recommendations to the secretary on alternative energy policies."

David Sandalow currently serves as the Assistant Secretary for Policy and International Affairs at DOE, where he acts as Secretary's Chu's principal adviser on energy policy as well as coordinates DOE's foreign policy involvement....Prior to joining the Obama Administration, Sandalow was a senior advisor to Good Energies, Inc., an energy-focused venture capital firm. Good Energies is an investor in SolarReserve, a solar power company that received a $737 million loan guarantee from DOE in September 2011.[VII]

But of course, not only Democrats reward their friends. Since 2000, farm subsidies of different kinds averaged around $18 billion a year. Total farm subsidies from 1995 through 2012 were a mammoth $292 billion.[45] Considering that in this period agribusiness spent less than 0.5% of that sum on lobbying—some $1.5 billion—this was a hell of a return on investment.[46] The distribution of these subsidies is also very telling. According to the Environmental Working Group, the top 10% of farmers collected 74% of all subsidies while 62% of farmers did not collect any subsidy payments at all. This top 10% included 50 billionaires or businesses in which billionaires have some form of ownership,[47] and a disheartening 15 members of Congress: 13 Republicans and 2 Democrats.[48] High on this list was a congressman from California. He and his wife, who own one-third of a family partnership, have received $188,570 in direct payments in 2012 and $5,132,156 in total since 1995.[49]

Last but not least, one more method of financial remuneration is through the tax code. The US tax code is almost 17,000 pages long;[50] the Constitution, by comparison, is less than 10 pages. As you can imagine, within those 17,000 pages there is a lot of space for special rules and treatment. They can target a specific company or industry and can reward individuals or groups. These rules also alter taxpayer behavior in ways that make little sense or that bring no economic value. They also typically benefit the haves. One example are the rules related to housing. While rent expenses are not tax deductible, mortgage interest payments are, despite the fact that the two are similar in nature since rent is the equivalent of an interest payment on a house. This tax deduction includes mortgage interest on

---

VII The list goes on and on. The full report can we found online at http://oversight. house.gov/wp-content/uploads/2012/03/final-doe-loan-guarantees-report.pdf

a second home (including vacation homes) and, in some cases, even applies to yachts. The higher is the loan, up to $1 million, the bigger is the tax benefit

Homeowners enjoy one more benefit that renters do not: an exemption from taxes on the first $500,000 of appreciation. If a couple's house appreciates by up to $500,000, than no capital gains taxes are due on the difference between the property's initial value and its increased one. Once again, the bigger the loan and the property, the greater the potential tax benefit. So, not only was the property purchased with the help of tax benefits as a result of interest deductions, gains are also partially exempt. This combination delivers more benefits the greater the loan.

Other popular deductions include charitable donations, which for the most *do not* go to programs which benefit low income groups, and many even go outside of the US, and employer-sponsored healthcare, as opposed to healthcare purchased individually. These and other special groups or special-interest deductions reduce the government's overall tax income and thus are indirectly financed by the broader taxpaying population. But special deductions go well beyond general yet discriminatory deductions.

In a 2008 research paper entitled "Lobbying and Taxes," three UCLA graduate students mathematically analyzed various cases and concluded that increasing lobbying expenditures by 1% appears to lower effective tax rates by somewhere between 0.5 to 1.6%.[51] The percentage may seem small, but it is actually quite substantial. If a company spends $10 million on lobbying and has a potential tax bill of $100 million, then increasing lobbying expenditures by 1% will cost $100,000, while the return on this investment will be $1 million in tax savings. This represents a 1:10 return on investment. In reality, companies invest less in lobbying and have higher tax bills so the actual numbers are even more dramatic.

Nor was this research the first of its kind: Donald Barlett and James Steele, who together comprise one of America's most prominent investigative journalism teams, reviewed the almost 900-page long 1986 Tax Reform Act for their 2000 book, *The Great American Tax Dodge*. They concluded that more than 650 tax exemptions where made for specific companies or individuals. That is 650 taxpayer subsidized rules written into law to serve the interests of private parties.

Such exemptions can take many forms, including escalated deductions, tax credits, R&D (Research and development) credits, exemptions, and others. As of 2004, there were around 10,000 companies in the US involved in R&D activities. About 100 of the companies (1%) received 54% of the $5.5 billion in tax benefits.[52] Given these circumstances, the absurdity of big corporations spending more money on lobbying than they do on paying taxes starts making sense. GE (General Electric) is a shining example of this behavior. Although the company was ranked fourth largest in the country by Fortune 500 in 2010 and although it netted $11.6 billion in profits, it paid zero taxes in 2010. In fact, GE ended 2010 with some $3.2 billion in tax benefits.[53] The same year, GE spent almost $40 million on lobbying.[54] GE was not alone in this funny tax game: 30 of the largest US corporations including Verizon, GP&E (Pacific Gas and Electric), Honeywell, Boeing, and FedEx, also made it in this "hall of shame."[55]

A final but important result of lobbying is that it provides some protection from government enforcement of many times purposely convoluted laws. Many different laws, and especially those targeting businesses, are confusing. Many claim, in fact, that the laws are purposely confusing in order to insure future potential revenues to lobbyists and politicians. Indeed, as former SEC (Securities and Exchange Commission) chairman put it, the 2,500 page Dodd-Frank Wall Street Reform and Consumer Protection Act would more aptly be named the "Lawyers and Lobbyist Full Employment Act."[56] In a research paper entitled "Political Contributions and the Severity of Government Enforcement," two scholars from Florida State University found that political contributions have a significant impact on reducing the severity of government enforcement outcomes. Moreover,

221

executives whose firms have made campaign contributions receive prison sentences that are 6 years lower than average and probation periods that are five years shorter than average.[57]

The net result of the expansion of lobbying, which grew alongside government and deficit spending, is clearly a growth in wealth disparity of our nation. In the words of the legendary lobbyist Gerry Cassidy, the lobby business led to "a huge redistribution of resources." This shift took place under Democratic and Republican Congresses and administrations alike.

The growth in government through the growth in debt had one more extremely severe impact: it corrupted the American political system like never before, especially on the federal level. It also created two groups of voters. The first group is composed of people who can pay for private access to be heard without making their privilege manifest; as reported from the Silicon Valley on May 2014 "The White House declined to identify the 20 high-rollers who paid $32,400 per head to sit at the Tech Roundtable."[58] Buying access comes in many other shapes. Some of the more creative ways include a sleepover at the White House in the Lincoln Bedroom.[59] The other group of voters are those who are hardly heard, and are even a targeted by the government using tools like the IRS (Internal Revenue Service) as a result of activism that threatens those in power.

The public has become so numb that few even ask themselves if there's anything inappropriate about Bill Clinton collecting more than $13 million a year in speaking fees while his wife is a top member of the administration.[60] Furthermore, it seems that this is a family business: 34-year-old Chelsea Clinton charges some $75,000 per appearance.[61] Hardly any public discussion or media outlet even questions who is paying these sums and what motivates them. Considering the fact that the Clinton family public speaking business generated more than $100 million over the past decade, while this power couple was (and still is) deeply and actively involved in politics, it's only fair to ask if this is only an entertainment operation. In contrast Harry Truman's or Dwight D. Eisenhower's life after the presidency was characterized by a retreat from public life, working their farms and writing their memories and not $500,000 per talk during endless speaking tours.

To fully understand the corruption of the elected institutions in the fiat money era, we need to take a closer look at the receiving end of the lobbying business: the elected officials. We have already touched upon the revolving door. The link between the lobbyists and politicians does not, however, just end with questionable hiring after or in between terms. The first goal of most elected officials is to get reelected. In the 2012 election cycle, an average winning Senate race cost around $10.2 million and an average House seat cost around $1.5 million.[62] Representatives, however, face elections every two years while senators do every six, so the real ongoing costs for staying in power need to be calculated accordingly. Keep in mind that these are average costs, with close races or races with formidable challengers costing much more.

The law imposes strict limitations on contributions made by individuals. As of early 2014, the limit stood at $2,600 per candidate per election, and $2,600 to $5000 per candidate per PAC, given that some PACs are affiliated with individual candidates and others support multiple candidates. These limitations mean that each candidate for Congress needs thousands of individuals, theoretically from their district, to willingly contribute significant amounts of money for their candidacy and reelection year in, year out. These contributions simply don't happen. Interest-free local supporters typically contributing $200 or less cover a very small part of the campaign cost, typically 5 to 20%. Nancy Pelosi, the former Speaker of the House, has a personal wealth of somewhere between $20 and $120 million. In the 2012 campaign cycle, she raised and spent around $2 million dollars. About 5% of this money came from small individual contributions, with the rest coming from PACs and large donors including law firms, health professionals, security firms, unions, retailers, real estate firms, and technology companies. Pelosi personally contributed zero dollars to her own election campaign.[63] The current speaker, John Boehner, raised some $9 million in the 2010 election cycle. A sizable amount of this money, an above-average 28%, came from small donors, while the rest came from large donors and PACs. Boehner also did not make any contribution to his own election, though he is far from having Mrs. Pelosi's wealth. Boehner's top contributors came from the security-investment industry, insurance, health care, law firms, energy and communications. One of his top single donors was AT&T, or to be more accurate, the telecom giant's executives.[64]

In his book *Extortion*, Peter Schweizer, a research fellow at Stanford University's Hoover Institute, reviewed these donations' provenance.

In the fall of 2011, AT&T and other wireless companies were awaiting the passage of the Wireless Tax Fairness Act. This bipartisan legislation would restrict any state or local jurisdiction from imposing certain new taxes on cell phone services, providers, or property. During the two months prior to the vote employees of AT&T and Verizon from all over the country wrote over two hundred individual checks totaling $180,000 to the campaign committees of different members of Congress. The day before the vote Speaker Boehner's campaign received thirty-three checks from wireless industry executives, totaling around $40,000. Twenty-eight of these checks came from AT&T executives. On the day of the vote, Verizon employees sent twenty-eight checks to different members of Congress.[65]

This case is, of course, just a tiny example. AT&T also has a PAC which in 2010 raised around $4.6 million from hundreds of AT&T executives and gave out almost $5 million to dozens of members of Congress, to election committees, and to other PACs. These contributions are split almost evenly between both political parties.

AT&T's PAC was just one of 3,557 registered PACs in 2010.[66]

As it turns out, lobbying money isn't raised only for elections; it also finds its way to more lucrative activities. One popular method of funneling money is paying relatives. Citizens for Responsibility and Ethics in Washington (CREW), a nonprofit nonpartisan organization dedicated to promoting ethics and accountability in government published a lengthy report[VIII] covering the 2008 and 2010 election cycles which found that:

> 82 members (40 Democrats and 42 Republicans) paid family members through their congressional offices, campaign committees, and political action committees (PACs);

> 44 members (20 Democrats and 24 Republicans) had family members who lobby or are employed in government affairs;

> 90 members (42 Democrats and 48 Republicans) had paid a family business, employer, or associated nonprofit;

> 20 members (13 Democrats and 7 Republicans) used their campaign money to contribute to a family member's political campaign;

> 14 members (6 Democrats and 8 Republicans) charged interest on personal loans they made to their own campaigns;

> 38 members (24 Democrats and 14 Republicans) earmarked to a family business, employer, or associated nonprofit.

There are, of course, some superstars:

> Rep. Howard "Buck" McKeon (R-CA) paid his wife and campaign treasurer a $238,438 salary;

> Rep. William Lacy Clay (D-MO) paid his sister's law office $292,557 in fees;

> Rep. Jerry Lewis (R-CA) paid his wife $512,293 to work in his congressional office;

VIII The full report can be found here: http://www.citizensforethics.org/page/-/PDFs/Reports/Family_Affair_House_2012_CREW.pdf?nocdn=1.

> › Rep. Grace Napolitano (D-CA) loaned her campaign $150,000 in 1998 and collected more than $94,000 in interest (62%) during the 2008 and 2010 election cycles alone;

> › Rep. Colleen Hanabusa (D-HI) loaned her campaign $125,000 and collected more than $31,000 in interest (24%);

> › Rep. Paul Broun (R-GA) loaned his campaign $309,000 and has so far collected nearly $29,000 in interest (9%), despite telling the Federal Election Commission (FEC) he wouldn't charge any interest on the loan at all.

Another popular method of pocketing money is reimbursement for expenses:

> › Rep. Rob Andrews (D-NJ) has in the past been cited by the FEC for illegal acts such as purchasing clothes with campaign money. Nevertheless, he has continued to use campaign funds for questionable expenses such as taking his family to a wedding at a luxury resort in Scotland;

> › Rep. Silvestre Reyes' (D-TX) reimbursements to himself and family members totaled more than $400,000 over the two election cycles. One particularly unusual entry included reimbursing his niece, a campaign staff member, for charitable donations;

> › Rep. Aaron Schock (R-IL) reimbursed himself more than $150,000, including more than $30,000 in hotel bills. His lodging ran the gamut from Hampton Inns to expensive five-star resorts in Miami and Athens, Greece.

This presumably legal yet sinister level of corruption contributes to cynical and deprecating views of our democratically elected institutions. This attitude, which is extremely hard to amend, is especially concerning because it is the first step towards the crumbling of democracy itself. From 2008 to 2013, according to Gallup polls, more than 70% of surveyed Americans said they disapproved of the way Congress was doing its job. In comparison, from 1974 to 1979 the disapproval rating reached 46%, meaning that the majority still approved.[67] It is worth mentioning that the identity of the majority party has little influence on public disapproval. In September 2010, when the Democrats were the majority, the disapproval rating was 77%. In September 2013 when Republicans were the majority, the disapproval rating was 76%.

The financing of Washington politics is an octopus that involves politicians, interest groups, wealthy individuals, and corporations trading in favors, protection, and lots of public money. Without a doubt, this destructive machine grew significantly and reflects the huge growth of reckless government spending, government overreach and government debt since the 1970s. If D.C. didn't have its hands on a money hose, and its pen on endlessly complex regulations, the army of lobbyists trying to steer money their way and ensure legislation benefiting them wouldn't exist. The fiat money era of government super-spending and increased D.C. presence led to this result, and there is only one obvious way to curb it.

Members of the legislative branch are not the only ones to enjoy the expansion in government spending. Those employed by the government have greatly benefited as well. According to a report by the Congressional Budget Office that covered the period from 2005 to 2012, the total compensation—wages and benefits—of civilian non-military federal employees, was higher than its equivalent in the private sector in three of four educational categories, leaving aside job security. In fact, if you have a high school diploma or less, you are significantly better off being employed by the federal government. The reason is simple: those with high school diplomas have a salary that is on average 36% higher than their private sector counterparts'. With some college education or a bachelor degree, the total compensation was 15% higher for federal employees. Only those with professional or doctorate degrees earn more in the

227

private sector than they would be in the public one. "Overall, the federal government paid 16% more in total compensation compared with that in the private sector."[68]

The issue of employee pay presents a good opening for a larger question: why is it that while GDP has grown more than 300% since 1971, and many other benchmarks have risen even more, the median household income has hardly changed? The absence of a proportionate growth in household income is significant because it means that even though the economy is producing three times more "stuff," the bottom half of American household are seeing none of this extra "stuff." When examining the winners and losers of the fiat money area, there is no doubt that the bottom 50% of American households are the biggest losers. Even more disturbing is that the lower you go down the income ladder, the greater the damage inflicted by the fiat money era. By this point, we have already examined and learned why financial markets and related industries grew so dramatically. Our next step, in order to better understand what happened to the average US worker, is to examine what the fiat money era did to US international trade and to US trade partners.

As previously discussed, commodity money—i.e. money backed by gold or silver—ensured balance of trade via the price–specie flow mechanism. However after the collapse of Bretton Woods and the introduction of the debt-money creation machine, the US could suddenly buy limitless products from overseas simply by creating dollars at will. As long as these dollars were accepted as money anywhere around the globe, the US could create more money at no apparent cost and could buy what it pleased.

Nixon was not only the president that removed the final obstacle to the debt-money creation machine, he was also the president who famously reestablished a diplomatic relationship with China. As the Chinese political and economic climate changed dramatically in the 1980s and 1990s, Nixon's two seemingly distinct actions integrated to help facilitate the rise of China and the crash of the American middle class.

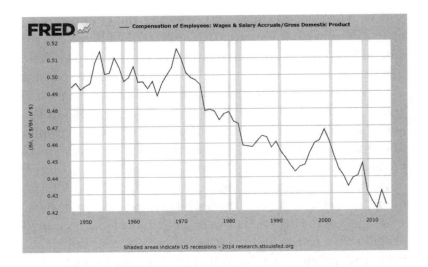

Employee compensation as percentage of GDP

1970 was the first year since the Second World War that the US ran a trade deficit. 1975 was the last time the US held a positive balance of payment, i.e. ran a trade surplus. Ever since 1996, this negative balance has been above $100 billion a year. In 2003, the annual trade imbalance grew to over half a trillion dollars. In the past three years (2011-2013) the number was around $700 billion.[69] This trade deficit has been paid for by debt-money creation.

In 1986, the US balance of trade with China passed the $1 billion deficit mark for the first time. Only 4 years later, this imbalance had reached $10 billion. By 2002, the deficit had surged to over $100 billion, and skyrocketed further to over $250 billion by 2006. In 2012 and 2013 the deficit reached an all-time high of $300 billion a year. In 2012, as in previous years, the US's top three trading partners were Canada, China, and Mexico, in that order. Each of these partners accounted for over 12.5% of US total trade. With all three, the US held a negative trade balance. However while the trade balance with Canada and Mexico was negative, it was relatively small: the US exported to Canada about 90% of what it imported and about

229

80% to Mexico. In China's case, however, the US exported a mere 25% of what it imported. Since 2000, the US has bought around $3 trillion more from China than it has sold to it. These imbalances are only a part of the US's overall negative balance of trade, which has totaled more than $10 trillion in the past 20 years.[70] Over the years, the US has come to depend on China's manufacturing for a large array of products, from electronics to toys to computers and apparel and even for big public works projects like the Bay Bridge. And because the US has sent all of its printed dollars to China, the US helped build China's robust manufacturing capacities while wearing down its own.

As most of the debt dollars were spent in the US, they caused overall prices to rise and the value of the dollar to fall almost 90%. The increase in prices, of course, was not equal across the whole economy. While financial assets, financial market employees, and public company executives could not be replaced by cheap labor from China, many average US employees could. The unlimited creation and the international purchasing power of those printed-debt dollars put massive ongoing pressure on the American workforce. If America (and Europe) could print and use unlimited amounts of money abroad without restrictions, the price–specie flow mechanism could no longer apply.

If the US had continued to back its currency with gold, as it had been until 1968, it just wouldn't have been able to run these types of trade deficits because it would have simply run out of money many years ago. The ability to create unlimited amounts of new money suddenly enabled ongoing and unlimited trade deficits. The existence of cheap labor markets in China and elsewhere that were willing to accept American dollars lessened the wage increase that would have occurred in the US if that new money had been spent locally. Thus the newly created money inflated prices of local products and assets without correspondingly raising labor costs. As a direct result, the income of the bottom 50% of households deteriorated in the face of such foreign competition. In the case of bottom 40% of American households, income did not even keep up with inflation, let alone stay on par with GDP growth. As of 2013, the bottom 40% of US households make about 12% less today than in 1970, adjusting for inflation.[71] The real purchasing power of the bottom 40% of households probably deteriorated by close to 20%, with their share in the "national pie," the GDP, dropping even more.

Salary levels in professions not subject to outsourcing clearly demonstrate the correlation between most American salary deflation and US–China trade relations. Lawyers and physicians serve as good examples of this truth. In 1979, lawyers made up 7% of the top 1% of earners, and medical professionals made up 16.8% of this group. Little had changed in 2005, with lawyers making up 8.4% and medical professionals 15.7%. This one per-cent's income doubled in inflation-adjusted rates, meaning that most lawyers and medical professionals whose jobs couldn't be outsourced saw their incomes grow in parallel with the increase in most price levels. Almost all physicians in the US fall within the top 5% of earners, a group whose income has grown by about 40% since 1975 in real inflation adjusted terms.[72]

While salaries for most American workers were pushed down by overseas competition made possible and paid for by the debt-money creation machine, the Americans with their income tied to the stock market experienced a very different reality. As we observed, the debt-money creation machine brought about an ongoing increase in asset prices, and along with it, four distinct bubbles. The 1995–2000 dot-com bubble, the 2003–2007 housing bubble, the accompanying 2003–2008 financial bubble caused by a surge in share prices, and the surge of financial assets since 2009 which is, as of December 2014, still in progress. This surge in asset prices is reflected in the S&P 500, which has risen almost fourfold since the 1970s, adjusting for inflation. The S&P 500 has also fluctuated wildly in the past two decades, as seen below:

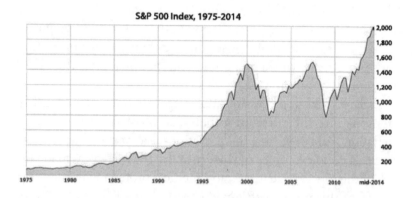

S&P 500, 1970-2014

This trend obviously benefited stockowners and those who derive significant income from capital gains. Stockowners are obviously disproportionately the nation's top earning group. According to Edward Wolff's research, 10% of Americans own about 80% of stock wealth with the top 1% owning about 38% thereof.[73] As for capital gains, on average, 45% of it went to the top 0.1% of earners.[74] It is pretty simple to understand now who gained from the dramatic stock price increase, one of the noticeable impacts of the money creation machine.

Income 1979– 2009, After Transfers and Federal Taxes

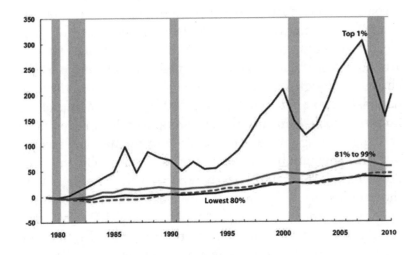

Source: Congressional Budget Office, Aug 2012

If we look at the graph above, which outlines the growth in after-tax income per group from 1979 to 2010, and compare it to the movement of the S&P 500, it is easy to see that the income of the top 1% shoots up in parallel with surges in the S&P 500. The income of the top 1% is heavily influenced by the top 0.1%, so the inequality in wealth distribution is even more extreme. Since the beginning of the fiat money era the wealth of the top 1% grew more than that of other income groups. This rate, however, has significantly accelerated since the stock market took off in 1995. Of course, the special tax treatment granted for capital gains further contributes to this phenomenon. This combination of increased incomes for the country's top earners and deflated pay for the country's bottom 40% set the stage for the country's current growth in inequality and for the deterioration of the middle class in America today.

Many scholars have devoted time to trying to explain America's income inequality. Though there are different opinions on the matter, two things are clear: first, that the gap has grown significantly since the late 1970s, and second, that the fortunes of the different sub-groups making up the top 0.1%, which accounts for about 10% of the national income, had their income change in tandem with their respective asset bubbles. For example, the sub-group within the 0.1% dealing in real estate grossed around 1% of the national income in 1979. This figure hardly changed through 1993, but shot up to almost 5.5% of the total national income between 2001 and 2005 around the time of the housing bubble. Similarly, the sub-group working in computers and engineering grossed around 1.5% of the national income in 1993. This number catapulted up to 5% in 2000 and back down to 2.25% in 2002, clearly reflecting the asset bubble in those industries.[75] Again, these are clear indications that the huge rises in income among the top 0.1, 1, and 10% are closely correlated to the big increase in asset-stock prices. This increase is a result of the fiat money creation machine.

Another way to measure income inequality is to look at the distribution of the national income. In 1979, the net (after taxes) income of the top 1% of households represented 8% of the national income. By 2007, that number had increased to 17%. The same demographic's net income in that same period multiplied threefold. Between 2005 and 2007, the net income of the top 20% of Americans eclipsed the total after-tax income of the bottom 80%.[76]

Growth in Real Household Income, 1979–2007 - After-Federal Taxes and Transfers

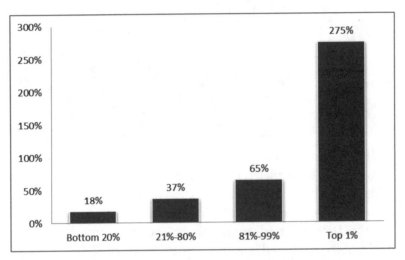

Source: Congressional Budget Office, Aug 2012

The above graph is of growth in real household income, 1979–2007. After-federal tax and transfers like food stamps and unemployment benefits, if these had been taken out of the equation, the results for the bottom 40% would have looked much worse.

This trend was slightly reversed in 2008 after the stock market collapse, but came roaring back during 2011-2014 stock market bonanza, a result of the $4 trillion of Wall Street bailout and QE programs. Most of the data isn't available yet as the big jump in asset prices occurred in 2012-2014, but in 2011, according to tax filing numbers released by the IRS, the top 1% was back on the pre-2008 track. That year, it grossed 18.7% of the total reported national income, more than 1.5 times the income of the entire bottom 50% combined.

2011 Gross Income Per Group

	Top 0.1%	Top 1%	Top 10%	Top 25%	Top 50%	Bottom 50%	Total
Percent of all earnings	8.86%	18.70%	45.39%	67.82%	88.45%	11.55%	100%
Number of Returns filled	136,500	1.36 Million	13.66 Million	34.14 Million	68.29 Million	68.29 Million	136.58 Million

If a situation where half the nation makes almost 90% of all income and the other half makes just above 10% seems troubling, just wait for the 2013 and 2014 numbers. If 2014 follows current stock market trends, it is reasonable to estimate that the top 10% will end up grossing about the same as the rest of the 90% combined, and the top 1% twice the entire bottom 50%. It is a naïve to believe that this situation can be healthy for the fabric of our society. One more result of the fiat money creation machine.

The net result of these income trends is simple, as the fiat money era and money creation wore on, the wealth (value of assets minus liabilities) gap between top 20% of households and the rest grew. It reached a pinnacle in 2013 following the massive $4 trillion money creation spree which began in 2009 and the ensuing stock market asset price increase. At the end of 2013, high income households had median wealth of 6.6 times higher than that of middle income households, which account for 47% of American households; and 70 times higher than the wealth of lower income households, which comprise 33% of American households, according to a Pew Research Center paper analyzing information release by the Federal Reserve at the end of 2013. This gap is double what it was in 1983, when the Fed started collecting this data, and, needless to say, the highest it has been ever since.[77] In the two decades prior to 1971 the wealth share of the top 0.1% was around 10% of all US wealth, by 2013 it shot up to 22%, a level never seen since the late 1920's. Since

1978 the real average wealth of the top 1% families grow three and a half-fold while that of the bottom 90% by 35 percent, from 1971 to 2013 for every $1 of new wealth accumulated by an average family from the bottom 90%, an average family of the top 1% acclimated $476.[78]

China, as it turns out, doesn't only trade with the USA. Europe's own debt-money creation machine ensured that it too ran a trade deficit with China for many years. In 2012, China was the EU's largest trading partner, with a deficit balance of around $200 billion. In the years prior to 2012 the deficit balance hovered between $100 and $200 billion. As a result, in 2012, China became the largest trading nation, surpassing the USA and trading about $3.8 trillion. On the way to the top, China accumulated a large trade surplus: an average of around $230 billion a year since 2005.[79] These huge trade credits forced China to decide how it would deal with the consequences of having an ongoing trade surplus and being the repository for foreign currency. After using part of the trade revenue to purchase materials, energy, and machinery abroad, China had to decide how to cover local expenses, mainly labor. China had two options when it came to making local payments in its currency, the yuan. The first was to have exporting Chinese companies exchange the foreign currency they accumulated into yuan on the open market. Doing so would have created strong buying pressure on the yuan, which would increase its price significantly due to huge ongoing demand and finite supply. Such an increase in price would make manufacturing relatively more expensive in dollars. More expensive manufacturing would severely hamper exports, a pillar of China's economy, since trading partners would seek cheaper options or cut back orders. The second option was for the government to buy the dollars and euros from exporting companies and pay them in new government-created yuan thus increasing the amount of yuan in the market. This solution would prevent the increase in price of the yuan and thus keep exporting momentum going. This solution, however, would simultaneously create local inflation as more and more newly created yuan entered the market. For the most part, China has selected the second option.

In 1994, China devaluated its currency sharply and then pegged the yuan to the dollar at the price of 8.28 yuan per dollar. This rate remained unchanged for more than 20 years, until July 2005. At that point, due to ongoing pressure by the US and the EU, China allowed some gradual appreciation in the yuan's price. This appreciation continued for only 3 years and was halted in 2008 due to the global crisis and its impact on China's exports. The process of gradual appreciation was allowed to continue once again in June 2010. In total, from 2005 and until June 2013, the period when yuan valuation was permitted, the currency appreciated by 34% against the dollar. It nevertheless did not reach its 1993 rate.[80]

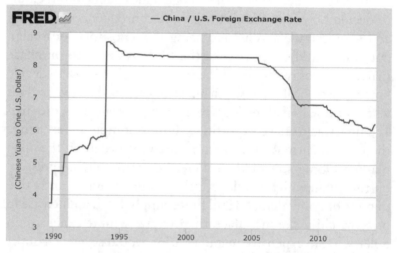

Value of one dollar in yuan; in 2013 the yuan's
exchange rate is still lower than in 1993.

The Chinese government's policy vis-à-vis its currency has had a significant impact on China and on the rest of the world. Obviously, one of its major impacts has been the huge growth in China's foreign currency reserves, also called forex reserves. When the Chinese government took the foreign currencies from its exporters and paid for them in newly printed yuan, the amount of dollars in the Chinese government's possession increased. Money created and sent by the US to pay for its trade deficit was accumulating in China's foreign currency reserves. In return, the Chinese printed their own yuan for use in the internal Chinese economy. In 1978, Chinese forex reserves stood at a dainty $1.6 billion. By the end of 2013, this number had swelled to a massive $3.5 trillion—a 2000-fold growth!

The printed yuan obviously created inflationary pressure and sent asset prices ballooning in China. China's *official* inflation rate for the past decade has been around 3% a year, with a specific surge in housing prices. As can be seen in the table below, salaries have increased almost threefold in less than a decade, and so have the price of many products on the market.

Average hourly compensation costs of manufacturing employees in China, U.S. Dollars, 2002-2009			
	Hourly Compensation per Employee		
	All Firms	Urban	Rural
2002	0.60	0.95	0.41
2003	0.68	1.09	0.46
2004	0.74	1.23	0.50
2005	0.83	1.35	0.57
2006	0.95	1.56	0.64
2007	1.21	1.96	0.80
2008	1.59	2.58	1.06
2009	1.74	2.85	1.15

Source: U.S. Bureau of Labor Statistics, International Labor Comparisons.

Though China's commercial housing market didn't really start developing until 1998, it has seen significant price increases ever since. A review of 70 large and midsize cities in China shows house price increases at an average annual rate of 5%. In the large cities, these price increases have been even higher.[81] In Shanghai, for example, the price of homes on the secondary market rose by 121% between early 2003 and mid-2008. In October 2013 alone, the price of homes in 100 large and midsize Chinese cities grew by 1.24%. The top 10 largest cities were up 15.7% from January through October 2013.[82]

Still, China's government is not the only one to employ this currency-buying policy. Many countries, when flooded with dollars and euros, preferred to print local currency instead of letting the former be exchanged on the free market. For example: since 1999, Switzerland forex reserves have been of around 90 billion Swiss francs. In 2008, frightened investors looking for refuge in the Swiss franc caused a sharp increase in demand for the currency. Rather than allowing the franc's price to rise, the Swiss government committed to holding it at a maximum rate of 1.20 francs to the euro. This meant that the Swiss government would buy up the inflow of foreign currencies with francs. As a result, the Swiss forex saw an almost five fold growth in its foreign-currency reserves. After the dust had settled, Switzerland held about 440 billion francs worth of foreign currency, equal to about three-quarters of the country's annual GDP.

The darkest part of this trade story, however, is still to come, and lies in the answer to the question of what China did with its dollars and euros. The simple answer is that China has bought up massive amounts of strategic assets from America and around the world. The US government and Federal Reserve debt-created money used by Americans to buy cheap plasma TVs, toys, computers, and clothing are now being used by China to buy America. The highest item on the list is US federal government debt, i.e. US government bonds. As of November 2013, China is the number-one foreign holder of US government debt, with holdings of a little more than $1.3 trillion. Hong Kong holds another $141 billion. Of all US foreign debt, about 36% is owed to China and Hong Kong. Second in line is Japan with $1.18 trillion in US government debt, followed by a long list of countries, none of which own more than $250 billion and most of which own below $100 billion dollars' worth of US debt. This list includes $53 billion owned by Turkey and $14 billion owned by Peru. This debt distribution means that China has a lot of power over the US. In fact, China can singlehandedly destabilize the US bond market and seriously hamper the federal government's policy of rolling over its debt, a devastating scenario for the US economy.

Of course, China is not likely to sabotage the US on a whim because both parties have a tremendous amount to lose in such a scenario. Nonetheless, having a finger on America's economy self-destruct button is a powerful tool in any relationship, one the Soviet Union never enjoyed during the Cold War. The situation also means that the US will have to pay China some $70–80 billion a year in interest when interest rates on the debt go back to their past 20-year average of around 5.5%.[83] This sum, by the way, is more than the Justice and Energy Department's budgets combined!

China's purchases haven't stopped at US debt. After reviewing World Bank data from 2000 to 2010, the *Economist* found that China led the world in cross-border mergers and acquisitions. These purchases targeted American firms, and with them the knowledge, systems, and intellectual property they own.[84] Thus, another noticeable result of the fiat money era is the economic, financial, and technological development of America's next international rival.

We cannot end this chapter without addressing a key question and an extremely important observation: why is it that the creation of $59 trillion in debt has not exploded into a devastating super-inflation spiral. Why has the consequence been the 90% loss in the dollar's value, as opposed to something more serious?

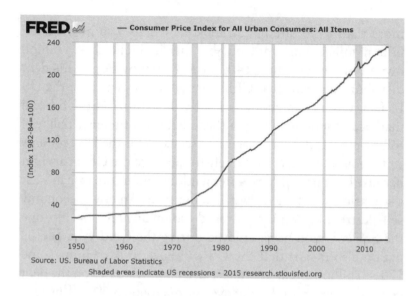

Source: US. Bureau of Labor Statistics
Shaded areas indicate US recessions - 2015 research.stlouisfed.org

The answer breaks down into a few parts.

First, as demonstrated above, the US was able to avoid high inflation by exporting some of its inflationary pressure to China and other developing markets by replacing US labor with cheap labor.

Secondly, we do not have full data on real inflation rates since, as previously discussed, the CPI does not reflect reality because of the way it is calculated, so it's reasonable to assume that deterioration of the value of the dollar is bigger than officially reported.

But the most important and significant element is far more hidden. The Industrial Revolution brought with it a huge growth in productivity. So much so that while in the 1700s some 90% of the population had to work in agriculture-food growing; today less than 2% of the population is occupied with this task. In an ecosystem with a limited amount of money, as it was throughout the 18th and 19th centuries, such a growth in productivity would cause prices to drop and living standards to rise. Such was the case during most of the 1800s, excluding the Civil War years. On average, between 1815 and 1895, prices went down 4% annually.[85] Meanwhile, annual per capita GDP went up around 1.5% a year, spelling a threefold increase in per capita GDP between 1820 and 1900.[86] So while prices were dropping sharply, output was skyrocketing, a combination that yielded an important improvement in most Americans' standard of living.

This kind of amelioration is, after all, the ultimate goal of human economic activity. After all, people do not eat gold, they eat products, hence what they need to improve their livelihood are more products not more coins. In the last thirty years of the 20th century, the world experienced a similar important shift: the Digital Revolution. This extraordinary technological milestone also brought huge improvements in productivity, so much so that we cannot even imagine running the world today without computers and the Internet. Yet prices for the most part did not go down. To the contrary, prices kept climbing. How can this be? Where did all this productivity growth go?

The simple answer is that money creation consumed this price reduction. All the productivity gains, which should have translated into society-wide improvements in living standards were instead eaten up by the flood of newly created money. Money creation produced inflationary pressure that pushed prices back up. Instead of lower prices and a higher standard of living for all people, the government got away with printing more money and the financial sector with taking on more leverage. In essence, the engines propelling the money creation—the oppressive costs of an increasingly complex society and government, the financial demands of a massive military-industrial complex, and the endless malinvestment bubbles—consumed the price reduction that would have otherwise been enjoyed by all the public. Hence, for all intents and purposes, our vast productivity gains were struck by a mammoth hidden tax, similar to inflation, yet even more subtle.

The fact that CPI increased by "only" an official average of 2.5% a year is not a result of some sort of miraculous new reality where unlimited money creation has no inflationary consequences. The reality is much bleaker than this fantasy. It was due to the Digital Revolution that such a super stealthy tax—an unthinkably huge seizure of resources and a transfer

243

of purchasing power from the masses to the few—could have occurred while producing a "reasonable" official rate of inflation.

The table below compares the real GDP per capita (per person) growth in four periods of 25 years each.

Period	GDP Per Capita Growth	Inflation	Comments
1825-1849	24.80%	- 10.80%	
1850-1874	36.71%	- 23.10%	The three years of the Civil War and greenbacks- excluded
1875-1899	52.67%	- 29.60%	
1989-2013	42.15%	+78.50%	

Source: Inflation: Federal Reserve of Minneapolis.
GDP: The Maddison Project

This table clearly demonstrates that growth and inflation rate have nothing to do with each other. As we can see from 75 years of data, an economy can grow significantly thanks to improvements in productivity, while prices constantly drop, which grants added purchasing power to the currency and people. Growth and deflation are only connected when prices drop sharply in a short period of time in response to drops in aggregate demand, commonly a response to the collapse of a financial bubble, as in 1929, 2000 and 2008. In the 25 years between 1875 and 1900, per capita growth dwarfed even that of the height of the fiat money era (52.7% vs. 42%). Prices simultaneously dropped by almost 30%. By contrast, prices increased by almost 80% between 1989 and 2013. If not for the fiat money era's money creation, we could have enjoyed the same economic bounty as in previous times of technological progress. The above table also disproves a commonly accepted "truth" of the fiat money era, namely that money creation and inflation lead to growth while price drops are indicators of depression and contraction. This fallacy mixes steady price drops due to productivity improvement with sharp price drops as result of quick disappearance of demand created by financial bubble's collapse. The Federal

Reserve Chairman vividly exemplified this fallacy:

"The source of deflation ... is in almost all cases a side effect of a collapse of aggregate demand... Likewise, the economic effects of a deflationary episode... recession, rising unemployment, and financial stress"

And thus the solution:

"...the U.S. government has a technology, called a printing press that allows it to produce as many U.S. dollars as it wishes [...] under a paper-money system, a determined government can always generate higher spending and hence positive inflation."

Deflation (price drops) is only a problem for debt-rigged economies as it increases the product-value of the debt and prevents central banks from inflating the debt away. For the citizenry, however, inflation, which is after all constant decrease of purchasing power, spells only a struggle to stay afloat.

Summary

On March 1968 at the request of President Jonson Congress eliminated the law which required that 25% of US money be backed by gold. In August 1971, President Nixon unilaterally canceled the Bretton Woods system which was the dominant monetary system since the end of the Second World War. These two acts started a new and unprecedented era in human history, a worldwide and exclusive fiat money regime, a monetary system with no real limitations on money creation.

The abandonment of any type of commodity money, even indirectly, came on the heels of previous inventions and institutions, among them fractional-reserve banking, the Federal Reserve as "lender of last resort," and government guarantee of bank failures via institutions like the FDIC. The combination of all of these removed the last breaks on the money creation machine. With no physical limitation dictated by linkage to the limited availability of a physical commodity like gold, and with the government basically covering significant parts of banks loan risks, all players and interests in the money creation ecosystem became aligned. Now the banks could constantly lower the reserve ratio and engage in ever-expanding lending schemes and government could get access to unlimited amounts of money well beyond its tax revenues through the creation of money in the form of debt. Furthermore, the public and corporations could now also access more and more newly created money in the shape of credit, if only the interest rates were low enough for them to believe that taking out these loans would be worthwhile. Throughout the fiat money era and especially since the late 1980s all these factors took on increasingly significant roles.

As a result, money was created on a historically unprecedented scale in the US and in Europe. During these decades the US created more than $56 trillion in the shape of debt, credit and liabilities taken on by all sectors of the US economy. This debt will reach $59 trillion by early 2015.

This new money and the debt-creation mechanism fundamentally changed the US economy and society. It reduced the value of the dollar by at least 85%, if not more; it also wasted the golden opportunity, afforded by the Digital Revolution, to further increase all Americans' living standards. This unlimited money funded endless trade deficits, which destroyed significant parts of US manufacturing capacity and of its labor force. This massive outsourcing in turn put ongoing pressure on and eroded the income of most American households. As a result of this mass outsourcing and debt-financed deficit in trade, China was able to accumulate huge dollar reserves and acquire not only American companies, know-how, and intellectual property, but also a strategic weapon in the shape of almost $1.4 trillion in US bonds.

The new money also brought about asset price increases and bubbles, mainly in the stock market, which enriched the holders of these assets: the rich, Wall Street, executives of publicly trading companies, and the well-connected. It simultaneously eroded the wealth, income, and livelihood of the majority of American households. This immense transfer of purchasing power, an inevitable outcome of massive money creation, from the masses to the lucky few, ended in unprecedented income inequality.

The debt-money creation machine enabled the government also to keep up unprecedented levels of spending and debt. It also enabled America to presumably "afford" the cost of its ever-growing complexity, web of bureaucracy, waste, corruption and crony capitalism. These corrupted Washington D.C. to its bones by creating the conditions in which lobbying could flourish, and made Washington connections a required asset for every industry and sector in America. The money generated by lobbying is funneled to politicians, staffers and members of executive and legislative branches. This corruption corroded public trust of and respect for its democratically elected institutions like never in American history.

Since 1968, America has become addicted to and dependent on debt and money creation. The dependence runs so deep that if the US did not increase its debt by some $1.5 to $2 trillion a year, the economy would fall into an immediate recession. At the same time, the annual cost of just paying the interest to maintain the nation's debts in all sectors at their current level takes up more than 10% of GDP. This 10% is more than 3 times the rate of GDP growth, which means that the debt maintenance alone occupies an ever-growing slice of GDP. As a consequence, the Federal Reserve has had to artificially force interest rates to almost zero, which has severely hampered the ability of retirees to live off their savings without taking serious risks in the volatile and unpredictable stock market. It has also made it nearly impossible for pension funds to accumulate the returns necessary to fulfill their commitments to their members.

The flood of money led to a series of booms and busts which are inherently economically wasteful. They left behind little more than debt in their wakes. These boom and bust cycles have destabilized the economy as people and resources rush in and then out of the malinvestments they create. They also enriched the lucky few in unprecedented ways, transferring purchasing power and further fueling the income gap and destabilizing America socially.

This new money also enabled both local and federal government to grow unchecked as it financed itself through debt rather than through taxes. As the government grew, so did the social complexity, red tape and bureaucracy, which increased dramatically the cost of almost any public and private economic activity, creating the conditions for even further debt creation.

If you look at every graph related to the US economy, from student debt to balance of trade and everything in between, you will easily see that 1971 was a meaningful turning point for the worse. The unleashing of tools that enabled endless money-debt creation set the US on a dead-end road. And though it has taken five decades or so, the course is set and the end inevitable.

In the prophetic words of John Maynard Keynes:

> Lenin is said to have declared that the best way to destroy the Capitalist System was to debauch the currency. By a continuing process of inflation, governments can confiscate, secretly and unobserved, an important part of the wealth of their citizens. By this method they not only confiscate, but they confiscate arbitrarily; and, while the process impoverishes many, it actually enriches some. The sight of this arbitrary rearrangement of riches strikes not only at security, but at confidence in the equity of the existing distribution of wealth. Lenin was certainly right. There is no subtler, no surer means of overturning the existing basis of society than to debauch the currency. The process engages all the hidden forces of economic law on the side of destruction, and does it in a manner which not one man in a million is able to diagnose.[87]

The M-bomb president Nixon and Johnson placed on the US economy had a long fuse, but as Herbert Stein, one of Nixon's advisers, famously said, "If something cannot go on forever, it will stop." Stop it did in late summer of 2008. This violent stop is the subject of our next chapter.

Chapter 11:
2008: A Peek at Hell

"Insanity is doing the same thing over and over again but expecting different results."

—attributed to Albert Einstein

The 2008 financial crisis was one of the most severe economic breakdowns in the history of the world. If it weren't for the swift reactions of central banks and governments, the world economy would have deteriorated rapidly to a state similar to that of the Great Depression, if not worse. During the Great Depression, about 40% of US banks went out of business. In 2008, 12 out the 13 largest financial institutions were on the brink of collapse.[1] Given the severity of the catastrophe, you would think that both Washington D.C. and the public would demand a deep and serious examination of exactly what happened. In reality, no such examination took place. Instead, Congress appointed the highly partisan Financial Crisis Inquiry Commission (FCIC) to investigate the matter, and then, without even waiting for the Commission's reports and findings, rushed to pass convoluted regulatory legislation. This 850-page bill along with its 14,000 pages of attached regulations is known as the Dodd-Frank Wall Street Reform and Consumer Protection Act.

When the FCIC's 500-page report came out in January 2011, the media coverage of the report's findings was somewhere between sparse and nonexistent. It seemed that the public's attention had already moved on to new big things like the Affordable Care Act, also known as Obamacare. This total disinterest in understanding the causes of the 2008 crisis is

249

mindboggling and represents a huge missed opportunity. How could so many affected people not demand an explanation for what had caused their misfortune considering that the crisis caused tens of millions of Americans to lose their homes, savings, and jobs, and ravaged economies worldwide?

On the bright side, the crisis provided a great opportunity to take a close look at the myths, beliefs, policies and organizations that run this country. The devastation caused by the crisis should have been a wake-up call for the American people to closely examine the leaders, press and pundits they had placed their faith in. After all, if we do not learn from such scarring events, what *are* the events that shape our beliefs and future actions? The 2008 crisis was also an appropriate moment to review the dangerous convictions underlying money creation policies and an opportunity to question the Federal Reserve's standing policy of solving the problems created by the collapse of one financial bubble by inflating an even larger one. Finally, America and the world could have faced the most difficult question of all: what will be the end result of this out-of-control debt-money creation machine put in place after Bretton Woods?

Instead, the public bought in to the false notion that this crisis was entirely unforeseen and just the work of "profiteers and speculators." Oh, those profiteers and speculators, again!

Instead of running out of town in shame, the same people responsible for the disaster became the leaders of the recovery, as if nothing had happened. They were cheered on by the same media pundits as they continued to rely on the same myths and policies that brought us to 2008 in the first place. Given that nothing has changed and nothing has been learned, what can we expect from the future?

The truth is that what happened in 2008 is very simple. As we will soon see, it is as basic and easy to understand as a children's story. The 2008 crisis, at its core, was neither complex nor an act of God. It was a classic financial bubble with all the classic attributes thereof: greed, misallocations, malinvestment and irrationality. The fall, too, evinced all the standard symptoms of the aftermath of a financial bubble collapse.

The story of the 2008 bubble and of the financial meltdown that followed is the story of the housing market in the US. In 1945, average inflated-adjusted housing prices in the US were more or less similar to what they had been 55 years earlier in 1890. For the next 55 years, home prices remained within a narrow band of plus or minus 12%, just slightly higher than the 1890 base benchmark. In fact, in 1995, prices were back exactly at the 1890 and 1945 levels. And then in the early 2000s prices doubled in a short period of time.

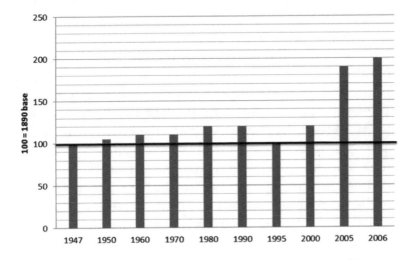

Housing pricing adjusted for inflation 1945-2006 (Case Shiller Index)

The foundations for this dramatic hike were laid many years prior. As we know by now, no inherent limits on money-debt creation have existed since 1971. With no fixed anchor limiting the quantity of money, the only tool that can impact the pace of money creation is interest rates. When interest rates are high, fewer businesses and people are willing to borrow. When interest rates are low, money creation machines click into high gear, pumping more debt-money into the marketplace, assuming of course that the borrowers believe they will see benefit from such lending.

There were many people, organizations, policies, and regulations involved in the creation of the housing bubble and the ensuing 2008 crash. Still the overriding issue, the "original sin," so to speak, was the incredible availability of cheap money for housing purchases. This huge abundance of money dedicated to housing powered the bubble and enabled Wall Street's dubious behavior. The story of this bubble starts therefore at the end of the previous one. After the collapse of the dot-com bubble, the US economy fell into a recession. It was time to pay for the hype and mass of poor investments, and so some painful corrections and reallocations took place. But the government and the Fed's long-standing policy was to avoid recessions and corrections at almost any price. This policy was also dressed up as patriotism after 9/11. To avoid a necessary economic correction, the Fed decided to come to the rescue and reduced the interest rate 11 times throughout 2001 until it fell to 1.75%, the lowest in almost 50 years. By November 2002, the interest dropped to 1.25%. This reduction was aimed at encouraging "liquidity," i.e. money borrowing and with it economic activity.

Although mortgage interest rates did not fall to this historic low, they did fall significantly compared to previous mortgage rates. The big difference created between the low mortgage rates and the Fed's near zero interest rates created a rush by Wall Street firms to lend money. Looking for better yields, they started pushing money into the mortgage market. This money, however, was not only US money. As we saw in the chapter dealing with currencies, many countries worldwide had significant dollar surpluses in their trade balances and thus were looking to invest in dollar-denominated assets. To them and to other international investors, nothing seemed more lucrative and safe than investing in US mortgages backed by collateral as solid as US homes.

The Fed's low interest rates were encouraging new debt-money creation, which, in the eyes of the Fed, meant economy stimulation. In his November 2002 testimony on economic outlook before the Joint Economic Committee of Congress, then Fed Chairman Alan Greenspan made all of this very clear:

Stimulated by mortgage interest rates that are at lows not seen in decades, home sales and housing starts have remained strong.[…].Besides sustaining the demand for new construction, mortgage markets have also been a powerful stabilizing force over the past two years of economic distress by facilitating the extraction of some of the equity that homeowners had built up over the years.

[…]

According to survey data, roughly half of equity extractions are allocated to the combination of personal consumption expenditures and outlays on home modernization.

[…]

It is important to recognize that the extraction of equity from homes has been a significant support to consumption during a period when other asset prices were declining sharply. Were it not for this phenomenon, economic activity would have been notably weaker in the wake of the decline in the value of household financial assets.[3]

The concept was pretty simple: the housing market would replace dot-com businesses as a generator of wealth and as a creator of a "wealth effect" (when the prices of assets rise, their owners feel more comfortable spending more). The rise in home prices would encourage not only more home building, but would also incite people to take loans out against their homes and use these loans for consumption, which would further stimulate the economy.

The Fed was delighted that the full impact of the end of the dot-com bubble was avoided. In a February 2004 meeting, then Fed Governor Ben Bernanke's mood was self-congratulatory. "The fact (is) that recessions have become less frequent and less severe. […] Whether the dominant cause of the Great Moderation is structural change, improved monetary policy, or simply good luck is an important question. […] This […] makes me optimistic for the future."[4]

While Bernanke blessed the Fed's good luck and improved monetary policies, here's what this policy looked like on the ground, according to the FCIC report:

> Money washed through the economy like water rushing through a broken dam. Low interest rates and then foreign capital helped fuel the boom. Construction workers, landscape architects, real estate agents, loan brokers, and appraisers profited on Main Street, while investment bankers and traders on Wall Street moved even higher on the American earnings pyramid and the share prices of the most aggressive financial service firms reached all-time highs. Homeowners pulled cash out of their homes to send their kids to college, pay medical bills, install designer kitchens with granite counters, take vacations, or launch new businesses. They also paid off credit cards, even as personal debt rose nationally. Survey evidence shows that about 5% of homeowners pulled out cash to buy a vehicle and over 40% spent the cash on a catchall category including tax payments, clothing, gifts and living expenses.[5]

As money rushed toward this newly discovered opportunity, prices started to rise fast, bringing in more new home buyers and encouraging more home construction:

> In Bakersfield, California, where home starts doubled and home values grew even faster between 2001 and 2006, wide-open farm fields were plowed under and divided into thousands of building lots. Home prices jumped 11% in Bakersfield in 2002, 17% in 2003, 32% in 2004, and 29% more in 2005.[6]

Home prices grew rapidly across the nation. Between 2000 and 2006, the median sales price of existing single-family homes rose by 56%, or 7.7% per year.[7]

In "hot" markets like Las Vegas, Florida and California, the jumps were much higher. As the buying frenzy spread, people started buying dozens of homes, not for the purpose of living in them or renting them, but rather with the goal of flipping them. Many houses had quickly become a commodity for trading, rather than properties where people lived. David Gussmann, the former vice president at Fannie Mae, told the Commission that in one package of 50 securitized loans his analysts found one purchaser who had bought 19 properties, falsely identifying himself each time as the owner of only one property, while another had bought five properties.[8]

In each of the years from 2002 to 2006, the number of new single family homes constructed grew to more than 1.4 million. The amount of new homes constructed peaked at 1.8 million in 2005 and 2006. This was 25 to 50%more than in the period between 1985 and 1998, In the 5 years between 2002 and 2006, 2.2 million more homes were built than in the preceding 5 years.[9]

This growth was in no way a response to a real shift in demand caused by something like population growth. Consequently, the housing inventory kept increasing. Builders and buyers were not the only participants. A new breed of mortgage broker joined the party as well. "According to an investigative news report published in 2008, between 2000 and 2007, at least 10,500 people with criminal records entered the field in Florida, for example, including 4,065 who had previously been convicted of such crimes as fraud, bank robbery, racketeering, and extortion."[10]

In the meantime, Washington was cheering, not only because a recession had been averted, but also because increasing home ownership by increasing loan accessibility had been a long-time official policy of all administrations. This policy somehow completely disregarded the question of whether the market and the people taking out the loans could handle the long-term burdens of such loans. Bill Clinton, in his charming way, shared with his audience this home-ownership-above-all policy, as if the average American was just like him:

When I was trying to coax my wife into marrying me, we were both living in Fayetteville, Arkansas, teaching at the University of Arkansas. And I had not gotten a definite answer; I think that's the most delicate way I can put this. [Laughter] And Hillary had to go away to somewhere—I can't remember where she was going now, but anyway she was taking a trip on an airplane, so I was driving her to the airport. And we drove by this wonderful old house. It was an old, old, very small house, and she said, "Boy, that's a beautiful house." And I noticed that there was a little "For Sale" sign on it. So I took her to the airport, went back, and bought the house. And when she came home after the trip, I drove by the house. I said, "See that house you liked? I bought it while you were gone. Now you have to marry me." [Laughter] And it worked; 20 years ago this fall, it worked. Most people do it the other way around[…]The goal of this strategy, to boost home ownership to 67.5% by the year 2000, would take us to an all-time high, helping as many as 8 million American families across that threshold.[11]

Deep into the bubble, President Bush reiterated this policy:

For millions of our citizens, the American Dream starts with owning a home. Home ownership gives people a sense of pride and independence and confidence for the future. When you work hard, like you've done, and there are good policies coming out of our nation's capital we're creating a home—an ownership society in this country, where more Americans than ever will be able to open up their door where they live and say, welcome to my house, welcome to my piece of property. [...]

   In 2002, I set a clear goal, 5.5 million minority home-owners by the end of the decade. [...]

   Some families are more than able to pay a mortgage, but just don't have the savings to put money down.[...]

So I'm asking Congress to pass my Zero Down Payment Initiative. We should remove the 3% down payment rule for first time home buyers with FHA (Federal Housing Administration) insured mortgages.[12]

This policy of increasing homeownership and putting home ownership at the center of the American Dream wasn't new. Fannie Mae and Freddy Mac, two government-sponsored enterprises (GSE), were formed for this exact purpose many years before Clinton or Bush took the oath of office. Fannie Mae was established in 1938 with the mandate to buy mortgages from lending banks that followed certain guidelines set by the FHA. The goal behind setting up Fannie Mae was to ensure that banks had an ongoing supply of money for mortgages. Fannie Mae then held the mortgages in its portfolio, or to a lesser degree, resold these mortgages to other investors. For the following thirty years, Fannie Mae was the only player buying mortgages from the mortgage originators, which are the organizations issuing loans to home buyers. The field Fannie Mae was operating in is known as the secondary mortgage market.

In 1968, Congress reformed the organization and turned it into a publicly traded company. Fannie Mae was still in the same business, but had become a GSE. In 1970, a second GSE, Freddie Mac, was set up. Together, they purchased more types of mortgages. Their conduct was governed by new internal guidelines concerned with mortgage size, loan-to-house value ratios, and debt-to-income ratios. The two GSEs were given a line of credit from the US government and some tax exemption benefits. Both were required to meet affordable housing mortgage purchase goals, set annually by the HUD (Department of Housing and Urban Development). The companies were also allowed extremely low reserve ratios. Although they had a mere 2.5% reserve on loans and 0.45% reserve on loans they repackaged and resold as securities— also known as the infamous "mortgage-backed security"—they still guaranteed these loans. Mortgage-backed securities are financial instruments that represent ownership of a debt secured by a group of mortgages. This debt gets its principle and interest payment from mortgage payments.

The two GSEs started to swell. In the late 1980s and 1990s, Fannie Mae grew rapidly into the largest firm in the US housing finance ecosystem. Correspondingly, their obligations and the mortgage-backed securities they guaranteed grew almost 350-fold in 20 years: from $7.59 billion in 1990 to $1.4 trillion in 1995 and then to $2.4 trillion in 2000. All of these obligations were backed by only $37.5 billion of shareholder equity, which was their cash on hand, amounting to only 1.5% of these companies' liabilities. Here fractional-reserve banking reached its high point. These two organizations practically held a license to print money and use it to buy mortgages from banks and other mortgage originators. This setup created a potentially endless supply of money for mortgages. There were at this point only two things that could prevent money from flooding the housing market: interest rates and stricter lending standards. Both of these controls, however, were rapidly loosening as the housing market went into hyper-drive in the early years of 2000s.

If unlimited money creation were not surreal enough, the Freddie and Fannie act becomes even more absurd when lobbying enters the scene. These two GSEs morphed into government-sponsoring enterprises, according to the FDIC's report

> "From 1999 to 2008, the two reported spending more than $164 million on lobbying, and their employees and political action committees contributed $15 million to federal election campaigns.[...] Former HUD secretary Mel Martinez described "the whole army of lobbyists that continually paraded in a bipartisan fashion through my offices. [...] It's pretty amazing the number of people that were in their employ."[13]

These efforts and monies were not spent in vain. As Fannie Mae COO Daniel Mudd wrote in a 2004 memorandum to

CEO Franklin Raines, the company "used to, by virtue of our peculiarity, be able to write, or have written, rules that worked for us."[14]

Even though Fannie and Freddie are GSEs, the executives' compensation packages didn't resemble government pay. Between the 1991 and 1998, the CEO of Fannie Mae earned a total of about $100 million. His successor from 1999 until 2005 grossed more than $90 million. Daniel Mudd, the following CEO who presided over the organization's demise in 2008, grossed more than $12 million dollars. Over at Freddie Mac, things didn't look much different: between 2003 and 2008 the CEO of Freddie Mac took home more than $38 million. The last year before the enterprise went into conservatorship in 2007—when a guardian was appointed to manage their matters—was especially lucrative: the CEO collected $19.8 million for that year alone.[15]

Even with the help of the low interest rates, the mortgage originators still had to bring in new borrowers to take out loans in order to continue growing the mortgage business. The market needed borrowers willing to take out new mortgages and buy all those newly built houses. So as the pool of traditionally qualified borrowers started to dwindle, mortgage originators became more and more forgiving in their requirements of borrowers.

In the market of mortgage originators, Countrywide Financial Corporation was among the most important, if not *the* market leader. In 2006, Countrywide originated around 20% of all mortgages in the United States. Countrywide was also deeply involved in approving and issuing nontraditional loans, i.e., loans that do not meet lending qualification standards. An inspection by the Banking Supervision division of the Federal Reserve found that in 2005 nontraditional loans made up 59% of originations at Countrywide, 58% at Wells Fargo, and 51% at National City. The inspection found that "two-thirds of the nontraditional loans made by the banks in 2003 had been what is known as 'liar loans'". [loans missing the basic documents needed to qualify for a mortgage].

Still, "originating what was sellable in the secondary market" was the business strategy of choice. Countrywide indeed proceeded to sell 87% of the $1.5 trillion in mortgages it originated between 2002 and 2005 to secondary buyers; Fannie Mae was one of its top buyers.[16] Like too many big companies in modern America, Countrywide also took care of its friends. Countrywide created a VIP loan unit with 13 full-time employees dedicated to winning over key politicians and executives. Benefits available to VIP borrowers included discounts—standard discount was 0.5 points/percent of interest cost and a waiver of so called junk fees—special service and speedy processing. Between 1996 and 2008, this VIP loan unit made hundreds of loans to members of Congress, congressional staff, White House staff, high-ranking government officials, and executives and employees of Fannie Mae. Among the Congress members the VIP handled was former Democratic Senate Banking Committee Chairman Christopher Dodd. This special treatment led to some special practices:

> Account Executives in the VIP unit had to fill in blanks on loan applications because "Friends of Angelo" (Angelo Mozilo, chairman and CEO of Countrywide) were reluctant or unwilling to provide basic information such as salary and employment information. They had already been promised specific loan terms and guaranteed approval, so efforts by VIP Account Executives to fill out fields on loan application documents amounted to "courtesy calls."[17]

As lending risk grew, so did the creativity involved in making loans available. Mortgage originators began introducing new sets of loans and Fannie and Freddie bought them up. These loans included interest-only loans, in which payment for the principal kicked in at a later stage; Alt-A loans, short for Alternative A-paper, a loan that does not even include the borrower's necessary financial documentation; and the now-infamous subprime loans, loans offered at rates above prime rates, which are rates offered to the most qualified borrowers. These subprime loans were offered to individuals who could not qualify for prime rate loans, typically due to low credit ratings. The latter two loans—Alt-A and subprime—are known as nonprime mortgage loans. According to the Government Accounting Office, in 2006 they accounted for 34% of the overall mortgage market. They grew from an estimated $171 billion in 2002 to $877 billion in 2005.[18] But Fannie and Freddie were by no means the only ones owning or guaranteeing mortgages.

By this time, pooling large collections of mortgages together into a bundle and selling the package to investors as a mortgage-backed security was standard practice. Hundreds of billions of dollars in mortgage-backed securities were thus packaged and purchased by financial investors and institutions the world over. Nowhere was a better home for these financially engineered assets than Wall Street. Many of these mortgage-backed securities were then insured against default by other large institutions like AIG, using a credit default swap which was essentially an insurance policy the holders of the mortgage-backed securities took out to insure the debt would paid in full. These complex financial tools were designed to evade insurance regulations that were meant to prevent insurance companies from insuring these types of liabilities.

In 2006, everyone, from the Fed to Wall Street, was happy. The economy was booming, mostly because of the housing market, and ongoing home construction and purchases added millions of jobs. Ever-increasing home prices created a wealth effect that enticed tens of millions of households to take out mortgages and spend them on consumption. The debt-money creation train was rolling full steam ahead, and the effect of that money was felt all across the economy. In January 2007, the Congressional Budget Office published a paper titled "Housing Wealth and Consumer Spending" which read:

The rise in real home prices between mid-1997 and mid-2006 added $6.5 trillion to consumer wealth. Combining that estimate with households' propensity to spend from housing wealth indicates that the rise in real home prices since mid-1997 has added between $130 billion and $460 billion per year to consumer spending. That estimate implies that consumer spending would be 1.4% to 5.0% lower than it is if real home prices had risen only at their trend rate since mid-1997, all else being equal.

Given that consumer spending significantly contributes to the economy, increased consumption had a tremendous impact on the economy.

It should come as no surprise that Christmas of 2006 was a happy time in Wall Street. According to the office of the New York State Comptroller, bonuses almost doubled in the two years between 2004 and 2006: they went from $18.6 billion in 2004 to $34.3 billion in 2006, averaging almost $200,000 per employee.

Wall Street's largest investment bank, Goldman Sachs, dedicated $16.5 billion to year-end bonuses. The chairman was paid a record $54 million in 2006, while top management received $25 million each. The CEO of Morgan Stanley, the country's second-largest investment bank, made $40 million in stock and options. Other financial institutions like Lehman Brothers and Bear Stearns paid out about $12 billion in compensation, averaging some $300,000 per employee.[19] Over at Merrill Lynch, the company disbursed $5 to $6 billion in bonuses. Analysts in their twenties making $130,000 a year got twice that sum in year-end bonuses; traders in their thirties got ten (or more) times this sum, somewhere between $3 and even $5 million in bonuses.[20]

Bonuses were almost three times the size they had been ten years prior, and almost ten times the size of 1990 bonuses.

Wall Street Bonus Payments

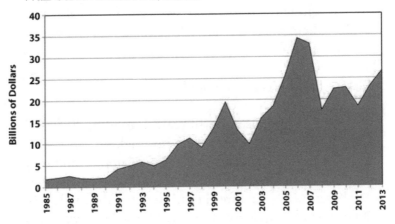

Source: Office of the New York State Comptroller March 12, 2014[41]

As usual, people believed the economy would continue to prosper because they wanted to believe and because it made lots of financial sense for them personally. From the home buyer in Bakersfield all the way to the chairman of the Federal Reserve, people simply shut out the thought that this rise in home prices and the ongoing demand for housing could one day end. An extremely dangerous megabubble was forming under the noses of the country's financial, political, and media leadership. No real attention was paid to the very few who realized that something was very wrong:

> J. Kyle Bass, a Dallas-based hedge fund manager and a former Bear Stearns executive, testified to the FCIC that he told the Federal Reserve that he believed the housing securitization market to be on a shaky foundation. "Their answer at the time was, and this was also the thought that was homogeneous throughout Wall Street's analysts— home prices always track income growth and jobs growth. And they showed me income growth on one chart and jobs growth on another, and said, We don't see what you're

263

talking about because incomes are still growing and jobs are still growing.' And I said, well, you obviously don't realize where the dog is and where the tail is, and what's moving what."[21]

Blatant fraud was also ignored:

Crabtree, an appraiser for 48 years, started in 2003 and 2004 to think that things were not making sense. People were paying inflated prices for their homes, and they didn't seem to have enough income to pay for what they had bought.[...] Crabtree began studying the market. In 2006, he ended up identifying what he believed were 214 fraudulent transactions in Bakersfield; some, for instance, were allowing insiders to siphon cash from each property transfer. The transactions involved many of the nation's largest lenders. One house, for example, was listed for sale for $565,000, and was recorded as selling for $605,000 with 100% financing, though the real estate agent told Crabtree that it actually sold for $535,000. Crabtree realized that the gap between the sales price and loan amount allowed these insiders to pocket $70,000. The terms of the loan required the buyer to occupy the house, but it was never occupied. The house went into foreclosure and was sold in a distress sale for $322,000. Crabtree began calling lenders to tell them what he had found; but to his shock, they did not seem to care. He finally reached one quality assurance officer at Fremont Investment & Loan, the nation's eighth-largest subprime lender. "Don't put your nose where it doesn't belong," he was told. Crabtree took his story to state law enforcement officials and to the Federal Bureau of Investigation. "I was screaming at the top of my lungs," he said. He grew infuriated at the slow pace of enforcement and at prosecutors' lack of response to a problem that was wreaking economic havoc in Bakersfield.[22]

By 2006, the economy was displaying all the classic characteristics of a financial driven bubble. The malinvestments and misallocations of all types of resources were extensive and far-reaching. Millions of unneeded houses— 15-20% larger than houses of the previous decade—were being built. At the bubble's peak, there were close to 3.5 million vacant houses.[23] In response to construction demand, millions of people changed jobs to unneeded positions. Residential construction jobs grew from 5.5 million in 1996 to 7.4 million jobs at the peak of the bubble in 2005. Had there not been a bubble, it is estimated that there would have been 1.7 million to 2.2 million fewer residential construction-related jobs in 2008.[24] Construction was not the only affected profession:

Business boomed for Christopher Cruise, a Maryland-based corporate educator who trained loan officers for companies that were expanding mortgage originations. He crisscrossed the nation, coaching about 10,000 loan originators a year in auditoriums and classrooms. His clients included many of the largest lenders—Countrywide, Ameriquest, and Ditech among them. "I was a sales and marketing trainer in terms of helping people to know how to sell these products to, in some cases, frankly unsophisticated and unsuspecting borrowers," he said. He taught them the new playbook: "You had no incentive whatsoever to be concerned about the quality of the loan, whether it was suitable for the borrower or whether the loan performed. In fact, you were in a way encouraged not to worry about those macro issues." He added, "I knew that the risk was being shunted off. I knew that we could be writing crap. But in the end it was like a game of musical chairs. Volume might go down but we were not going to be hurt."[25]

The financial markets were creating more financial tools to streamline the flow of more money to the housing market and to Wall Street's trading games. These tools did not reflect market reality or borrowers' ability to undertake more debt.

Most home loans entered the pipeline soon after borrowers signed the documents and picked up their keys. Loans were put into packages and sold off in bulk to securitization firms including investment banks such as Merrill Lynch, Bear Stearns, and Lehman Brothers, and commercial banks [...] such as Citibank, Wells Fargo, and Washington Mutual. The firms would package the loans into residential mortgage backed securities that would mostly be stamped with triple A ratings (i.e. best creditworthy loans) by the credit rating agencies, and sold to investors. In many cases, the securities were repackaged again into collateralized debt obligations (CDOs)—often composed of the riskier portions of these securities which would then be sold to other investors.[...]

The instruments grew more and more complex [...] when firms ran out of real product, they started generating cheaper-to-produce synthetic CDOS—composed not of real mortgage securities but just of bets on other mortgage products. Each new permutation created an opportunity to extract more fees and trading profits. And each new layer brought in more investors wagering on the mortgage market—even well after the market had started to turn. So by the time the process was complete, a mortgage on a home in south Florida might become part of dozens of securities owned by hundreds of investors—or parts of bets being made by hundreds more. Treasury Secretary Timothy Geithner, the president of the New York Federal Reserve Bank during the crisis, described the resulting product as "cooked spaghetti" that became hard to "untangle."[26]

The stock market also reflected the housing bubble and the overheating economy as it continued to climb. The Dow Jones and S&P 500 almost doubled between late 2002 and late 2007. Like the techies of the dot-com bubble, hundreds of thousands of people close enough to the source of the housing bubble or stock market were prospering in unimaginable ways, first and foremost financial institutions. The Congressional Budget Office estimated that between 2003 and 2005, the richest 3 million people in America saw their income increase from $1.3 trillion to $1.8 trillion, equal to the combined total income of the bottom 166 million Americans.

By December 2007, the collapse had begun: the value of financial institution shares dropped and financial companies posted large losses. Still Wall Street's five biggest firms were paying out $39 billion in bonuses, up from $36 billion the previous year. These bonuses averaged at $219,198 per employee, more than four times the 2006 median household income.[27]

By early 2008, more and more loans were in default, Wall Street was posting dismal results and financial institutions stock prices were declining sharply. Still, these huge losses did not affect the departing management of these collapsing companies. The removed CEO of Merrill Lynch was awarded more than $161 million in a retirement package. Similarly, the resigning Citigroup CEO received an exit package worth $95 million. Even as the economy was crumbling, the golden parachutes reached dizzying heights.

As Wall Street executives cashed out with massive bonuses, the burden of debt taken on by the American public grew at an unprecedented rate: "Overall mortgage indebtedness in the United States climbed from $5.3 trillion in 2001 to $10.5 trillion in 2007. The mortgage debt of American households rose almost as much in the six years from 2001 to 2007 as it had over the course of the country's more than 200-year history."[28]

Still, the country's political, financial, business, and media leadership saw, heard, and said nothing, even when financial institutions' practices were brought to their attention:

Ruhi Maker, a lawyer who worked on foreclosure cases at the Empire Justice Center in Rochester, New York, told Fed Governors Bernanke, Susan Bies, and Roger Ferguson (other top ranking Fed officials) in October 2004 that she suspected that some investment banks—she specified Bear Stearns and Lehman Brothers—were producing such bad loans that the very survival of the firms was put in question. "We repeatedly see false appraisals and false income," she told the Fed officials, who were gathered at the public hearing period of a Consumer Advisory Council meeting. She urged the Fed to prod the Securities and Exchange Commission to examine the quality of the firms' due diligence; otherwise, she said, serious questions could arise about whether they could be forced to buy back bad loans that they had made or securitized.

Maker told the board that she feared an "enormous economic impact" could result from a confluence of financial events: flat or declining incomes, a housing bubble, and fraudulent loans with overstated values.

[...]The Fed governors politely listened and said little, she recalled. "They had their economic models, and their economic models did not see this coming,"[29]

[...]

In that same month [August 2005], a conclave of economists gathered at Jackson Lake Lodge in Wyoming. It was a "who's who of central bankers," recalled Raghuram Rajan, who was then on leave from the University of Chicago's business school while serving as the chief economist of the International Monetary Fund. Greenspan was there, and so was Bernanke.

Jean-Claude Trichet, the president of the European Central Bank, and Mervyn King, the governor of the Bank of England, were among the other dignitaries.

Rajan presented a paper with a provocative title: "Has Financial Development Made the World Riskier?" He posited that executives were being overcompensated for short-term gains but let off the hook for any eventual losses[...] Rajan added that investment strategies such as credit default swaps could have disastrous consequences if the system became unstable, and that regulatory institutions might be unable to deal with the fallout.

He recalled to the FCIC that he was treated with scorn. Lawrence Summers, a former U.S. treasury secretary who was then president of Harvard University, called Rajan a "Luddite," implying that he was simply opposed to technological change. "I felt like an early Christian who had wandered into a convention of half-starved lions," Rajan wrote later.

In late 2005, regulators decided to take a look at the changing mortgage market. Sabeth Siddique, the assistant director for credit risk in the Division of Banking Supervision and Regulation at the Federal Reserve Board, was charged with investigating how broadly loan patterns were changing. He took the questions directly to large banks in 2005 and asked them how many of which kinds of loans they were making.

Siddique found the information he received "very alarming," he told the Commission[...] [The review Siddique wrote] found that two-thirds of the nontraditional loans made by the banks in 2003 had been of the stated-income, minimal documentation variety, known as liar loans, which had a particularly great likelihood of going sour.

The reaction to Siddique's briefing was mixed. Federal Reserve Governor Bies recalled the response by the Fed governors and regional board directors as divided from the beginning. "Some people on the board and regional presidents... just wanted to come to a different answer. So they did ignore it, or the full thrust of it," she told the Commission. [...]

"The bankers pushed back," Bies told the Commission. "The members of Congress pushed back. Some of our internal people at the Fed pushed back."[30]

Both political and financial leaders chose to keep their heads in the sand. By the beginning of 2006, the bubble had grown so much that it could no longer support its own mass. As collapse became imminent, the people on the ground became aware that something was wrong:

> Warren Peterson, a home builder in Bakersfield, felt that he could pinpoint when the world changed to the day. Peterson built homes in an upscale neighborhood, and each Monday morning, he would arrive at the office to find a bevy of real estate agents, sales contracts in hand, vying to be the ones chosen to purchase the new homes he was building. The stream of traffic was constant. On one Saturday in November 2005, he was at the sales office and noticed that not a single purchaser had entered the building. He called a friend, also in the home-building business, who said he had noticed the same thing, and asked him what he thought about it. "It's over," his friend told Peterson.[31]

But higher up on Wall Street, in Washington D.C. and at the Federal Reserve, business was running as usual. The debt-money machine plowed ahead as changing course was not an option.

> Despite all the signs that the housing market was slowing, Wall Street just kept going and going—ordering up loans, packaging them into securities, taking profits, earning bonuses. By the third quarter of 2006, home prices were falling and mortgage delinquencies were rising, a combination that spelled trouble for mortgage-backed securities. But from the third quarter of 2006 on, banks created and sold some $1.3 trillion in mortgage-backed securities and more than $350 billion in mortgage related CDOs.
> [...]
> At Citigroup, meanwhile, Richard Bowen, a veteran banker in the consumer lending group, received a

promotion in early 2006 when he was named business chief underwriter. He would go on to oversee loan quality for over $90 billion a year of mortgages underwritten and purchased by CitiFinancial. These mortgages were sold to Fannie Mae, Freddie Mac, and others. In June 2006, Bowen discovered that as much as 60% of the loans that Citi was buying were defective. They did not meet Citigroup's loan guidelines, and thus endangered the company—if the borrowers were to default on their loans, the investors could force Citi to buy them back. Bowen told the Commission that he tried to alert top managers at the firm by "email, weekly reports, committee presentations, and discussions"; but though they expressed concern, it "never translated into any action." Instead, he said, "there was a considerable push to build volumes, to increase market share." Indeed, Bowen recalled, Citi began to loosen its own standards during these years up to 2005: specifically, it started to purchase stated-income loans. "So we joined the other lemmings headed for the cliff," he said in an interview with the FCIC.

He finally took his warnings to the highest level he could reach— Robert Rubin, the chairman of the Executive Committee of the Board of Directors and a former U.S. treasury secretary in the Clinton administration, and three other bank officials.

He sent Rubin and the others a memo with the words "URGENT—READ IMMEDIATELY" in the subject line. Sharing his concerns, he stressed to top managers that Citi faced billions of dollars in losses if investors were to demand that Citi repurchase the defective loans. [...]

Bowen told the Commission that after he alerted management by sending emails, he went from supervising 220 people to supervising only 2, his bonus was reduced, and he was downgraded in his performance review.[32]

Wall Street was not simply turning a blind eye to its unethical and financially insane practices, it was actively discouraging internal questioning.

It took more than a year for the news to receive the attention it merited. By mid-2007 the entire scheme started to unravel entirely. By the time the Fed finally was willing to recognize that something was wrong, it was far too late:

> Then, in July 2008, long after the risky, nontraditional mortgage market had disappeared and the Wall Street mortgage securitization machine had ground to a halt, the Federal Reserve finally adopted new rules to curb the abuses. [...]By that time, however, the damage had been done. The total value of mortgage backed securities issued between 2001 and 2006 reached $13.4 trillion.[33]

Throughout 2007 and into 2008, housing prices fell and foreclosures rose. This slowdown placed growing pressure on all financial sectors involved in holding, guaranteeing and insuring mortgages and their derivatives. The first strong warning sign of financial trouble came in July 2007 when Bear Stearns, one of Wall Street's largest investment banks, announced that its two subprime hedge funds had lost nearly all of their value amid a rapid decline in the market value of subprime mortgages. By mid-March 2008, Bear Stearns had hit a brick wall. With the help of the Federal Reserve—in the form of $30 billion—JP Morgan agreed to acquire the company. The price was set at $2 a share, a stunning fall from its $172 share price just four months prior. It seemed at the time to all in the financial community that a major catastrophe had been narrowly averted.

As the bubble entered its final stage in late 2007 to early 2008, Fannie Mae and Freddie Mac owned or guaranteed some $5.3 trillion of mortgages while holding barely 2% of this sum in capital. Fannie and Freddie were not the only ones. All major financial institutions had bought large quantities of mortgage-backed securities, and thus were inherently exposed to great risk. The mortgage-backed securities were also insured by the largest insurance companies via the credit default swap, spreading the risk around even further. The stage was set for a major collapse that would ripple on all sides of the globe. The only thing missing was a spark to set things off. It took the form of widespread borrower default on their mortgages.

In late 2007, and to an even great extent in 2008, the bubble had begun collapsing: housing prices plummeted 18% between mid-2007 and mid-2008, and defaults on mortgage loans and foreclosures were piling up. These defaults created mounting losses for the GSEs holding or guaranteeing these mortgages. In time, these losses wiped out the GSEs' entire capital. By September 2008 the companies were practically insolvent.

On September 6, 2008, the Federal Housing Finance Agency (FHFA) placed Fannie Mae and Freddie Mac into conservatorship, practically taking over the two companies. Although both companies' CEOs were sent home, the financial problems remained. From January 2008 through the third quarter of 2010, the two GSEs lost $229 billion. $77 billion of this sum was their own capital and $151 was paid with government support. The Congressional Budget Office has projected that the cost of the GSEs' failure could reach $389 billion by 2019.[34]

In the months leading up to August 2008, the Fed was scrambling to get a handle on the situation and better understand the extent of the problem. Despite these efforts, the Fed still had no idea of the magnitude of the crash on the horizon. The attendees of the Open Market Committee meeting held in the offices of the Board of Governors of the Federal Reserve System on Tuesday, August 5, 2008 showed no signs of concern with a looming disaster. Rather, the members discussed growth, inflation, and commodity pricing. Alarm bells were not ringing.

At the time, Chairman Bernanke predicted:

Housing, of course, remains very uncertain. We don't really know when the bottom will be, although I would add [...] that there seems to be a growing confidence that when we have reached the bottom in housing, whenever that may be, we will see a very quick improvement, both in the financial markets and then, presumably, in the economy as well.[…]So just looking at the traditional indicators of growth and production, I think the best guess is for a slow second half, a slow beginning of 2009.

[…]

On inflation, I do have concerns, as everyone else does. I think that the commodity price movements we have seen are good news.[35]

Such were the optimistic observations of the Chairman of the Federal Reserve a month before the total collapse of the US financial market.

The failure of the mortgage market's two behemoths, Fannie Mae and Freddie Mac, at the beginning of September made it clear that the problems springing up were grave. As a result, investors and institutions scrambled to take cover, sell toxic assets, and pull their money out of risky institutions.

The next fortress to fall was Lehman Brothers, the fourth largest investment bank in the US with almost $20 billion in revenue, 28,000 employees, and $600 billion in assets and liabilities. On September 10, just 4 days after Fannie Mae and Freddie Mac were placed in conservatorship, Lehman Brothers announced its financial results: huge, panic-inducing losses. A hasty attempt to put in place a fire sale, as in the case of Bear Stearns, failed. Secretary of the Treasury Paulson made it clear that government assistance that had been offered to Fannie and Freddie was out of the question. The company was doomed. Harvey Miller, Lehman's legal counsel at the time, told the FCIC

"We went back to the headquarters, and it was pandemonium up there.[…] paparazzi running around. There was a guy there …in a sort of a Norse god uniform with a helmet and a picket sign saying "Down with Wall Street."

... There were hundreds of employees going in and out.... Bart McDade was reporting to the board what had happened. Most of the board members were stunned. Henry Kaufman, in particular, was asking "How could this happen in America?"[36]

This was how one of the country's most venerable and largest financial institutions, formed in 1850, met its ignominious end. On September 15, Lehman Brothers filed for bankruptcy. Wall Street was stunned.

On that same day, another Wall Street powerhouse was virtually dead. Merrill Lynch—with 64,000 employees and $64 billion in revenue, ranked number 70 in the Fortune 500 list of largest global companies for 2007— was also posting large mortgage losses and was unable to finance its short-term debts. That same day, Bank of America announced that it would buy Merrill Lynch. It did not make this offer of its own volition: the federal government threatened the CEO of BofA, saying that he and other top executives could be removed if they did not go through with this deal.[37]

Another financial giant brought to ruin was AIG. AIG was one of the largest insurance companies in the US and was the largest issuer of the credit default swaps, insuring some $441 billion worth of mortgage-backed securities. As more and more mortgages defaulted, AIG was increasingly called on to pay out the insurance claims. To make matters worse, the downgrade of the rest of the securities, which hadn't defaulted yet, required AIG to come up with additional collateral reserves as insurance for those securities. AIG was hanging on by a thread. Luckily for AIG, the government concluded that AIG could not be allowed to go the way of Lehman and thus, on September 16, committed $180 billion to its rescue.

This whirlwind of events in mid-September 2008 provoked widespread panic. Secretary Treasurer Timothy Geithner, then head of the Federal Reserve Bank of New York, told Bloomberg TV: "The entire U.S. financial system and all the major firms in the country, and even small banks across the country, were at that moment at the middle of a classic run. [...] None of them would have survived a situation in which we had let that fire try to burn itself out."

Hedge funds, banks, and investment banks all came under huge pressure from investors trying to get their money out of harm's way. In the next 10 days, the Fed provided $300 billion to commercial and investment banks in hopes of stemming the tide. These frantic attempts did little to help, as nobody knew the scale of the "surprises" and capital losses that were still to come. Fed Chairman Ben Bernanke told the commission, "I honestly believe that September and October of 2008 was the worst financial crisis in global history, including the Great Depression. If you look at the firms that came under pressure in that period ...only one ...was not at serious risk of failure....So out of maybe the 13, 12 of the most important financial institutions in the United States, 12 were at risk of failure within a period of a week or two."

So on September 20, in reaction to this crisis, the Treasury sent Congress a proposal for a piece of historic legislation known as TARP (Troubled Asset Relief Program). TARP would authorize the spending of $700 billion to buy the toxic mortgage-related assets (i.e. the packaged and securitized dubious mortgages) from financial institutions. This convenient initiative would remove the toxic assets from the financial institutions' balance sheets and replace them with freshly printed dollars. These toxic assets would now become the property of the American taxpayer. On October 3, 2008, TARP was signed into law by President Bush. In the following months, TARP's hundreds of billions of dollars were given to more than 700 institutions and companies nationwide, including $81 billion to automobile manufacturers and auto financing companies.

TARP wasn't the only relief program. Some of the other programs included: the Primary Dealer Credit Facility (PDCF), which aided financial institutions listed as primary dealers; the Term Securities Lending Facility (TSLF), which offered Treasury securities for loan over a one-month term; some new FDIC programs; and more.

The damage of the financial crisis quickly spread to Main Street. Credit froze almost overnight, causing disruptions in the day-to-day operations of businesses throughout the economy. This credit-freeze was followed by a sharp drop in consumer spending, as the rapid decline in housing prices made millions of households realize that they were not so wealthy after all.

All the symptoms of a bubble collapse were now unraveling in full force while the workers previously engaged in the unnecessary construction and financing were laid off. A quick downturn was in motion: rising unemployment led to further cutbacks in consumer spending, which led to more layoffs, which in turn led to more consumer spending cuts and so on. By December 2009, the US economy had lost some 8 million jobs, and the number of unemployed and under-employed reached some 17% of the workforce.

The American Dream of home ownership was now turning into a nightmare for tens of millions of people. With unemployment spreading, many people could not afford their mortgages, but due to the state of the housing market, they could not get rid of their homes either. Some 8 million families had their homes foreclosed or put in the foreclosure process. This situation further pushed down housing prices. Prices plummeted 32% nationwide, and in the previously "hot" markets like Nevada, Florida and California, prices tanked nearly 50%.

State and local governments also felt the pain of the crisis. For one, as property and sales tax incomes fell, so did tax revenues. While the incoming money dwindled, the demand for government assistance such as unemployment benefits, welfare, Medicare, and Medicaid sharply rose.

The stock market followed the overall decline. The Dow Jones Industrial Average, which was trading at around 14,000 in mid-2007, fell to a low of 6,600 by March 2009. Simultaneously the S&P 500 fell almost 60% from 1,560 to close where it had been in 2002, pre-bubble: 680 points. This sharp and rapid decline put unbearable pressure on retirees who saw their 401(k)s shrink dramatically, and with that, their daily livelihood. The crisis was a repeat of the dot-com bubble, but on steroids: the economy was correcting all the malinvestments, inefficacies and misallocations of resources. Naturally, since the housing bubble was larger and wider in scope than the dot com bubble, so was the subsequent correction process. It was very painful and its effects were felt everywhere. Unfortunately, little could be done to remedy the situation. After all, the crisis of 2008 was a classic credit-created bubble, and these bubbles, whether we like it or not, have very distinct outcomes, as we already know.

Faced with a growing crisis the Federal Reserve and the federal government turned once again to what they knew best: printing and creating money. This time, however, they engaged in this practice on an unprecedented scale. Following the hundreds of billions of TARP relief dollars, Congress enacted a $700 billion American Recovery and Reinvestment Act, better known as the stimulus package. It was not enough, however, so starting in 2009, the Federal Reserve embarked on a series of programs known as Quantitative Easing (QE). Through three QE programs, the Federal Reserve created about $3.5 trillion in new money and "lent" it to the Treasury and to financial institutions. The program would end, at least for the time being, in November 2014.

The bailout, the stimulus, and QE programs opened the gates to a new level of government deficit. In the four years prior to the crisis, the average federal budget deficit stood at $300 billion a year. After the financial meltdown, the deficit shot up more than fourfold: to $1.4 trillion in 2009, $1.3 trillion in 2010, $1.3 trillion in 2011, $1.1 trillion in 2012, and $680 billion in 2013 increasing the debt from $10 trillion dollars in September 2008 to $18 trillion by December 2014.[38]

The Fed not only flooded both US and international markets with trillions of new dollars, but it also pushed interest rates down to zero, literally. In June 2012, the interest (aka yield) on 10-year government bonds fell to a 200-year low. This QE program, described by the person who managed it as "the greatest backdoor Wall Street bailout of all time," pushed the stock market up dramatically to new record levels

Once again, as if 2000 and 2008 never happened the bells were and still are (as of early 2015) ringing on Wall Street and in Silicon Valley. In the 5 coming years, the Dow and S&P 500 would rise well beyond their 2006-2007 heights and even the NASDAQ would return to 2000 territory. With the IPO market humming, companies are once again traded on abstract and wild valuations and promises. Once again, tech companies are being acquired, but this time not for hundreds of millions, but rather for billions of dollars, mostly based on projected growth expectations and the faith that "this time it'll be different." Politicians are once again talking about the importance of buying a home: in August 2013, President Obama spoke of the "most tangible cornerstone at the heart of middle-class life: the chance to own your own home." Even the surviving bankers are back to receiving their famous bonuses, which totaled to $27 billion (or an average of $164,500 per employee) at the end of 2013.[39] Like in 2004-2005 when the housing bubble was forming, everything seems to be going quite well now. That is at least the sentiment on Wall Street, in Silicon Valley, at the Fed, and among its trusty media pundits.

In the public arena a storm of useless noise overpowers the voices asking the most vital questions of our economy's future. Can constant printing of money and debt really solve this country's systematic problems and create lasting prosperity out of thin air? Can there really be no consequences to dumping almost $5 trillion of TARP, stimulus, and QE money into the market? Who will the losers of such massive money creation be? And last but not least, can we really do the same thing over and over again and expect different results?

These questions were never addressed before things settled back to the "normalcy" of mass debt-money-printing and huge Wall Street bonuses. This time around, however, the massive money production is having mixed results, at best. While asset prices, and especially the visible stock market, have more than tripled benefiting mostly the most wealthy, the unemployment rate and income of the median American household remains far from perfect. While the official unemployment rate has been dropping since 2009, giving much reason for cheer in the media, a look at reality, as indicated in the attached graph, clearly paints a more accurate picture. In reality, the drop in the official unemployment number is more a reflection of the number of people who gave up looking for work all together.

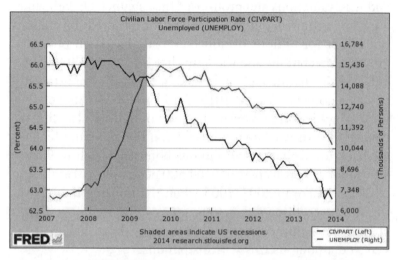

Graph by FRED showing the ratio between labor participation and employment. The drop in unemployment (top line in the graph) has been closely followed the drop in labor participation (people who are employed or looking for work).

September of 2008 saw the violent collapse of the mother of all economic bubbles. Although this event wrought havoc on both the national and international economy, no one involved took any responsibility. At the same time, the public did little to demand a show of leadership from those sworn to serve our nation. The government's principal economic representatives, Ben Bernanke and Tim Geithner, continued serving as heads of the Fed and the Treasury, respectively. Needless to say, no legal action has been taken against any bank or other financial institution, or their top executives, not even to recoup some of the massive losses from the extravagantly remunerated executives.

Given our acceptance of the Fed and Wall Street dodging responsibility, it should come as no surprise that none of the financial media felt the need to seriously inquire how all this could have happened under their "watchdog" eyes. In fact, the only noticeable reaction to this massive crisis was the establishment of the Financial Crisis Inquiry Commission (FCIC), which in January 2011 submitted a detailed and lengthy 500-page report on the causes and details of the crisis. This report got very limited attention from the public and the press. The *Wall Street Journal* stashed an article on the report on page A4, and put it sixth in the Business & Finance column, right below some news about Amazon's mixed earnings. The *Washington Post* concluded that "the report does not contain any major revelation that would fundamentally alter popular perceptions of the crisis." The *New Yorker* went down a similar path, covering the report with an article titled "Crisis Panel's Report Parsed Far and Wide" which was placed on the *New Yorker* website below stories like: "US Approves Genetically Modified Alfalfa."[40]

As 2008 fades into history, let us depart from it with the words of Richard Breeden, former chairman of the Securities and Exchange Commission. Breeden shared the following thoughts with the FCIC: "Everybody in the whole world knew that the mortgage bubble was there.[…] This was not some hidden problem. It wasn't out on Mars or Pluto or somewhere. It was right here. …You can't make trillions of dollars' worth of mortgages and not have people notice."

Will we be hearing one day similar thoughts regarding the more than $20 trillion printed by governments worldwide since 2008, through the stimulus, zero interest policies and QE programs?

Chapter 12:
What's Next?

"Better is it that thou shouldest not vow, than that thou shouldest vow and not pay"

(Ecclesiastes 5:5)

This book is not a prophesy trying to predict the future, nor is it an investment strategy guideline. At its core, this is a history book aiming to illustrate humanity's gradual path to the fiat money era, what this era entailed, and what the future likely holds. If history teaches us anything, it is that unexpected outcomes prevail. It is not unreasonable to assume that almost no one in Europe in May 1914 could have imagined how the European continent would look in May 1916. There were no experts recorded in 1987 that predicted the collapse of the Soviet empire just 4 years later. And on the morning of September 9, 2001, very few Americans imagined that within two years the US would be engaged in a full-fledged war in Afghanistan and Iraq and that the World Trade Center would be nothing but a heap of rubble. The unimaginable happens and only in retrospect do historians talk about the writing on the wall. The termites eat away at the castle's foundation in dark stealth, until things reach a tipping point and the walls come crumbling down with great force.

Not only are humans incapable of predicting the future, they also lack the capacity to imagine anything distant from the reality they're experiencing in the moment. The weather in the San Francisco-Bay Area serves as a nice example. Typically, the weather in the South Bay in July and August averages around 85 degrees Fahrenheit, or more. Forty miles north, in San Francisco, the weather is typically 20 to 25 degrees colder in the summer. San Francisco is, in fact, the coldest city in the US in the summer and is also typically foggy and cloudy. Still, come summertime, under-dressed and freezing South Bay residents visiting San Francisco can be seen all around the city. Everyone knows it's colder in San Francisco, and yet when a person steps out of his South Bay home on a warm sunny day, it's hard to imagine that 60 degree cloudy weather is only a 50 minute drive away.

Now imagine the same phenomenon applied to changes of historical magnitude. Even those who rationally understand the fundamentals can't really internalize and comprehend the consequences and imagine the way things will actuality play out.

In this chapter I will try to describe the course and its probable outcome, yet any attempt to pinpoint future events and attach them to dates, though popular and in high demand, will not only be probably wrong but also misleading. It is impossible to pinpoint the exact start of an avalanche: the last snowflake that brings the mountain to a roar bears no traits that make it different form the millions of previous flakes. The only thing you can point out is the mountain's condition and the probability of such conditions causing an avalanche.

If we look at the situation on the ground, it's clear that the American economy is heading towards a perfect storm, the 3D Hurricane, to be exact: Demographics, Debt, and Deficit. The latter two, debt and deficit, are a direct result of the fiat money era. Demographics refers to America's aging population: the result of spectacular scientific advances and the fall in American fertility rate. Together, these three will pull the US into a crisis that the country is not prepared to weather.

Let's take a deeper dive into the components of the 3D Hurricane by beginning with demographics. In 1900, about 3 million Americans (or 4% of the population) were over the age of 65. By 1950, the number of Americans over 65 had climbed to 12 million (around 8%), and by 2010 the number stood at around 40 million (13%).[1] By 2030, this number is expected to swell to around 70 million (or 20% of the population). Of this 20%, 40% will be 75 and older.[2] This segment of the population is growing at a faster rate than the rest. Between 2000 and 2010, the over-65 population grew by 15%, while the total US population grew by 9.7%. Meanwhile, due to medical advances, the fastest growing group within the older population is the 85- to 94-year-old group. Between 2000 and 2010, this group grew by 29.9%, increasing from 3.9 million to 5.1 million.[3]

Total US population 65 and older 1900-2050

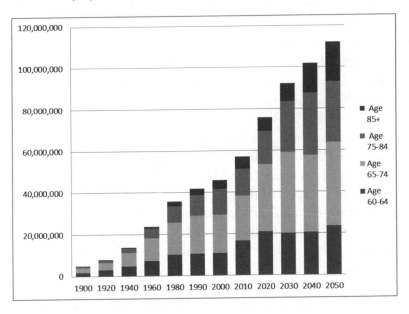

Source: US Bureau of Census. Data for 2010 to 2050 are from the Census2008 national projections, issued August 14, 2008.

This unprecedented growth in the elderly population will produce ongoing and increasing stresses on government programs that aid the elderly, such as Social Security (SSA) and Medicare. To make things even more complicated, these programs, which are funded through employment taxes, do not actually have any assets to their name. All the money collected over the years has been lent to the federal government. The Social Security Administration's $2.8 trillion dollars in "assets" is nothing more than an IOU from the federal government, part of the $18 trillion federal debt. In order to pay back this IOU, the federal government will have to increase its income through higher taxes or take on even more debt. Since 2010, the benefits that the SSA has paid out are greater than the money it collects. As such even if the government paid back the $2.8 trillion it owes, the program could only survive for a maximum of two more decades after which it would run out of all of its assets and reserves. From that point on, SSA would only be able to honor, via ongoing collection, at most 75% of its commitment to retirees. It is worth mentioning that these estimates are based on a full economic recovery and pre-2008 SSA income. Given recent drops in labor participation, as mentioned in the previous chapter, this prospect seems particularly doubtful.

Some of the SSA's funds will run out even earlier: according to its own estimates, the funds of the Social Security's Disability Insurance (DI) program will run out by 2016.[4] Medicare's funds are in no better shape: the Medicare Hospital Insurance (HI) trust fund is expected to run out of money by 2026.[5]

Meanwhile, until 2033, Social Security and Medicare will continue withdrawing their funds from the Treasury. Until 2018, both programs will withdraw an average of $75 billion a year. Their withdrawals will climb significantly thereafter, creating permanent pressure on the federal budget.[6]

Both programs are obviously critical for those depending on these payments. Amongst the recipients of social security today, 53% of married couples and 74% of unmarried persons receive 50% or more of their income from Social Security. For about half of those people, social security comprises 90% or more of their income.[7] By the same token, both state and local public pension funds are also deeply underfunded. The Congressional Budget Office estimates that such state pension funds are missing $3 to $4 trillion, while other organizations estimate an even higher number.[8]

The depletion of both Social Security and state pension funds means that the government will likely be called to the rescue. In fact, we don't even need to wait until 2025 or 2030 to test this assumption. Even today, union leaders are asking to use federal emergency fund money originally slated for Michigan homeowners, to help pay pension funds in Detroit.[9] 401(k) accounts will not be a source for salvation: as of late 2013, the median 401(k) account balance of 55 to 65-year-old Americans was around $75,000-$165,000, depending on the source. Assuming a 20-year retirement, this balance translates into a yearly income of $4,000 to $10,000. Clearly, for most Americans, 401(k) can be regarded only a supplements to Social Security. With this, the bottom line is clear: social security payments are, and will continue to be, critical sources of income for the vast majority of an ever-growing population of retirees. Taking into consideration the Social Security and Medicare obligations, and other federal expenses, the Congressional Budget Office estimates that in the decade between 2015 and 2024, the budget deficit will grow by an additional $8 trillion. This colossal deficit growth is only a single decade's worth. This brings us to the next D—the deficit.

An important reminder: the deficit and surplus refer to the bottom line of the annual budget, whereas the debt is the sum of all deficits and of the unpaid interest they have accrued over time.

In the first 200 years of the US's existence, the federal government's budget was neatly balanced, save for a few periods of war and one economic depression. Between 1789 and 1849, the government ran a surplus of $70 million, an average of $1.1 million a year, around $30 million in today's money, annually. The Civil War created a large deficit, totaling almost $2.7 billion during the war years.[10] The debt accumulated from this deficit was paid down using budget surpluses year after year until 1914.

Although the debt would never again fall below $1 billion, the growth of the economy and population would bring the accumulated debt to hover around 3% of the GDP before WWI.

Between 1901 and 1917—the year the US entered WWI—the budget was, on average, balanced: the government ran a small surplus for 10 of those years and a small deficit for 6 of them. In 1909, for example, the government had a deficit of $89 million, or about 12% of the budget. In 1907, on the other hand, the government saw a surplus of $87 million, or about 15% of the budget.

Participation in WWI caused a big jump in annual deficits: almost $23 billion in 1918 and 1919 combined. This deficit was about 250 times the size of prewar deficits and caused the debt to jump from a little over $1 billion to around $25 billion, or about $338 billion in 2014 dollars. The debt now represented about 33% of the GDP at the time. After the war ended, however, the government cut the budget by almost 80% and once again achieved surpluses. Throughout the Roaring Twenties, the budget was in surplus. These surpluses were used to pay off about a third of the outstanding WWI debt, decreasing it to around 15% of GDP.

During the Great Depression, the budget started running deep, and ongoing deficits grew, averaging $3 billion a year from 1932 until the US joined World War II in 1941. When the US entered the war after Pearl Harbor at the end of 1941, the yearly deficits jumped 5-fold and then 10-fold. After the end of WWII, the deficit subsided and the budget reached a small surplus in 1947. The ongoing deficits that had begun in the early 1930s pushed the debt up to $240 billion (about $2.9 trillion in 2014 dollars) by the end of WWII. This debt set a historical record, representing 109% the size of GDP, compared to only 16% in 1930.

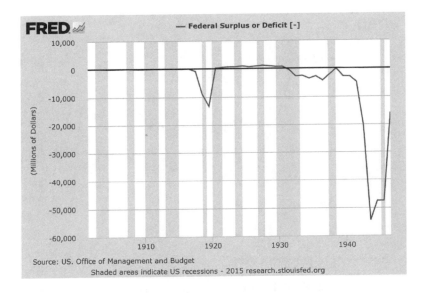

Federal deficits and surpluses: 1900-1946

While the US debt would never again be paid off in any significant way, the debt's share of GDP would shrink significantly due to the growth of the US economy after the war. In 1974, the debt fell to a low of 30% of GDP.

Although 1947 saw the budget return to surplus, 11 of the 15 years between 1950 and 1965 averaged deficits of $3 billion a year, around 4.5% of the budget. With the outbreak of the Vietnam War, deficits grew again, peaking in 1968 at $25 billion, or 14% of the budget.

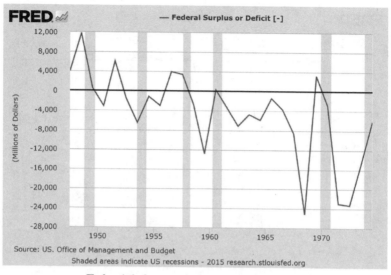

Federal deficits and surpluses: 1947-1975

Even though the entire previous decade was made up of deficits, 1975 set a new record: a $53 billion deficit. This despite the fact that the Vietnam War was over. From then on and until 1998, the federal government ran increasingly large budget deficits. In 1982, the deficit crossed the $100 billion mark for the first time in history. In 1983, this number reached the $200 billion mark and peaked at $290 billion in 1992. Thereafter, the deficit started to decline, and even turned into a surplus in 1998. 1998 to 2001 saw a 4-year break in government deficits, with sizable surpluses in 1999 and 2000. However, in 2002, the budget returned to deficits once again, hovering up and down around $300 billion a year. In 2008, after the crash of the housing bubble, TARP and the stimulus plans sent the deficit skyrocketing. For the first time in US history, the deficit for a single year climbed above $1 trillion. In 2009, the deficit totaled to $1.4 trillion dollars, then $1.3 trillion in 2010, $1.3 trillion in 2011, $1.1 trillion in 2012 and then $680 billion in 2013.[11]

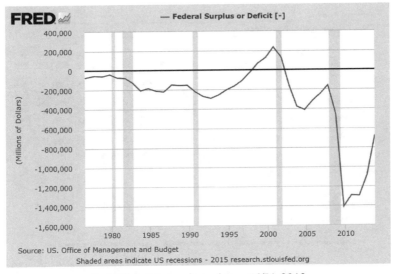

Federal deficits and surpluses: 1976-2013

These ongoing unpaid deficits, combined with the constant accumulation of compounding interest, have brought the US federal debt (as of late 2014) to a whopping $18 trillion.

The years ahead do not look any more promising: according to CBO budget projections the annual deficits will continue to persist. In 2015, the deficit is expected to fall to $470 billion, and then climb to $750 billion by 2019 crossing the trillion dollar mark again in 2022. Overall, between 2015 and 2024, according to CBO projections, the total deficit will equal to almost $8 trillion, pushing the national debt to around $26 trillion by 2025. All of these numbers are based on assumptions, and as we will see, may actually end up being much higher.

Summary Table 1.

CBO's Baseline Budget Projections

	Actual, 2013	2014	2015	2016	2017	2018	2019	2020	2021	2022	2023	2024	Total 2015-2019	2015-2024
						In Billions of Dollars								
Revenues	2,774	3,029	3,305	3,481	3,631	3,770	3,932	4,104	4,288	4,490	4,702	4,926	18,120	40,630
Outlays	3,454	3,543	3,783	4,020	4,212	4,425	4,684	4,939	5,200	5,522	5,749	6,000	21,124	48,534
Deficit (-) or Surplus	-680	-514	-478	-539	-581	-655	-752	-836	-912	-1,031	-1,047	-1,074	-3,005	-7,904
On-budget	-720	-553	-504	-555	-583	-641	-719	-775	-821	-907	-886	-871	-3,001	-7,261
Off-budget[a]	40	38	26	16	2	-14	-34	-61	-91	-124	-160	-203	-3	-642
Debt Held by the Public at the End of the Year	11,982	12,717	13,263	13,861	14,507	15,218	16,028	16,925	17,899	19,001	20,115	21,260	n.a.	n.a.
						As a Percentage of Gross Domestic Product								
Revenues	16.7	17.5	18.2	18.2	18.1	18.0	18.0	18.0	18.1	18.1	18.2	18.4	18.1	18.1
Outlays	20.8	20.5	20.9	21.1	21.0	21.1	21.4	21.7	21.9	22.3	22.3	22.4	21.1	21.7
Deficit	-4.1	-3.0	-2.6	-2.8	-2.9	-3.1	-3.4	-3.7	-3.8	-4.2	-4.1	-4.0	-3.0	-3.5
Debt Held by the Public at the End of the Year	72.1	73.6	73.2	72.6	72.3	72.6	73.3	74.2	75.3	76.8	78.0	79.2	n.a.	n.a.

Source: Congressional Budget Office.

Note: n.a. = not applicable.

a. Off-budget surpluses or deficits comprise surpluses or deficits in the Social Security trust funds and the net cash flow of the Postal Service.

Congressional Budget Office, February 2014 -The Budget and Economic Outlook: 2014 to 2024 (assuming current laws governing federal taxes and spending generally remained unchanged)[12]

All of this discussion of deficits now leads us to the final of the three Ds, the debt, which in this context refers to the accumulated combination of all unpaid deficits and loans of all sections of the US economy, government, financial sector, corporations and households. This grew from around $1.5 trillion at the beginning of the fiat money era to $16 trillion in 1994 and to $58.5 trillion by end of 2014.

If this total debt continues growing at the same rate as in the last 20 years (from $17 T to $58 T or x 3.39) the debt will reach around $200 trillion by 2035.

In the same 20 year period, GDP has grown around 163% ($9.9 T to $16.2 T). If GDP continues growing at the same pace, it should reach around $26.5 trillion by 2035. The debt-to-GDP ratio will therefore be around 740%; that is, more than seven years' worth of the entire economy's output. With interest rates of 5% (which has been the average over the past 20 years), the interest payment alone on the economy's $200 trillion debt will be around $10 trillion, or approximately 37% of the expected GDP in 2035.

Almost anyone can understand that debt becomes unmanageable when income doesn't keep pace with the debt's growth.

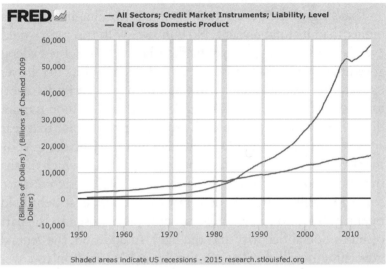

FRED: Growth in All sectors liabilities (top line) Vs. in GDP (bottom line) (1950-Q3-2014), the gap is ever widening.

The big question is what will happen when debt maintenance (paying interest) and debt growth (taking on new debt to finance more deficits) becomes impossible. This moment is hard to pinpoint and predict. First and foremost, it depends on what potential lenders think of the borrower, how long the lenders are willing to loan new money, and, as they assess the risk, what interest they will require for their loans.

If the US economy were another entity and were trying to get a loan from the US government today, it would be turned down, and so would the US government itself. Both the economy and the government would be deemed too risky. The Federal Housing Administration (FHA) requires a debt-to-income (DTI) ratio of a maximum of 43% to qualify for its mortgage loan.[13] Both the government and the economy have a much higher DTI than the FHA would accept. In fact, according to the Office of Debt Management, the federal government's debt payment in 2013 was almost $4 trillion, while its annual income, which comes from tax revenue, was around $2.9 trillion. This means the federal government has a DTI of around 140%.[14]

That's right: the government's annual debt due in 2013 was higher than its total revenue. No borrower with this ratio would even be considered for a loan by the FHA. In 2018, the Federal government will need to raise at least $6 trillion in order to roll over its maturing past debt (i.e. borrow new money to pay its due debt) together with its ongoing budget deficit. This $6 trillion is more than 1.5 times the government's projected revenues for that year.

As of the end of 2012, the average maturity of the government's outstanding debt was around 65 months,[15] which means that in the coming 5 years, the government will need to re-raise some $12 trillion in new debt just to roll over past debt held by the public and foreign governments (as opposed to the part owed to Social Security and the like). In addition, the federal government will need to raise at least $2-3 trillion to cover ongoing projected budget deficits, totaling altogether around $14-15 trillion. Only if it manages to raise these $14-15 trillion, would the government be able to avoid defaulting on its debt within the coming six years.

If the US government decides to lengthen its debt maturity range, taking advantage of the low interest rates lenders are currently willing to accept, the government would reduce the risk of encountering the potential problems involved in raising such large amounts of money in a short period of time. Consequently, however, the government will have to agree to increase its interest payments to lenders significantly, since short-term 12-month bonds have interests as low as 0.1% whereas long-term 30-year bonds currently have 3.6% interest on them. If the federal government attempts to move $10 trillion of debt to long-term bonds, it will instantly increase its interest payments by around $280 billion dollars per year,[16] thus growing total interest payments from around $221 billion paid in 2013 to around three-quarters of a trillion by 2018.

In its February 2014 10 year budget and economic outlook, the CBO calculated interest cost based on 10-year treasury notes with 3.6% yields and assumed that interest on those notes would increase by about 0.6% every year from 2015 until 2018, and remain at 5% thereafter between 2018 and 2024. With these interest rates, the deficits are projected to reach more than $26 trillion by 2024. Interest payment, by this projection, will reach around half a trillion dollars by 2018, compared to $221 billion in 2013. By 2024, interest payments are assumed to reach $880 billion, eating up about 18% of all tax revenue. However, if the markets force the Treasury to pay an increase of 1% above CBO projected interest, then the accumulated debt will grow by an additional $2 trillion. Debt would increase from $18 trillion to around $28 trillion dollars within a short 10-year period. It's terrifying to imagine the outcome if rates get back to 1995 levels of 7.5%. The CBO also doesn't assume any noticeable downturn, or takes into account the consequences on revenue and expenses alike a market crash of the type we saw in in 2000 and 2008.

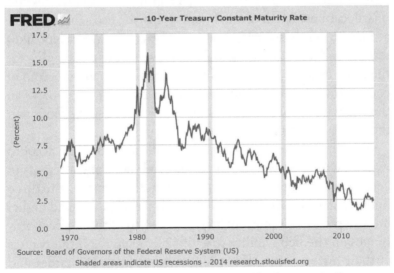

FRED 10-Year Treasury Maturity Rate, as of 11/2014: 2.34 Percent

But as we saw earlier in this chapter, it is not only the federal government that is deeply indebted. The entire US economy is indebted as well, with about $42 trillion in debt owed by all *other* sectors, including households, local governments, corporations, and the financial sector. This debt will have to be rolled over in the coming 7-10 years in order to keep the economy going.

The question, of course, is whether the lending markets will go along with these numbers, and if so, what interest rates will in order be necessary to make it possible raise these sums.

As discussed, keeping interest rates at their current historic lows is critical for the federal budget and also for the economy at large, given the current level of debt. In order to keep rates on Treasury bonds down, the Fed has to continue its QE or similar money creation programs, which purchase securities from the Treasury at current low rates, thus keeping interest down. By continuing this process, however, the Fed is also constantly increasing the money supply, which significantly increases the risk of inflation and of dollar devaluation. In addition, this injection of new money, as we have covered thoroughly, constantly destabilizes the market through ever-growing asset bubbles and misallocations. At the same time, keeping the Fed's interest rates at next to zero also severely harms the economy's savers, likes retirees and pension funds, making it even more challenging for the latter to meet their commitments to their members. And of course, low interest rates further widens the income gap between the real winners of the asset bubbles and the misallocations and the losing majority of Americans.

There is one more critical consideration to take into account regarding near-zero rates: even if the Fed wants and attempts to keep rates low, there is no assurance that it will manage to do so in the long run, as investors could very plausibly demand higher interest rates. At its current state, the health of the US economy hinges on the Fed's ability to artificially keep the interest rates at their historic lows. This task, however, becomes harder and harder to manage as time goes on.

It is quite common to encounter commentators and politicians who explain that the government debt is not a problem because a) we have been in large debts before, like during World

War II and b) the government can tax and print money at will in order to pay its debt. For these reasons, these people claim, the US will never default on its debt obligations. These claims are misleading at best. Comparing the US economy today to its position at the end of WWII is like comparing an obese old lady to an overfed young boxer. At war's end, the US was the only game in town in terms of manufacturing, infrastructure, food production, gold reserves and even natural resources like oil. In 1946, the US was producing more than China and Europe *combined*; in late 2014, according to the IMF, the US didn't even manage to out-produce China. Similarly, in 1947 the US was pumping 20 times more oil than Saudi Arabia and 120 times Kuwait's production.[17] At the same time, all other former economic powers were trying to start rebuilding their destroyed cities, scarred societies and burned down factories.

Furthermore, not only is there historical evidence that dozens of governments *have* defaulted on their debt, including the US government, but also, printing money to pay debt obligation is in itself a form of default. Making a currency less valuable through massive money printing, as will be required here if the Fed would try to pay the debt through printing, would inflate the debt, which is in itself a type of default. Furthermore, as we know, the US economy has a much bigger debt than only the federal government's debt, so the question of whether the Fed will be able to print away the other sectors' $42 trillion debt remains.

Taxation to pay the federal debt is not a practical solution either, as it would require increasing astronomically all tax rates. Such an increase would affect not just the top 1% but would act as a shock to the economy. The impact of such tax increases would make tax collection even more complicated and expensive, which would require even higher tax rates.

Currently, the US government's revenue comes from four main sources: 1) income tax, which accounts for around 43-45% of revenue; 2) payroll taxes paid by employees and employers, mainly for funding of Social Security and Medicare, making up 36-38% of revenue, 3) corporate taxes, around 10% of tax revenue; and 4) other tax sources like excise taxes and custom duties, which account for around 9% of government revenue.

Imagine a tax increase targeting only the top 5% of earners, who pay about 55% of all income tax. In order to pay off the interest on the national debt and to cover ongoing deficits, the top 5% total federal tax payments would have to increase by around 40%. On top of that payroll taxes would also have to grow by 20% all across the board on all employees and employers. A similar growth in corporate and duty taxes would also be necessary. Such a huge increase in taxes would raise the cost of employment and slow the economy down as the government takes control of more and more resources to pay off its debt. Moreover, if such changes were put into effect, they would still be inadequate should expenses and interest exceed the CBO's projections, or should tax collection efforts yield diminishing results due to the overall costs of raising taxes. As we saw, the deficits are only expected to grow over time, so such taxes would have to constantly increase well beyond this level if they are to have a chance to cover the growing deficits.

While taxes grow dramatically and the share of available resources shrinks, all other sectors of the economy will have to somehow deal with their own $42 billion debt and its interest burden. This task will prove even more unfeasible if all accessible resources are diverted to paying off government debt. It is therefore clear that although increasing taxes will eventually have to be part of the debt's restructuring, taxes alone will not be able to cover even the interest on deficits, let alone make any serious dent in the debt's principal. The government debt and the growing government deficits alone are just too serious to be taxed away.

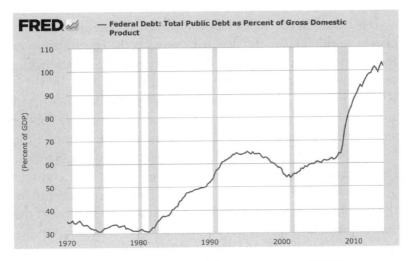

Total federal government debt as percentage of GDP

It is very common to talk about the ratio of government debt to GDP. This comparison, however, misses a point. The GDP is the total "pie" of all goods and services and of all players in the market, including households, companies and the government. Since the government cannot take in 100% of GDP, a more correct measure would be the ratio of all-sector debt to all-sector income, i.e. GDP. The ratio between these two is currently around 4 to 1. Meanwhile, government debt should be compared to government income from taxes. Currently, that ratio is 5.5 to 1. Measuring the ratio between government debt and GDP may make the problem look a little smaller, but it does so by comparing two things that are only remotely connected, at least as long as the entire market and citizens are not enslaved by the government, and even then most of the GDP will not be available for the government.

This discussion now arrives at some big questions: How long will the fiat money era go on? How long can this debt cycle go on? Why and how will it end? What will the outcome of such an ending be? And what will replace it? We will try and answer these fundamental questions as we make our way to the book's end.

It is clear that the fiat money era will not go quietly. The ruling classes worldwide are too deeply invested in the continuation of the fiat money era not to resist the massive policy changes that its removal would entail. Furthermore, in our current state, ,in which all debt is somebody else's asset, a simple and consensus-based solution seems entirely impossible. Throughout the years, the world economy has become addicted to, and structured around, the fundamental principles of the fiat money era, a kind of Keynesianism on steroids: an ever-growing money supply and debt, constant government deficits, and welcomed inflationary targets. For more than a generation, western economies, and with them most of the world, have absorbed the ways of fiat money in academia, politics, investment, media, and finance circles. Very few people remember a different system, let alone believe in the possibility of other economic principles like sound money, a true market economy, responsible consumption, and limited government.

The US, and the western world, is not unlike a person who has decided to live on a 4000-calories daily diet, instead of the recommended 2,000. After years of overindulgence our economy is fundamentally dysfunctional; addicted to debt and money creation.

There is no simple way out. We can either continue "feasting" and face deadly consequences down the road, or we can undertake serious long and painful treatments. This path calls for an understanding of our situation and a strong desire to solve the problem. Unfortunately, we are far from the place of understanding and acknowledgment. With no simple way out, and with a very small chance of convincing a skeptical, ignorant, entitled public that has long been fed promises and fallacies, the political, media, and financial class choose the easiest path forward, business as usual. This is assuming that the ruling class even knows what the economy's condition is, and is not as clueless as they were on the eve of the summer of 2008. The fundamentals of the fiat money era will inevitably continue down their unsustainable path until reality will allow them no longer.

There will be no simple or quick fix, however, no matter how agonizing. The crash of the fiat money era will also be far from a Hollywood happy ending. The risk to the very fabric of our society will be enormous and the challenges to the institutions of this country huge. Big unknowns will have lasting impacts on this nation's future. For example: Who will occupy the White House? Will it be a president with the tenacity and moral compass of Lincoln or of his predecessor, Buchanan? Who will hold the torch for us in a time of such darkness and obscurity? Will it be an engaged leader like FDR or an unengaged one like Obama? The answer to these questions could determine the future of the United States, and indeed, the world, for the next century or more. As in most historical crossroads, the end of this period will also be comprised of pain, anxiety, misery, blame, violence, demagoguery, ignorance, and deep and legitimate concerns. At the same time, it will also present opportunities and hope and some valuable lessons for humanity to carry with it as it moves to the next chapter in its history.

The fiat money era is now in its final stages: the machine is spinning at full force with diminishing results. The central banks and other financial institutions are being forced to pump ever-growing amounts of money to keep things afloat. As a result, central banks are also increasing the risks, damages, and unintentional consequences to society and the world economy.

The collapse of this house of cards will inevitably come when investors and institutions lose trust in the fiat money era fundamentals and rush to try and save their money and assets.

A final blow to the fiat money era could come from a few different potential places. Let's call these places the triggers that could serve as the nails in the coffin of this era. Some of these triggers are:

The bond market fails to raise enough money. As the US debt grows, investors "would demand," in the words of the CBO, "high interest rates to buy the government's debt." Rates could also increase in response to inflationary pressures or in reaction to a fall in the value of the dollar. Given that the US government needs to raise some $16 trillion in the next 7 years to roll over past debt and to cover ongoing deficits, the bond market could become very vulnerable and reach a breaking point. If the government is unable to raise this money, or if its cost, i.e. interest rates increases to '80s and '90s levels, the entire US economy could spin out of control, collapsing layer after layer. The first to fall would be the financial markets, and with them the entire world economy.

As time goes on and we move into the 2020s and 2030s, such risks will rapidly increase, as the debt continues to grow. With the government needing more and more money just to keep itself upright, the government's wiggle room will grow ever smaller. If the bond market fails to deliver the money the government needs in order to roll over the debt and finance the deficits at an affordable price, the Fed would inevitably start printing money. This hypothetical is now a complete reality: since 2009, the Fed has actually created and "purchased" around $2.5 trillion in government debt. It is hard to imagine and predict the myriad consequences and repercussions of this policy, should the Fed really attempt to replace the $16 trillion of bond market debt with money printed from thin air. Such an exercise will have huge and lasting impact on inflation, the dollar, other sectors' debts, and social stability. This, of course, will not solve the overall $42 trillion debt problem of other sectors.

Social unrest. Though the political and media establishments did a remarkable job of delegitimizing and suppressing the two social rebellious movements that sprung in the wake of the 2008 crisis: Occupy Wall Street and the Tea Party, it's reasonable to assume that there will come a point when the fiat money losers—the "bottom 60%," college students, millennials or even retirees—will not be willing to pay the price anymore.

Social movements and unrest can erupt overnight; sometimes from individual acts like refusing to take a seat in a bus. Yet once they are unleashed, it's hard to imagine where they go and how fast they move. After its control of the legislator and executive branches between 2009 to 2011, only the most naïve can still believe that the Democratic Party is really the protector of the poor and underprivileged. And following the reception the Republican establishment gave the Tea Party, few can believe that the Republican Party is the real protector of free markets and sound money principles.

As the prices paid for the fiat money era would continue to mount—in terms of rising food prices, mounting cost of living, student loans, cuts in social security benefits, real unemployment, and growing income inequality—the field will become more and more ripe for revolt. It may require one more Wall Street president in disguise, but eventually the American masses could revolt even if they do not fully understand the ways in which the system is rigged and corrupt. Who will lead this revolt and where will he or she take it? Will it be students fed up with the burden of college tuition and student debt? Or minimum wage employees disgusted with Wall Street billion-dollar bonuses? Or will it be perhaps a revival of the Occupy movement or of the Tea Party? It's impossible to foresee. It is impossible to predict, but it is such events that could mark the end of the fiat money era.

The abandonment of the dollar as the international reserve currency. One of the US economy's key assets is the status of the dollar as the world reserve currency. As such, the dollar is the currency used for international transactions and by central banks and others to keep reserves. Since the dollar is the international currency, the US can constantly print dollars, go out to the international markets and buy commodities and products with no limitations and no real regards of its ever-growing trade deficit. This status also enables the US to print the money it needs to pay its debt.

The big danger is that, as the US creates more and more dollars and the value of the dollar consequently deteriorates, other nations, financial markets, and trading entities could very well have a change of heart about the dollar. An editorial in China's official state-run news agency Xinhua News suggested in late 2013 that the world should consider a new reserve currency "that is to be created to replace the dominant US dollar."

One article doesn't make the change, but it does serve as a clear indication of a new frame of mind. This call to replace the dollar was not unique.

There is support for a super currency to replace the dollar coming from the IMF and prominent economists like Nobel Prize–winner Joseph Stiglitz. In fact, the IMF already has the infrastructure in place for such a move. The Special Drawing Rights (SDR) are a potential super currency blueprint created by the IMF in 1969 with roots in the Bretton Woods system. Though not considered a currency, but rather a means of exchange between the IMF members' central banks, the SRD is based on a basket of main currencies, and can easily adopt the role of an actual super currency. Indeed, in March 2009, in a release on the People's Bank of China's website, China's central bank governor, Zhou Xiaochuan, called for a new "super-sovereign reserve currency" that would replace the dollar.

> Back in the 1940s, Keynes had already proposed to introduce an international currency unit named Bancor, based on the value of 30 representative commodities. Unfortunately, the proposal was not accepted. The collapse of the Bretton Woods system, which was based on the White approach, indicates that the Keynesian approach may have been more farsighted. The IMF also created the SDR in 1969, when the defects of the Bretton Woods system initially emerged, to mitigate the inherent risks sovereign reserve currencies caused. Yet, the role of the SDR has not been put into full play due to limitations on its allocation and the scope of its uses. However, it serves as the light in the tunnel for the reform of the international monetary system.[...] Special consideration should be given to giving the SDR a greater role. The SDR has the features and potential to act as a super-sovereign reserve currency.[18]

Because SDR would delay the collapse of the fiat money era, its adoption as a super currency, or indeed, the very notion of a super currency, is growing in popularity. Switching away from the dollar, however, would deliver a significant blow to the US economy and to the American's global power.

China has even began acting on its desires. As of October 2013, the UK and China have agreed to allow direct trading between the sterling and the Chinese yuan, rather than via the dollar. This agreement made the pound sterling the fourth currency to trade directly with the Chinese yuan, with the others being the US dollar, the Australian dollar, and the Japanese yen.[19] Furthermore, in May 2014 China and Russia signed a significant 30-year deal to deliver gas to China, and though the contract was to be paid in US dollars, Russian Energy Minister hinted that the Russian Finance Ministry was working on transferring this and other contracts into Russian rubles.[20] And in November 2014 China and Canada signed a deal which allows direct dealing between the Chinese yuan and the Canadian dollar making it the fifth currency to trade directly with the yuan.

The elimination of the dollar as the world's reserve currency will severely impact the US economy in multiple ways. The first would be an increase in the cost of maintaining the federal debt and a general interest increase. Because the dollar is the world's reserve currency, central banks invest sizable parts of their reserves in dollar-denominated bonds, mainly treasury securities. If central bank demand for US treasury bonds drops, not only will it be much harder for the government to raise the trillions needed to roll over the debt, but the price to secure such funding will be significantly higher, with obvious consequences.

The loss of reserve currency status will leave the US unable to control its debt. Today, even the external debt—the 35% owed to foreign governments, not to US citizens—is denominated in US dollars. This denomination means the US is not exposed to an increase in the debt due to changes in exchange rates. If the debt were denominated in a different currency, however, it would grow in dollars if the dollar fell against the other currency. It would also prevent the US from paying the external debt with self-printed dollars and thus inflate the debt away.

One more impact, though not necessarily all that negative, would be the disappearance of the unlimited ability to print money and import goods. Once the US has to pay for its imports with currency it cannot fabricate, the capacity to run constant large deficits in the balance of payment will be severely diminished. This will have a significant short-term impact on the price of foreign labor and of imported products, which will increase dramatically.

Last, but clearly not least, the value of the dollar will be affected. Once the status of the US dollar as the world's reserve currency is over, its value will plummet, as demand for dollars would drops dramatically. The desire to hold dollar-denominated assets—mainly US treasury bonds at low interest rates—will also decrease, placing further pressure on the bond market and on the value of the dollar. This cycle could very possibly end with the collapse of the dollar and the bond market in tandem. When external non-US demand for the dollars drops, the inflationary impact of money creation would be much stronger. When almost all printed dollars would cycle only within the local US economy, its value would dive further.

The abandonment of the dollar as the world reserve currency does not have to happen as a matter of international policy. It can come about gradually as governments and multinational companies react to the dollar's deteriorating value. Just as with the sterling during and after WWI, the dollar could be left behind in a natural progression. The abandonment could also be the result of a political move, like a reaction to an international conflict in Eastern Europe or in the South China Sea.

Once this rapid decline starts, it can gain momentum and become a self-fulfilling prophecy. Like with the bond market, a rapid decrease in the value of the dollar would not be able to be contained. By nature, the impact would travel across the economy and have wide and destructive implications for interest rates, inflation and the bond market. Thus, what may look like a modest slide in the value of the dollar could trigger the "big bang."

Inflation. Inflation could well be the trigger that sets off the "big bang." As mentioned in earlier chapters, one of the biggest reasons that inflation has remained relatively under control over the course of the fiat money era was the drastic productivity boost brought on by the Digital Revolution. The Information Age saw productivity improve by leaps and bounds, which would have, if it weren't for money creation, translated into significant drops in prices and cost of living. This huge productivity gain could be nearing its end, and its deflationary contributions as well. Thus the massive dollar creation in the decades ahead could lead to meaningful inflation.

Furthermore, the use of inflation as a tool to wear away the debt is actually one of the goals of the central banks money printing. In a rare candid TV interview, Benoît Cœuré, an executive board member of the European Central Bank actually admitted "low inflation is as bad as deflation in terms of the capacity of our economy to grow out of debt. We don't need to meet deflation to be worried. Low inflation is a concern."[21]

The US experienced high inflation in the late 1970s when inflation topped 14% and interest rates 19%. This episode had a damaging impact on the economy at the time, but it is not even close to what would happen today if inflation came close to these numbers.

Bond prices and inflation move in opposite directions. To explain why, let's revert to a simple example. Let's say I hold a $100 bond with a 3-year maturity date, which means that the government will pay me $100 for that bond, interest included, in three years. Now let's say the inflation for each of the next three years will be of 100%. This means that $100 in cash today will be worth, in today terms, $50 next year, $25 in two years, and $12.5 in three years. So if I have a $100 bond with a three-year maturity date, which is really like today's $12.5, it's worth it to sell this bond today for, say, $50 and instead invest the money in some asset that will not deteriorate as badly, like gold. After all, losing 50% of the bond's value is better than losing 87.5%.

Of course, in reality things are a little more complicated and people have different expectations and assessments of future inflation. The relationship, however, is always the same: a rise in inflation sends the bond market down. Furthermore, the higher the inflation, the sharper the decline in bond prices, as people discount the future maturity value of those bonds.

As we saw previously, the US government needs to raise some $16 trillion in the coming years to cover its ongoing deficits and to roll over past debt. In order to do this in an inflationary environment, the government will have to significantly increase the interest it pays for those securities. As inflation rises, there will come a point when the bond market cracks and controlling the hole in the ongoing budget and the ability to roll over the previous debt will be all but impossible.

A bust. A seemingly moderate bust could also act as the "big bang" trigger. As previously discussed, the debt-money creation system is prone to ongoing asset bubble creations. As the market becomes more extreme, these bubbles become larger and their effects harsher. The dot-com bubble was focused, for the most part, around the tech sector. When it burst, the pain in the tech industry and in the Silicon Valley was very real and definitely severe. However, other Main Street industries and even the financial sector were much less harmed. The shock waves of the 2008 housing bubble spread much wider, reaching the financial sector and practically bankrupting Wall Street, almost bringing down the entire US economy.

In the same vein, the amount of new money needed in order to remedy each subsequent bust continues to grow. In 2002, post dot-com, sharply reducing the interest rates was enough to get the housing bubble going. In 2009-2013, interest rates were at zero, and the markets still needed the trillions of printed QE dollars to get started and keep going. As we know by now, if only from experience, these asset bubbles never last forever. All the explanations claiming that "this time is different" eventually turn out to be no more than those of Ponzi scheme peddlers. One such burst of a periodic bubble could easily get out of hand and morph into the big bang.

How many more 2008s can the Fed save before the creation of trillions of dollars translates into rampant inflation, a crisis in the bond market, or a sharp dive in the value of the dollar?

Private sector default. A default on private sector debt could just as easily trigger a "big bang" situation. As we have seen, while the government owes $18 trillion, all other sectors owe (as of end of 2014) a whopping $42 trillion. While the government debt's risks are easy to follow, as the debt is concentrated in a single sector, the $42 trillion in private debt is much more spread out and hard to track. This however, does not make the situation any less risky or explosive. Remember that the 2008 crisis ensued from a debt collapse of the over-leveraged financial sector. It was not caused by government debt. If a similar debt crisis develops in one of the many indebted sectors, it could easily expand into an economy-wide event. One of the riskiest sectors remains the financial sector, which is still highly leveraged in the stock, bonds and derivatives markets.

The collapse - or mass default - of a debtor-nation. The question of the solvency of Greece and of other European nations that faced severe pressures in summer of 2010 remains open. And though the European central bank managed to create liquidity (i.e. money) and thus delay an immediate European debt crisis, the fundamental issues remain. Furthermore Europe is not alone when it comes to debt problems. Japan, for example, has a public debt higher than Greece. The Japanese government debt is now above 240% of GDP and the government continues to run ongoing deficit budgets. Increasing debt (and thus money supply) took an unprecedented turn after 2008, not only in the US.

According to a research paper by McKinsey & Company from February 2015, global debt grew more than 40%, by $57 trillion, between 2007 and mid-2014, and as of mid- 2014 world debt stood at $200 trillion. By mid-2014, the debt of Japan's economy stood at 517% of its GDP, Spain's at 401% and China's at 282%. China's total debt has, in fact, quadrupled since 2007, rising from $7 trillion in 2007 to $28 trillion by mid-2014. About half of China's new debt was linked to real estate. Almost half of the world debt increase came from governments, $19 trillion in advanced economies and $6 trillion in developing countries. This huge indebtedness in such a short period of time , especially while the world economy is slowing down, increases the risk of a collapse of one, or more, over-leveraged nations. Japan and China, especially the Chinese real-estate market, together with Greece, Spain, Portugal and Italy, are prime candidates.

Political turmoil and/or natural disaster. Even unpredictable events beyond our control could serve as the trigger. Many historical events have been put in motion by the random acts of individuals or small groups. This was the case in June 28, 1914, when a Serb shot the Archduke Franz Ferdinand of Austria in Sarajevo, setting in motion the events that led to WWI. This was also the case in September 11, 2001, and the wars that followed. As high debt levels deplete resources, the economy becomes more prone to stressful events. Under such conditions, even a relatively small event that could otherwise be easily weathered in better days might become a serious challenge. With US financial resources basically confined to the Fed's printing press, a large scale natural catastrophe like the 1906 San Francisco earthquake or Hurricane Katrina, or an international conflict could start a chain of events that will bring about the "big bang."

While the above scenarios assume a big event that would signal the end of the fiat money era, there is another possibility. This second possibility is slower and more drawn-out. In it, the economy continuously deteriorates over a long period of time, similar to Japan's "lost decades." This period would be marked by high unemployment, low labor participation numbers, growth in the number of low paying jobs, a decrease in the standard of living, periodical cycles of booms and busts, a restructuring of social programs, the erosion of savings by inflation, a growing income gap, and social unrest. Then one morning, our grandchildren would wake up and look around, not even realizing that all of America's greatness and majesty has withered away.

This scenario is quite probable; after all, a slow decline was the fate of the great Roman Empire and of the more recent British Empire. Though completely feasible, a continuous decline is probably less likely in the modern world given its sophisticated and interconnected financial markets and the speed at which information travels. These factors tend to accelerate any sign of crisis, especially when dealing with the world largest economy.

The answer to the looming question of when the "big bang" will occur is quite unclear; it is nearly impossible to say with real accuracy anything more than any day between tomorrow and thirty years from now, or maybe even more. Although the risk increases over time as the termites continue to eat at the foundations of the castle, it is still impossible to time an avalanche. When the conditions are ripe, it is typically a random event that tips the balance and starts the unimaginable.

On Thursday, December 16, 2010, President Hosni Mubarak was the "king" of Egypt, if not of the entire Arab world. A personal relationship with him was the best thing any person in Egypt could pray for. The next morning, one street vendor 1,300 miles away in Tunisia decided to set himself on fire, setting the Arab Spring into motion. Six months later, the once-king found himself caged and dressed in rags, and all those who had previously been his friends and acquaintances disappeared as quickly as they could. When the conditions are right, you can never time when the termites will eat through the final supporting piece. One thing's for sure: that tipping point moment is always a big surprise, regardless of whether one understands the process or not.

How would the "big bang" look? Based on past crashes, it is likely that we won't know what is happening until we are suddenly faced with the unbearable reality of massive financial market collapse and escalating business shutdowns. Thereafter, what will follow is widespread unemployment and a wave of hyper chatter as the media and the political class scrambles to assign blame and come up with real or imaginary solutions. The 2008 meltdown started in late 2007, and for long months it was not clear what was really going on. It is right to assume that few will realize and even less public attention will be given when the fiat money era breathes its last breath.

In October 1929, the New York stock market crashed, but this didn't happen overnight. The process of the crash was long, with stocks shooting up and down over time. In fact, on the infamous Black Thursday, stocks lost 11% of their value. It took from September 1929 until July 1932, almost three years, for the Dow Jones index to reach its bottom, falling from 381 to 41 and losing 89% of its value. It was only over time that the Great Depression truly became "great."

When the collapse begins, it is reasonable to assume that it would gravitate towards the bond market or around the value-exchange rate of the dollar. Thereafter, the waves will quickly crash onto the shores of other sections of the highly leveraged financial sector, dragging them towards bankruptcy in a replay of 2008. With the bond, financial, and credit markets out of commission, the highly leveraged government, banks, and corporations will soon reach a standstill, and with them sizable parts of the economy.

It is also reasonable to believe that governments will try to aggressively intervene in an attempt to salvage the situation. Based on past events, such interventions could include short- and long-term steps like temporary market shutdowns, urgent capital control measures, emergency taxes and levies, and further injections of cash even at the cost of more inflation. All of these actions would be trumpeted as necessary evils. After all, why is a 2% inflation goal today deemed "positive inflation" and 10% inflation not?

Capital control measures, one of the expected government reactions, are worth further investigation. Capital controls are acts taken by the government or Federal Reserve to limit the free movement of capital or to force certain capital activities, all with the intention of achieving certain fiscal or monetary goals. These acts can also include taxes, penalties, and financial enticements. A possible potential capital control measure introduced in response to a crisis in the bond market would be formulated along these lines: "To protect the savings of retirement programs from the volatility we are experiencing in the bond markets, the government will issue 'specially protected' bonds with durations of 20 years that will bear a set 'special and fair' fixed interest. These bonds will not be tradable. All persons under age 55 will be required to place a quarter of all 401(k), pensions, and other retirement plans in these bonds in order for these plans to maintain their tax-exempt status. This initiative is good for savers, for America, and the markets in general." Such an act is so close to reality that you can almost hear the president or secretary of the Treasury making this speech at a post-crash press conference.

Considering that total retirement assets stood at $22 trillion at the end of 2013,[22] such an act could almost instantly yield trillions of dollars in long-term savings, forced into overpriced government bonds and locked for a long period of time.

Many different capital control steps can be taken. All of them, however, will prove to be nothing more than a frail attempt to handle the crisis, curb the panic, and conduct an orderly and maximally inconspicuous default. After all, the hidden fourth D stands for Default. And it is default that is the key to untangling the mess of the fiat money era we're currently in.

Default can come in many shapes and forms, including:

> **Inflation**: massive devaluation of the dollar which deflates debt away by returning the owed nominal sums but with significantly reduced purchasing power.
> **Taxes**: High and arbitrary taxes, especially on inflationary gains, which, of course, are not real gains
> **Capital controls**: including forms of default that are disguised as mandatory savings with the government, or banks acting as the government's long arm.
> **The restructuring of programs**: using fancy names to reduce or delay in meaningful ways the debt obligations the government has to such programs as social security.

> And above all, **the restructuring of the debt itself**, including canceling or significantly delaying payment obligations.

All of these potential faces of default serve the same purpose: to fundamentally and significantly shrink the burden of government debt by effectively allowing the government to avoid paying back its obligations as originally committed, or at least by delaying the problem until it becomes another generation's problem. Default, however, is no magic cure. There is no such thing as default without massive loss of wealth and savings by holders of the debt. And it is not only the government debt which will have to go this way; all $42 trillion of debt belonging to other sectors, which by then will be much higher, together with the trillions of unfunded and currently not recorded liabilities, will have to be addressed in the same manner. Detroit's Grand Bargain of November 2014 which led to the city's exit from bankruptcy procedures, provides a glimpse into the kind of default discussed above. The agreement forgave (i.e. wiped out) 74% of the city's unsecured debt and allowed the city to pay the pensions it owed its employees only thanks to a deal involving the city's art treasuries. The money for the pensions was raised through a complex deal: in an effort to prevent the sale of the Detroit Institute of Arts' collection, the museum, private foundations and the state would raise over three-quarters of a trillion dollars. This money would go to Detroit's depleted pension fund. In exchange, ownership of the DIA would be transferred from the city to an independent charitable trust.

Eventually, there will be no way around this forth D, with its massive wealth destruction and societal destabilization. When the fiat money era comes to its brutal end it will be marked by an unprecedented global default.

Restructuring and eliminating the debt and the consequent massive wealth destruction will be one side of the story; the other will be how to get the economy going again. After the burst of the mother of all bubbles, the economy will experience massive unemployment, especially of people previously-employed by the industries which owed most of their existence to the debt–money creation cycle.

Many otherwise-sound industries will of course also be affected by the dramatic drop in demand for their products as well as in credit and liquidity. This necessary massive reallocation of resources, capital, and people will be extremely painful. It is not unreasonable to imagine that these events will dwarf the Great Depression. The pressure on civil society and its institutions will be immense, and all along demagogues will try to promote their "magic" remedies.

"Desperate times call for desperate measures" will be the catchphrase of the day, and the measures will indeed be very special. The past will quickly be forgotten as no one takes responsibility, exactly as in the events of 2008. Pundits and politicians will once again jump to blaming one another and, of course, the speculators and profiteers. Hopefully this blame game will not become religiously, ethnically, or racially charged as it has in humanity's not-so-distant past. While rolling out various draconian measures, the system will try to somehow hold things together and conduct a smooth and elegant default while at the same time putting economic activities back into action.

The Great Depression lasted for almost 10 years and really didn't disappear until the outbreak of WWII and the massive government spending that followed. The magnitude of the problems this time around, however, will dwarf those of the Great Depression, while the then-new magic cure of massive government spending followed by the total destruction of all other industrialized economies will not be available again.

The times at the end of the fiat money era will be ones of anxiety and crisis and of emotions and prophets. They will see sound thinking and rational thought drowned out by illusory promises and easy-fix schemes. Powerful voices will adopt techniques from the playbooks of previous masters. They might even cull from an adept manipulator and demagogue like Adolf Hitler, who wrote in *Mein Kampf*:

"The whole art [of propaganda] consists in doing this [calling the masses' attention to certain facts, processes, necessities] so skillfully that everyone will be convinced that the fact is real, the process necessary, and the necessity correct.[...][Propaganda] consists in attracting the attention of the crowd and not in educating those who are already educated or who are striving after education and knowledge, its effect for the most part must be aimed at the emotions and only to a very limited degree at the so-called intellect.[...] All propaganda must be popular and its intellectual level must be adjusted to the most limited intelligence among those it is addressed to. Consequently, the greater the mass it is intended to reach, the lower its purely intellectual level will have to be."[23]

People crave certainty, and thus in times of crisis, they often seek authoritarian figures with decisive ideas who are quick to promise simplicity, certainty and future stability. Such figures and ideas become accepted, as strange as they might appear in more normal days. In his 1841 book *Extraordinary Popular Delusions and the Madness of Crowds*, Charles MacKay, a Scottish writer pointed out: "during the Great Plague of London, in 1665, [...] people were more addicted to prophecies and astronomical conjurations, dreams and old wives' tales than ever before or since."

Regarding this tendency to be drawn to presumed comfortable certainties, Benjamin Franklin warned that "those who would give up essential Liberty, to purchase a little temporary Safety, deserve neither Liberty nor Safety."

When the fiat money comes to an end, there will be many promises of future safety in exchange for much liberty in the present day.

The powerful voices calling for even more limited economic freedom as the solution to the problem will join the voices of those calling for limited liberty in general. After all, there is direct correlation between personal liberty and economic freedom. The most common and basic of human activities involve managing physical needs and pursuing resources to satisfy those. People desire food before play, and seek shelter before noble social ideas; they also devote much more time to basic needs. Therefore, being for liberty but against economic liberty is an oxymoron because economic liberty deals with the most common and basic activities in people's lives. Political freedom and economic freedom are two sides of one coin; one cannot exist without the other. It is no coincidence that the ultimate deprivation of freedom, slavery, is the actual act of "owning" a person, his property, and the fruits of his labor through tyranny and coercion. Where a culture of economic freedom does not exist, all other liberties eventually break apart.

It is no accident that the regimes that most deprive people of economic freedom are also those who deprive them of every other form of freedom, including human rights. It is no fluke that one of the most murderous and internally oppressive governing system so far on earth, Soviet Communism, had its core ideology based on state control of all means of production and the central planning of resource and gain distribution.

Liberties are not only a right that people strive for, they are also a precondition for the existence of a prosperous economy. People's free choices are not only "inalienable rights", but are also the fundamental base of a functioning market. Meddling with these freedoms is one of the underlying reasons the fiat money era's bitter destruction will come about in the first place.

Oppression does not just mean throwing millions into forced labor camps as in the Soviet Union or seizing people's riches. Our liberty is curbed every day in America even today. When the city of New York forbids by law the rental of residential units for less than 30 days, it is aggressively breaching the basic rights of property ownership and individuals' freedom of occupation. This situation is especially ugly when you consider that one of the main reasons for this restraint is the protection of the rich and lobbyist-equipped hotel industry. As a result, this ruling also financially harms tens of thousands of visitors and local business owners that could have enjoyed the money spent by those visitors.

Strangely, the first two cities to fight the basic freedom of property owners to rent their property to short-term renters are the same two cities leading the charge to legalize the use of marijuana under the banner of protecting personal freedom, reducing black market activity, and contributing to the economy. The division of liberties into "good" liberties— activities we personally and socially approve of and perhaps like to do—and "bad" liberties—activities we do not personally and socially approve of, is not less a flaw of Social-Conservatives. Liberty is obviously not about only permitting the things we all like and approve of, just like freedom of speech is not about the freedom to voice only the things we favor. The framework of society should not support only what the majority finds fit or what happens to be the current convention.

The separation of church and state didn't come about because most Americans in the days of Thomas Jefferson were non-religious, quite to the contrary. The *enlightened* concept of liberty exists to enable individuals to act freely as long as their actions don't infringe upon the same rights of others. As stated by Thomas Jefferson: "rightful liberty is unobstructed action according to our will within limits drawn around us by the equal rights of others. I do not add 'within the limits of the law' because law is often but the tyrant's will, and always so when it violates the rights of the individual."[24]

Liberty, like resources, is limited in terms of access. It cannot exist in two places at once: When we give the government the monopoly on using force and violence, we mostly remove this right from individuals. If we forfeit the right to control economic resources to the government, we deprive private individuals and institutions of these resources. Still, giving power to the government is not always wrong, and is some areas— especially protecting the free markets from monopoly seeking corporation—it is a necessity for keeping society together.

The risk of losing our liberties, the cornerstone and foundation of these United States, will be the most significant long-term risk and challenge brought by the end of fiat money era. It is the liberty-repressing big government philosophies, shared by "rights-seeking" Democrats and "pro-business" Republicans alike, which brought about the fiat money era and its impending catastrophic end. The risk of the adoption of an even more controlling government in the face of the crisis is a risk to the actual foundation of this country, which was born not around a race, religion, or ethnic group, but rather around the simple idea of "liberty and justice." Trying to resolve the crisis of the end of the fiat money era with a bigger government will result in additional complexity, and will require even more resources, and limitations on personal liberties, and though no long-term remedy will result from such a path, substantial long-term damage to society and personal liberties surely will. Liberty, this country's biggest contribution to the human race, will need our protection more than ever before, when the fiat money era comes to its brutal end. It is for this reason that it is critical that enough people realize and understand what Democratic President Woodrow Wilson so concisely stated: "The history of liberty is a history of the limitation of governmental power, not the increase of it."[25]

Otherwise, the end of the fiat money era, brought about almost entirely by an overreaching government, will result in an even more overreaching government, which will inevitably lead to the exchange of even more liberties today for a promised future safety. This outcome would not only be ironic, but also extremely counterproductive, and would result in many more years of misery before the era's final demise.

What should be done?

America is one of the greatest nations on earth; it has vast and rich lands, immense amounts of water, gas, and oil, and possesses many other natural wonders and resources. Its history includes innovation, entrepreneurship, ingenuity, and hard work. Among its foundations is the Constitution, one of the most important documents in the history of mankind. The notions of freedom and liberty are cornerstones of America's identity. America's institutions include the Supreme Court, a branch with the power to enforce basic human rights and curb an overreaching government. American universities are some of the best research institutions on earth. The country's innovation and technologies can constantly grow productivity, hence providing more goods for the American people and supporting an ever-growing and aging population. America can make it again, and stand once more as the "city upon a hill, the eyes of all people [...] upon us."

Relative to the utter devastation that most of Europe experienced during and after WWII, the end of the fiat money era will be far from total destruction. In fact, this forced one-time jubilee—an ancient biblical decree which called for the forgiveness of all debt every 50 years—should be warmly welcomed as a fresh start and new beginnings. To achieve this, however, America will have to do much more than just restructure its debts, government, and other sectors.

To once again be a beacon of hope to its people and the world, America will have to go back to the values that made her so great in the first place. We must have to get rid of the underlying reasons for the debt along with the debt itself. We will have to transform the conduct and culture that brought us to this point. We will have to rid ourselves of the complex society, to "de-complex" in a meaningful way. And we will need to build mechanisms that constantly ensure that we do not slide back down a slope of complexity. We will have to eliminate dozens of unnecessarily convoluted laws that cost us fortunes to implement, and deliver no real value. We will have to abolish all the corruption, subsidies, waste, and structural fraud which are so ingrained in the federal and some state budgets. At the same time, America will need to completely redo its tax system, which presumably finances these budgets, and in doing so, also take into consideration the paradigm shift that would be created by the breakthrough technologies awaiting ahead.[IX]

We will have to close myriad federal government agencies and make national issues local once again and out of the hands of unwieldy bureaucracies located thousands of miles away. We will have to make Wall Street once again accountable for its actions. We will have to get back to free market principles and abandon crony-capitalism, which, at this current state, resembles Leonid Brezhnev's Russia more than the system envisioned by our Founding Fathers. We will have to scale down our military footprint around the world. This military-industrial complex we cannot afford and its human and capital investments we too often cannot justify. We will have to agree to endure and communally share the inevitable temporary pains, as the consequences of the collapse of the fiat money era play out. We will have to put our heads down and march forward as we pass through the tough process of reorganization, reallocation and restructuring.

And above all else, we will have to go back to a sound money system, which will mean living according to our means as a state, as a society, and as individuals. This will require an educational and psychological transformation. The culture of impulsive consumption paid by debt, regardless of real need and of the impact on the environment, will have to be seriously reconsidered. Happiness will again have to be found from within, from personal interactions, and from nature. People will have to stop

IX Historically, wealth and resources were distributed by work, i.e. the key to being fed was contributing some type of labor (looting and managing included). As technology continues to flourish, it will render many occupations increasingly obsolete, just as the Industrial Revolution reduced the number of people needed in agriculture production from 90% of population to 2%. As a result, the country's necessary labor force will shrink. Thus, keeping the old model of resource distribution will ensure, at least in the short term, the immense concentration of all wealth in the hands of the very few (like inventors or financiers of new technologies), while the masses whose labor is made unnecessary will be condemned to starvation for no apparent reason. This immoral model is socially unsustainable as well as unneeded. The technological breakthroughs that await us will require totally new thinking regarding wealth and resource distribution. The old "socialist" or "capitalist" models, created in the nineteenth century will simply no longer be good enough when it comes to a future world where robots and technology will do much of the work previously done by humans.

believing that the government can solve all their problems, and politicians will have to stop falsely promising they can provide all the answers. We will have to, as President Woodrow Wilson said,

> Remember that America was established not to create wealth—though any nation must create wealth which is going to make an economic foundation for its life—but to realize a vision, to realize an ideal. America has put itself under bonds to the earth to discover and maintain liberty now among men, and if she cannot see liberty now with the clear, unerring vision she had at the outset, she has lost her title, she has lost every claim to the leadership and respect of the nations of the world.[26]

Such a spirit of liberty and such leadership and respect cannot start but from within.

There shines a ray of hope through the tough times ahead. If as a result of the crisis, America is able to rediscover its way and return to its original values of liberty and justice, then there is a bright silver lining to these stormy clouds.

If America, after coming through this crucible, returns to its core ideals of small government, personal responsibility and self-reliance, and above all else, of living within its means; then the crisis, with all its pains and adjustments, will actually forge renewed thinking and provide the start of a new morning in America -- a morning bright and clear, that will find America, once again, simple, honest, humble, and free.

Join my mailing list and receive updates on current events, recommended reads, financial alerts and more at: www.us2025.com

NOTES

Chapter 2: Bigger is Better, or Is It?

1. Omur Harmansah, Cities and the Shaping of Memory in the Ancient Near East, Cambridge University Press, 2013
2. Leo A. Oppenheim and Erica Reiner. *Ancient Mesopotamia: Portrait of a Dead Civilization,* University of Chicago Press, 1977
3. Hammurabi Laws text, Cornell University Library
4. Joseph A. Tainter, *The Collapse of Complex Societies,* (Cambridge University Press) 1988, 91-92.
5. Idem pg. 188.
6. The Waste book 2012 and 2013 http://www.coburn.senate.gov/public/index.cfm?a=Files.Serve&File_id=d204730e-4a24-4711-b1db-99bb6c29d4b6
7. John Frydenlund, *Sugar's sweet deal,* Forbes, June 2008 - http://www.forbes.com/2008/06/27/florida-sugar-crist-biz-beltway-cx_jz_0630sugar.html
8. *The Waste book* 2013 #16 Pg. 30 http://www.coburn.senate.gov/public/index.cfm?a=Files.Serve&File_id=d204730e-4a24-4711-b1db-99bb6c29d4b6
9. *Reuters,* Oct 24, 2013 - http://www.reuters.com/article/2013/10/24/us-usa-sugar-forfeit-idUSBRE99N1GD20131024
10. *"Hoeven Supports No-Cost Sugar Program in farmer Bill"* Senator Hoeven web site, June 13, 2012 - http://www.hoeven.senate.gov/public/index.cfm/2012/6/hoeven-supports-no-cost-sugar-program-in-farm-bill
11. *Span Design Displeases East Bay Leaders,* SF Gate, June 11, 1998.

http://www.sfgate.com/bayarea/article/Span-Design-Displeases-East-Bay-Leaders-call-3003659.php

12. http://earthquake.usgs.gov/earthquakes/states/10_largest_us.php

13. Uniform California Earthquake Rupture Forecast (UCERF) http://www.scec.org/ucerf2/

14. Mercury News Bay Bridge 1930's vs. today http://www.mercurynews.com/breaking-news/ci_23833904/building-bay-bridge-1930s-vs-today

15. http://www.cnbc.com/id/47631526

16. USA Today Mistakes made on bay Bridge – January 2014 http://www.usatoday.com/story/news/nation/2014/01/24/bay-bridge-hearing/4846375/

17. NY Times, *Review of Bayonne Bridge* http://www.nytimes.com/2014/01/03/nyregion/long-review-of-bayonne-bridge-project-is-assailed.html?_r=0

18. Delaware River port authority www.drpa.org/bridges/bridges_bf.html

19. California Biomedical Research Association http://ca-biomed.org/pdf/media-kit/fact-sheets/cbradrugdevelop.pdf

20. http://www.nytimes.com/2013/07/01/health/american-way-of-birth-costliest-in-the-world.html?pagewanted=all&_r=1&

21. Amy S. Oxentenko, MD; Colin P. West, MD, PhD; Carol Popkave, MA; Steven E. Weinberger, MD; Joseph C. Kolars, MD, *Time Spent on Clinical Documentation-A Survey of Internal Medicine Residents and Program Directors* http://archinte.jamanetwork.com/article.aspx?articleid=774409#ref-ioi90169-4

22. http://www.airlines.org/Pages/Government-Imposed-Taxes-on-Air-Transportation.aspx

23. http://www.iata.org/services/finance/Pages/tax-list.aspx

Chapter 3: Cash or Credit?

1. Day Glyn Davies, *A History of Money: From Ancient Times to the Present*, (2002), 71
2. Idem, 74
3. Michael Hudson, *How Interest Rates Were Set, 2500 BC – 1000 AD, Journal of the Economic and Social History of the Orient 43* (Spring 2000), 132-161
4. Jane McIntosh, *Ancient Mesopotamia:* New Perspectives (2005), 167
5. David Wayne Jones, *Reforming the Morality of Usury: A Study of Differences that separated the protestant reforms* (2005), 34
6. Simon Smith Kuznets, *The Doctrine of Usury in the Middle Ages*, transcribed by Stephanie Lo, An appendix to Simon Kuznets: Cautious Empiricist of the Eastern European Jewish Diaspora. University of Chicago
7. John H. Munro, *Usury, Calvinism, and Credit in Protestant England: from the Sixteenth Century to the Industrial Revolution*, 2011
8. Henry Dunning Macleod, *The Theory and Practice of Banking*, Volume 1, (1855), 357
9. Henry Harrisse, *Christopher Columbus and the bank of Saint George*, University of British Columbia Library
10. *PBS Public broadcasting services*, The Medici's

Chapter 4: The Secret Weapon: Not All Taxes Are Created Equal

1. John Maynard Keynes, *The Economic Consequences of the Peace* (Harcourt and Howe Inc, 1920), Chapter VI, section VI. 13 http://www.econlib.org/library/YPDBooks/Keynes/kynsCP6.html
2. *Forbes magazine*, 11/2010 and http://money.howstuffworks.com/question213.htm

3. Georgios Plavoukos, *THE SENSITIVITY OF NORWE-GIAN HOUSE PRICES TO CHANGES IN OIL PRICES*, http://csb.uncw.edu/imba/annals/PlavoukosG.pdf
4. Joseph Tainter, *The Collapse of Complex Societies* (Cambridge University Press, 1988), 134
5. Idem, 147
6. Carmen M. Reinhart, Kenneth Rogoff, *This Time Is Different: Eight Centuries of Financial Folly* (2009), 176
7. Idem, 175
8. Idem, 183

Chapter 5: The Birth of the Money Creation Machine

1. Tim Congdom, *Central banking in a free society, London institute of economic affairs* (2009), 180
2. Detlev S. Schlichter, Paper Money Collapse (2011), 60
3. The New York Times http://www.nytimes.com/2006/11/19/opinion/19summers.html?_r=0
4. CEO Compensation, Forbes List, April 2008, http://www.forbes.com/lists/2008/12/lead_bestbosses08_Richard-S-Fuld-Jr_A9P0.html
5. Carmen M. Reinhart Kenneth Rogoff, *This Time Is Different: Eight Centuries of Financial Folly* (2009), 152
6. Jeremy Atack, Larry Neal, *The Origins and Development of Financial Markets and Institutions* (2010), 14
7. Niall Ferguson, *The Ascent of Money* (2009), 143
8. Antoin E. Murphy, *John Law: Economic Theorist and Policy-maker* (1997),205
9. Niall Ferguson, *The Ascent of Money* (2009), 150
10. Antoin E. Murphy, *John Law: Economic Theorist and Policy-maker* (1997), 6
11. John Law, *Money and Trade*, copy of document available at https://ia700304.us.archive.org/7/items/moneytrade-consid00lawj/moneytradeconsid00lawj.pdf

12. Antoin E. Murphy, *John Law: Economic Theorist and Policy-maker* (1997), 94

Chapter 6: The Illegitimate Child: Lender of Last Resort

1. Paul Warburg, *"Defects and Needs of Our Banking System,"* The New York Times, January 6, 1907. https://archive. org/stream/jstor-1171781/1171781_djvu.txt
2. President Jackson's *Veto Message Regarding the Bank of the United States*; July 10, 1832" In a Compilation of Messages and Papers of the Presidents (New York: Bureau of National Literature, Inc., 1897), http://avalon.law.yale. edu/19th_century/ajveto01.asp
3. *The Saturday Evening Post*, February 1935. Pg. 25 and pg.70.
   http://www.saturdayeveningpost.com/wp-content/ uploads/satevepost/18227040.pdf
4. *Closed for the holiday - the Federal Reserve Bank of Boston*, pg. 10
5. Milton and Rose Friedman, *Free to choose, a personal statement* 1990 pg. 83
6. *Remarks by Chairman* http://www.federalreserve.gov/ boarddocs/Speeches/2002/20021108/default.htm
7. Anthony Saunders, and Berry Wilson, *The impact of consolidation and safety net support on Canadian*, US and UK banks, Journal of banking and finance, 1999, Vol. 23 pp 537-51
8. James R. Barth, Tong Li, Wenling Lu, Triphon Phumiwasana, and Glenn Yago, *The Rise and fall of the US mortgage and credit markets*, Milken Institute, 2009, page 18. http://www2.owen.vanderbilt.edu/lukefroeb/USN. econ.week.6.2009.Milken.Crisis.overview.pdf
9. *FDIC Final Rule* 11/18/2104 https://www.fdic.gov/news/ news/financial/2014/fil14057a.pdf
10. *Federal Reserve* Act section 2 A

11. *The Federal Reserve* - http://research.stlouisfed.org/fred2/series/DISAMBSL

12. Chairman Ben S. Bernanke, Oct 2009, *The Federal Reserve's Balance Sheet: An Update* http://www.federalreserve.gov/newsevents/speech/bernanke20091008a.htm

13. http://www.democraticwhip.gov/content/hoyer-audit-federal-reserve-bill-misguided-policy-inserts-politics-monetary-policy

14. *Wall Street Journal* http://online.wsj.com/news/articles/SB10001424052702303763804579183680751473884

15. *United States Government Accountability* Office http://www.sanders.senate.gov/imo/media/doc/GAO%20Fed%20Investigation.pdf

16. *The Federal Reserve* http://www.federalreserve.gov/releases/h41/current/

17. *Vice Chairman Stanley Fischer*, October 11, 2014 http://www.federalreserve.gov/newsevents/speech/fischer20141011a.htm

18. *World Bank Food Price* Index-http://siteresources.worldbank.org/DEVCOMMINT/Documentation/22887406/DC2011-0002(E)FoodSecurity.pdf

1. *The Intelligent Woman's Guide to Socialism and Capitalism* (1928), 263
2. *A history of sterling,* The Telegraph http://www.telegraph. co.uk/news/1399693/A-history-of-sterling.html
3. *Bank of England, Banknotes,* History. http://www.bank-ofengland.co.uk/banknotes/pages/about/history.aspx
4. Federal Reserve of San Francisco, *American currency exhibit*
5. Jane Kamensk, *The Oxford Handbook of the American Revolution*, 334
6. *The Economic History of Britain Since 1700: Volume 1: 1700-1860,* (Cambridge University Press, 1981), 362
7. Angus Maddison, *Historical Statistics for the World Economy: 1-2003 AD.* http://www.ggdc.net/maddison/historical_statistics/horizontal-file_03-2007.xls
8. Ron Paul, *The Case for Gold, Second Edition,* 100
9. *The New York Times,* Sep 19, 1873, can be found at http://query.nytimes.com/mem/archive-free/pdf?res=9D05E-1D81239EF34BC4152DFBF668388669FDE
10. James Ford Rhodes, *History of the United States from the Compromise of 1850* (1906), Volume 7 Pg. 45
11. *The New York Times:* http://cityroom.blogs.nytimes.com/2008/10/14/learning-lessons-from-the-panic-of-1873/?_php=true&_type=blogs&_r=0
12. *Joint Discussions Between Gen. Thomas Ewing, of Ohio, and Gov. Stewart L Woodford of New York* (1876), available online at https://archive.org/details/jointdiscussion00woodgoog

1. Jim O'Donoghue, Louise Goulding, and Grahame Allen, *Consumer Price Inflation Since 1750* (ISSN 0013-0400, Economic Trends No. 604) pp 38-46 http://safalra.com/other/historical-uk-inflation-price-conversion/
2. William Silber, *When Washington Shut Down Wall Street: The Great Financial Crisis of 1914 and origins of America's monetary supremacy* (Princeton Press), 168
3. Idem, 2
4. http://www.historylearningsite.co.uk/rationing_and_world_war_one.htm
5. *What's a little debt between friends?* BBC Magazine, http://news.bbc.co.uk/2/hi/uk_news/magazine/4757181.stm
6. Leo Grebler, Wilhelm Winkler, *The Cost of the World War to Germany and to Austria-Hungary* (Yale University Press, 1940), 9
7. Feldman, *Army, Industry, and Labor in Germany*, 1914-1918, 117
8. Idem, 86
9. Idem, 90
10. http://www.pbs.org/greatwar/resources/casdeath_pop.html
11. Angus Maddison, *Historical Statistics of the World Economy: 1-2008 AD*
12. Richard Burdekin , Farrokh Langdana, *Confidence, Credibility and Macroeconomic Policy Routledge* (1995), 92
13. Costantino Bresciani-Turroni, *Economics of Inflation: A Study of Currency Depreciation in Post-War Germany (1931)*, 404
14. HENRY HAZLITT, *Lessons from the German Inflation*, http://www.fee.org/the_freeman/detail/lessons-of-the-german-inflation
15. Phillip Coggan, *Paper Promises* (2012), 80 note # 1
16. Hugh Rockoff, Until its over: *The us economey in world war I* (June 2004) - http://www.nber.org/papers/w10580.pdf

17. *The Measurement and Behavior of Unemployment* http://www.nber.org/chapters/c2644.pdf

18. http://www.usgovernmentspending.com/fed_spending_1924USmn

19. Quartz http://qz.com/74271/income-tax-rates-since-1913/

20. Martha Olney, *Buy Now, Pay Later*, 1991

21. http://web.bryant.edu/~ehu/h364/materials/cars/cars%20_30.htm

22. Martha Olney, *Buy Now, Pay Later*, 1991

23. Natacha Postel-Vinay, *Debt Dilution in 1920s America:Lighting the Fuse of a Mortgage Crisis European Historical Economic Society*, March 2014, http://www.ehes.org/EHES_No53.pdf

24. Kenneth A. Snowden Bryan, *The Anatomy of a Residential Mortgage Crisis: A Look Back to the 1930s*, School of Business and Economics UNC Greensboro, NC June, 2009

25. Eugene N. White, *The Great American Real Estate Bubble of the 1920s: Causes and Consequences Rutgers University and NBER*, Department of Economics , Pg. 8,9 http://economics.rutgers.edu/dmdocuments/White1920sReal-Estate.pdf)

26. Kenneth A. Snowden, *The Anatomy of a Residential Mortgage Crisis: A Look Back to the 1930s Bryan School of Business and Economics UNC Greensboro, NC June, 2009* https://sedonaweb.com/attach/schools/NCBEfaculty/attach/chapter-297.pdf

27. Tobias F. Rötheli, *Innovations in Banking Practices and the Credit Boom of the 1920's*, Department of Economics, University of Erfurt, Germany

28. Joseph S. Davis, *The Worm Between the* Wars, 1919-1939: An Economist's View (The Johns Hopkins Press, 1975), 99

29. Board of Governors of the Federal Reserve System, Banking and Monetary Statistics (Washington: National Capital Press, 1941). *Quoted at: Margin Purchases, Brokers'*

Loans and the Bull Market of the Twenties, Gene Smiley , Marquette University , Richard H. Keehn , University of Wisconsin- Parkside http://www.thebhc.org/publications/BEHprint/v017/p0129-p0142.pdf

30. http://library.brown.edu/cds/mjp/render. php?view=mjp_object&id=mjp.2005.01.055

31. http://www.nytimes.com/learning/teachers/featured_articles/19991018monday.html

32. Eugene N. White, *LESSONS FROM THE GREAT AMERICAN REAL ESTATE BOOM AND BUST OF THE 1920'S* Working Paper 15573. NATIONAL BUREAU OF ECONOMIC RESEARCH https://www.clevelandfed.org/research/seminars/2010/white.pdf

33. Timothy Cogley, *Monetary Policy and the Great Crash of 1929: A Bursting Bubble or Collapsing Fundamentals?*, Federal Reserve Bank of San Francisco, http://www.frbsf.org/economic-research/publications/economic-letter/1999/march/monetary-policy-and-the-great-crash-of-1929-a-bursting-bubble-or-collapsing-fundamentals/

34. Office of personnel management- http://www.opm.gov/policy-data-oversight/data-analysis-documentation/federal-employment-reports/historical-tables/total-government-employment-since-1962/

35. http://en.wikipedia.org/wiki/U.S._Automobile_Production_Figures

36. Nicholas Wapshott, *Keynes vs. Hayek, The clash that defined modern economies* (2011), 158-160

37. Milton Friedman and Anna J. Schwartz, *A Monetary History of the United States*, 1867-1960, Pg. 300-301.

38. Ben Bernanke, *Money, Gold, and the Great Depression*, http://www.federalreserve.gov/boardDocs/speeches/2004/200403022/default.htm

39. Marriner S. Eccles, *Beckoning frontiers: Public and personal recollections*, Alfred A. Knopf, 1951 ,

40. Elmus Wicker, *The Banking Panics of the Great Depression*, Cambridge University Press, 1996

41. *Federal Deposit Insurance Corporation: The First Fifty Years.* http://www.fdic.gov/bank/historical/managing/Chron/pre-fdic/

42. Elmus Wicker, *The Banking Panics of the Great Depression* (Cambridge University Press, 1996), 146-7

43. *Federal Deposit Insurance Corporation: The First Fifty Years.* http://www.fdic.gov/bank/historical/managing/Chron/pre-fdic/

44. http://www.investopedia.com/terms/g/gold-reserve-act-1934.asp

45. US department of Treasury http://www.treasury.gov/resource-center/international/ESF/Documents/Trunc%20+%20Notes.pdf

46. http://www.newyorkfed.org/aboutthefed/fedpoint/fed14.html

47. *Farm Economics, Department of Agriculture*, Cornell University Dec 1957 http://fraser.stlouisfed.org/docs/meltzer/peawar57.pdf

48. Robert A. Margo, *Employment and Unemployment in the 1930s*, Table 1: http://fraser.stlouisfed.org/docs/meltzer/maremp93.pdf

49. http://www.treasurydirect.gov/govt/reports/pd/histdebt/histdebt_histo3.htm

50. *$1 of debt from 1930-* https://www.edwardjones.com/groups/ejw_content/@ejw/@us/@graphics/documents/web_content/web226225.pdf pg. 5

Chapter 9: The Golden Dollar, the Bretton-Woods System

1. William Safire, *Before the Fall: An Inside View of the Pre-Watergate White House*

2. http://www.presidency.ucsb.edu/ws/index.php?pid=3115#axzz1UZnES7PMon

3. Paul Volcker, Toyoo Gyohten, *Changing fortunes: the world's money and the threat to American leadership* (1992), 77

4. William Safire, *Before the Fall: An Inside View of the Pre-Watergate White House*

Chapter 10: Bye-Bye, Gold; Hello, Fiat Money

1. http://research.stlouisfed.org/fred2/series/TCMDO
2. US Census Bureau, March 2014. http://www.census.gov/foreign-trade/statistics/historical/gands.pdf
3. http://www.census.gov/foreign-trade/statistics/historical/gands.txt
4. Commerce department
5. Edward Nelson, *The Great Inflation of the Seventies: What Really Happened?* Federal Reserve of St. Louis., Paper 2004-001 http://research.stlouisfed.org/wp/2004/2004-001.pdf
6. Idem, 3
7. Has the BLS removed food or energy price- http://www.bls.gov/cpi/cpiqa.htm
8. http://www.bls.gov/cpi/cpiqa.htm Q # 3
9. Keynes, *The General theory of employment interest and money*, Chapter 2, II – available online at http://gutenberg.net.au/ebooks03/0300071h/chap02.html
10. http://www.nytimes.com/2012/12/14/business/colleges-debt-falls-on-students-after-construction-binges.html?pagewanted=all
11. The Project on Student Debt, *Student debt for the class of 2012*, http://projectonstudentdebt.org/files/pub/classof2012.pdf
12. Consumer Financial Protection Bureau
13. FRED http://research.stlouisfed.org/fred2/series/SLOAS http://libertystreeteconomics.newyorkfed.org/2012/03/grading-student-loans.html
14. United States Government Accountability Office, September 2014. http://www.gao.gov/assets/670/665709.pdf

15. Lindsey Burke, *How Escalating Education Spending Is Killing Crucial Reform*, Oct 2012, http://www.heritage.org/research/reports/2012/10/how-escalating-education-spending-is-killing-crucial-reform

16. University of California annual accountability report 2011, Pg. 87 http://accountability.universityofcalifornia.edu/documents/accountabilityreport11.pdf

17. Flashbacks of the 1970s for Stock-Market Vets, 2009, The Wall Street Journal. http://online.wsj.com/news/articles/SB124001598168631027

18. US census, department of commerce

19. Lisa Endlich, *Goldman Sachs, The Culture of Success*, 1999, chapter 1

20. Federal Reserve Economic Data (FRED)

21. *Too Big to Fail after All These Years*, Federal Reserve Bank of New York, Staff Reports, 2005 pg. 62

22. Carola Frydman and Raven Saks, *Historical trends in executive compensation* 1936-2005, 2007, Pg. 3 - http://web.mit.edu/frydman/www/trends_rfs2010.pdf

23. Idem Pg. 63

24. Jenny Anderson, *Alfa list, The New York Times*, April 27, 2007

25. The Financial Crises Inquiry Report, 2011, Pg. 37

26. *Too Big to Fail after All These Years*, Federal Reserve Bank of New York, Staff Reports, 2005

27. CEO pay and the top 1%, economic policy institute brief 331, May 2012 http://s4.epi.org/files/2012/ib331-ceo-pay-top-1-percent.pdf

28. http://usatoday30.usatoday.com/money/companies/management/2011-03-31-ceo-pay-chart-total.htm

29. Bloomberg technology, January 2014, http://www.bloomberg.com/news/2014-01-15/yahoo-chief-operating-officer-de-castro-to-leave-web-portal.html

30. SF Gate, June 24, 1995 - http://www.sfgate.com/business/article/Netscape-Will-Go-Public-With-Stock-Sale-in-August-3030632.php

31. *The Monthly Fool*, July 1999. http://www.fool.com/dtrouble/1999/dtrouble990723.htm
32. *Hale & Dorr* The IPO Report 1999 http://www.ipoguidebook.com/files/upload/99_ipo_report.pdf
33. Alexander P. Ljungqvist, *IPO pricing in the dot-com bubble*, Stern School of Business New York University, 2002
34. New York City Securities Industry bonus pool. http://www.osc.state.ny.us/press/releases/feb13/avgbonus.pdf
35. http://www.businessweek.com/bwdaily/dnflash/dec1999/nf91222c.htm
36. The $1.7 trillion dot.com lesson, CNN Money, Nov 2000, http://money.cnn.com/2000/11/09/technology/overview/
37. Federal Reserve Economic Data (FRED) http://research.stlouisfed.org/fred2/series/SLGSDODNS
38. US Census Bureau, U.S. *Neighborhood Income Inequality* in the 2005–2009 Period, October 2011, Pg. 5
39. http://www.washingtonpost.com/blogs/wonkblog/wp/2014/12/12/enough-is-enough-elizabeth-warrens-fiery-attack-comes-after-congress-weakens-wall-street-regulations/
40. http://act.credoaction.com/sign/dunn_kxl?sp_ref=13466206.4.882.f.3712.2&referring_akid=9161.3325844.R1oi7U&source=fb_share_sp2
41. *Exchange during CNBC debate*, Nov. 9, 2011 - http://www.washingtonpost.com/blogs/fact-checker/post/newt-gingrich-and-freddie-mac-is-he-being-misleading/2011/11/16/gIQAiAvNSN_blog.html
42. http://www.nytimes.com/2011/10/28/us/politics/obama-bundlers-have-ties-to-lobbying.html?pagewanted=1&_r=2
43. http://www.newyorker.com/online/blogs/johncassidy/2013/05/tom—wheeler-federal-communications-commission.html
44. http://blog.washingtonpost.com/citizen-k-street/chapters/introduction/

45. The Environmental Working Group, *EGW Farm subsidies*-http://farm.ewg.org/regionsummary.php

46. http://www.opensecrets.org/lobby/indus.php?id=A&year=2010

47. The New York Times, Nov 2013. http://www.nytimes.com/2013/11/07/us/billionaires-received-us-farm-subsidies-report-finds.html?_r=0

48. *Law makers farm subsidies*, The Wall Street Journal May 2013 http://www.wsj.com/articles/SB10001424127887324682204578517670331693946

49. http://farm.ewg.org/persondetail.php?custnumber=A09247988

50. US government printing office

51. Lobbying and Taxes, http://papers.ssrn.com/sol3/papers.cfm?abstract_id=1082146

52. The Wall Street Journal, May 30, 2007 http://online.wsj.com/news/articles/SB118048308219917822

53. GE paid no Federal taxes in 2010, ABC News, March 2011 - http://abcnews.go.com/Politics/general-electric-paid-federal-taxes-2010/story?id=13224558

54. http://www.opensecrets.org/lobby/clientsum.php?id=D000000125&year=2010

55. http://www.ibtimes.com/30-major-us-corporations-paid-more-lobby-congress-income-taxes-2008-2010-380982

56. *The Daily Beast*, July 13, 2010 http://www.thedailybeast.com/articles/2010/07/14/a-failed-financial-bill.html

57. Sarah Fulmer, April Knill, *Political Contributions and the Severity of Government Enforcement*, Florida State University, http://business.nd.edu/uploadedFiles/Faculty_and_Research/Finance/Finance_Seminar_Series/2012%20Fall%20Finance%20Seminar%20Series%20-%20April%20Knill%20Paper.pdf

58. http://politics.slashdot.org/story/14/05/11/035236/silicon-valleys-love-hate-relationship-with-president-obama

59. http://www.cnn.com/ALLPOLITICS/1997/02/26/clinton.lincoln/
60. CNN, *Former President Bill Clinton commanded the largest speaking fees of his career in 2011*, http://www.cnn.com/2012/07/03/politics/clinton-speaking-fees/
61. The New York Times, *Chelsea Clinton Follows Parents*, http://www.nytimes.com/2014/07/10/us/politics/chelsea-clinton-follows-parents-lead-as-a-paid-speaker.html?_r=0
62. Center for Responsive Politics http://www.opensecrets.org/news/2013/06/2012-overview.html
63. http://www.opensecrets.org/politicians/summary.php?cycle=2012&type=I&cid=N00007360&newMem=N
64. http://www.opensecrets.org/politicians/summary.php?cycle=2010&type=I&cid=N00003675&newMem=N
65. Peter Schweizer, *Extortion*, 2013, Pg. 26-27
66. CFI- the campaign finance institute http://www.cfinst.org/data/pdf/VitalStats_t9.pdf
67. Gallop, *Congress and the public*, http://www.gallup.com/poll/1600/congress-public.aspx
68. Congressional Budget Office Report, *Comparing the Compensation of Federal and Private-Sector Employees*, Jan 2012 http://www.cbo.gov/sites/default/files/cbofiles/attachments/01-30-FedPay.pdf
69. US Census Bureau http://www.census.gov/foreign-trade/balance/c0015.html
70. U.S. trade in goods with World, Not Seasonally Adjusted, US Census Bureau, http://www.census.gov/foreign-trade/balance/c0015.html
71. US census, *Historical income* http://www.census.gov/hhes/www/income/data/historical/household
72. Jon Bakija, Adam Cole, Bradley T. Heim, *Jobs and Income Growth of Top Earners and the Causes of Changing Income Inequality: Evidence from U.S. Tax Return Data.* April 2012 http://web.williams.edu/Economics/wp/BakijaColeHeimJobsIncomeGrowthTopEarners.pdf
    And Forbes magazine, Who actually are the 1% http://

www.forbes.com/sites/timworstall/2011/12/28/who-actually-are-the-one-percent
And Top 1% Historic perspective http://pubs.aeaweb.org/doi/pdfplus/10.1257/jep.27.3.3

73. Brad Plumer, *Who benefits from stock market boom*, March 2013 - http://www.washingtonpost.com/blogs/wonkblog/wp/2013/03/11/graph-of-the-day-who-actually-benefits-from-a-stock-market-boom/

74. Robert Lenzner, *The top 0.1% eran half the capital gains*, Forbes, 11/2011- http://www.forbes.com/sites/robertlenzner/2011/11/20/the-top-0-1-of-the-nation-earn-half-of-all-capital-gains/

75. Jon Bakija, Adam Cole, Bradley T. Heim, *Jobs and Income Growth of Top Earners and the Causes of Changing* Income Inequality: Evidence from U.S. Tax, April 2012. Pg. 62- http://web.williams.edu/Economics/wp/BakijaCole-HeimJobsIncomeGrowthTopEarners.pdf

76. CBO Trends in the Distribution of Household Income between 1979 and 2007, October 2011- http://www.cbo.gov/sites/default/files/cbofiles/attachments/10-25-HouseholdIncome.pdf

77. Richard Fry, Rakesh Kochhar, *America's wealth gap widest on record*, Pew Research center, Dec 2014, http://www.pewresearch.org/fact-tank/2014/12/17/wealth-gap-upper-middle-income/

78. Emmanuel Saez (UC Berkeley) Gabriel Zucman (LSE), *Wealth Inequality in the United States since* 1913 October 2014, slide 40. (calculate: $10M/$21K) http://gabriel-zucman.eu/files/SaezZucman2014Slides.pdf

79. The World bank http://data.worldbank.org/indicator/BN.GSR.GNFS.CD

80. Marc Labonte, *Congressional Research Service China's Currency Policy*, 2013. https://www.fas.org/sgp/crs/row/RS21625.pdf

81. Marie-Theres Stohldreier, *The Determinants of House Prices in Chinese Cities*, Department of Economics of

the University of Zurich, 2012 http://www.econ.uzh.ch/ipcdp/theses/MA_MarieStohldreier.pdf

82. *China property boom continues relentlessly*, Dec 2013 http://www.globalpropertyguide.com/Asia/china/Price-History

83. FRED, *10 year treasury maturity rate average and US Treasury* http://www.treasury.gov/resource-center/data-chart-center/tic/Documents/mfh.txt

84. Forbes magazine, *The Foreign Companies That Are Buying Up America* June 2013- http://www.forbes.com/sites/kenrapoza/2013/06/27/the-foreign-companies-that-are-buying-up-america

85. Federal Reserve Bank of Minnesota, *consumer price index* 1800. http://www.minneapolisfed.org/community_education/teacher/calc/hist1800.cfm

86. Maddison Angus, *The World Economy Historical Statistics,*. Pg. 247
Plus, Economic History Association http://eh.net/encyclopedia/a-history-of-the-standard-of-living-in-the-united-states

87. John Keynes, *The Economic Consequences of the Peace*, 1920, Harcourt and Howe Inc. Chapter VI, section VI. 13-http://www.econlib.org/library/YPDBooks/Keynes/kynsCP6.htm

Chapter 11: 2008: a Peek at Hell

1. *Financial Crisis Inquiry Commission* (FCIC) report, Ben Bernanke, page 354
2. Governor Ben S. Bernanke, *Remarks before the National Economists Club*, Washington, D.C. November 21, 2002
3. *Federal Reserve Board*, http://www.federalreserve.gov/BoardDocs/Testimony/2002/20021113/default.htm
4. Governor Ben S. Bernanke, *The Great Moderation*, Remarks at the meetings of the Eastern Economic Association, Washington, DC. February 20, 2004.. http://www.federalreserve.gov/Boarddocs/Speeches/2004/20040220/
5. *The Financial Crisis Inquiry Commission* Report ("FCIC") page 5 (hereafter Commission report)
6. Commission report. p. 14
7. *CBO Housing Wealth and Consumer Spending* 1/2007 http://www.cbo.gov/sites/default/files/cbofiles/ftp-docs/77xx/doc7719/01-05-housing.pdf
8. Commission report P. 161
9. NAHB/Wells Fargo Housing Market Index and U.S. Census Bureau.
10. Commission report, P. 14 footnote 64
11. William J. Clinton, *Remarks on the National Homeowner-ship Strategy,*June 5, 1995
12. President G.W. Bush, *Remarks to the National Association of Home Builders in Columbus*, Ohio, October 2, 2004
13. Commission report P. 42-43
14. Report of OFHEO *Special Examination of Fannie Mae* May 2006
15. *Committee on Oversight and Government Reform*, Darrell Issa, Chairman COMPENSATION AT FANNIE MAE AND FREDDIE MAC, , Nov 2011
16. Commission report P. 20
17. Staff Report Prepared for Chairman Darrell Issa, *How Countrywide Used its VIP Loan Program to Influence Washington Policymakers.* U.S. House of Representatives Committee

on Oversight and Government Reform July 5, 2012

18. Jason Thomas, *A Closer Look at Fannie Mae and Freddie Mac: Department of Finance*, George Washington University

19. The Associated Press, Tuesday, December 19, 2006

20. On Wall Street, Bonuses, Not Profits, Were Real, The New York Times Dec 2008 http://www.nytimes.com/2008/12/18/business/18pay.html?pagewanted=all&_r=0

21. Commission report, P. 19

22. Commission report, P. 15

23. Andrew Haughwout, *The Supply Side of the Housing Boom and Bust of the 2000's*, Federal Reserve Bank of New York, August 21, 2012

24. Bureau of labor statistics, *The U.S. housing bubble and bust: impacts on employment Monthly Labor Review*, December 2010

25. Commission report, p. 35

26. Commission report, P. 8

27. Jan. 17, 2008. Bloomberg news

28. Commission report, P. 7

29. Commission report, P. 16

30. Commission Report, P. 21

31. Commission report, P. 24

32. Commission report, P. 19

33. Commission report, P. 22

34. Commission report, P. 321

35. Federal Reserve Minutes http://www.federalreserve.gov/monetarypolicy/fomcminutes20080805.htm

36. Commission report, P. 338

37. *Secretary Paulson to the House Oversight Committee*, Dec 2009

38. Treasury Direct, http://www.treasurydirect.gov/NP/debt/current

39. NY State Comptroller http://www.osc.state.ny.us/press/releases/mar14/031214.htm

40. Colombia Journalism review, http://www.cjr.org/the_
    audit/financial_crisis_inquiry_commi.php?page=all
41. *New York City Securities Industry Bonus Pool,* Office of the
    New York State Comptroller http://www.osc.state.ny.us/
    press/releases/mar14/wall_st_bonus_pool.pdf

Chapter 12: What's Next?

1. Department of health and human resources, *Administration of aging.* Older Population by Age Group: 1900 to
   2050, http://www.aoa.acl.gov/Aging_Statistics/future_
   growth/future_growth.aspx#age
2. Department of health and human service http://www.aoa.
   gov/Aging_Statistics/future_growth/future_growth.aspx#age
3. The Census Bureau https://www.census.gov/newsroom/
   releases/archives/2010_census/cb11-cn192.html
4. *A summary of the 2014 annual report,* Social security
   administration http://www.ssa.gov/oact/trsum/
5. *Status of social security and Medicare programs,* summary of
   2013 annual report http://www.socialsecurity.gov/OACT/
   TRSUM/tr13summary.pdf
6. *A summary of the 2014 annual report,* Social security
   administration http://www.ssa.gov/oact/trsum/
7. *Social Security administration,* Social Security basic facts.
   http://www.ssa.gov/pressoffice/basicfact.htm
8. The Congressional Budget Office, *The Underfunding of
   State and Local Pension Plans,* May 2011
   http://www.cbo.gov/sites/default/files/cbofiles/ftp-
   docs/120xx/doc12084/05-04-pensions.pdf
   And: Harvard Kennedy School, unfunded pensions in the Untied States http://www.hks.harvard.
   edu/var/ezp_site/storage/fckeditor/file/pdfs/
   centers-programs/centers/mrcbg/publications/fwp/
   MRCBG_FWP_2012_08-Healey_Underfunded.
   pdf And: http://reason.com/archives/2013/09/06/

taxpayers-on-the-hook-for-trillions-in-u/print

9. The Wall Street Journal, *Unions Want Federal Money to Plug Detroit Pension Hole*, April 2014 http://online.wsj.com/news/articles/SB10001424052702 30462630457950626092360530

10. *The Bureau of public debt*, history, http://www.publicdebt. treas.gov/history/history.htm

11. Historical tables, *Budget of the U.S. government*, Office of management and Budget http://www.whitehouse.gov/ sites/default/files/omb/budget/fy2012/assets/hist.pdf

12. The Congressional Budget Office, *The Budget and Economic Outlook: 2014 to 2024* - http://www.cbo.gov/sites/ default/files/cbofiles/attachments/45010-Outlook2014_ Feb.pdf

13. http://archives.hud.gov/offices/hsg/sfh/ref/sfhp2-12.cfm

14. Office of Debt Management report, http://www.treasury. gov/resource-center/data-chart-center/quarterly-refunding/Documents/TBAC%20Discussion%20Charts%20 Feb%202012.pdf

15. Idem, 15

16. John H. Cochrane, *Having your cake and eating it too: The maturity structure of US debt.* University of Chicago Booth School of Business, Nov 2012, http://faculty. chicagobooth.edu/john.cochrane/research/papers/Maturity_of_debt.pdf

17. US energy information administration - http://www.eia. gov/dnav/pet/hist/LeafHandler.ashx?n=pet&s=mcrf-pus1&f=a
And http://www.country-data.com/cgi-bin/query/r-7587. html
And http://www.bechtel.com/BAC-Chapter-3.html

18. Zhou Xiaochuan, Zhou Xiaochuan's *Statement on reforming the International Monetary system*, March 2009 - http://www.cfr.org/china/zhou-xiaochuans-statement-reforming-international-monetary-system/ p18916

19. The Guardian http://www.theguardian.com/business/2013/oct/15/london-china-investment-rules-yuan

20. *RIA Novosti* http://en.ria.ru/russia/20140523/190068675/China-to-Pay-for-Russian-Gas-in-US-Dollars—Russian-Energy.html

21. Bloomberg, Nov 24 - http://www.bloomberg.com/news/2014-11-24/coeure-says-draghi-clarified-why-we-re-doing-what-we-re-doing.html

22. http://www.ici.org/policy/retirement/plan/401k/faqs_401k

23. Adolf Hitler, *Mein Kampf*, Chapter VI: War Propaganda

24. Thomas Jefferson, *Political Writings by Thomas Jefferson to Isaac Tiffany*. Pg. 224

25. Address to New York Press Club September 9, 1912 Wilson Center. www.wilsoncenter.org/about-woodrow-wilson

26. *"The Coming On of a New Spirit"*, speech to Chicago Democrat's Iriquois Club (12 February 1912), The Politics of Woodrow Wilson, p. 180

Acknowledgments

The journey which ended with the publication of this book started in September 2008, when Wall Street crashed, and the entire financial market and world economy seemed on the verge of collapse. As I felt the conventional media didn't seem to deliver answers, I set out to find them myself. Although many books provided detail on specific events, I could not find a comprehensive yet simple overview that drew links between past and present and made a clear connection between all the elements that shape our current reality.

I would like to therefore first thank the thinkers and writers that took the time to thoroughly highlight different aspects of the history of money. Their names can be found within the notes section.

On a personal note, I would like to thank my brother Yishai for endless hours of discussion, debate, and thought, and for his intimate involvement in the intellectual creation, as well as editing, of this book. Many thanks to my son Aylon for countless hours of researching, editing, writing and for many useuful ideas. Thanks to David Drum, a good friend who took the time to read and critique the first draft, and Jesse Allread who provided good advice. I have greatly benefited from the solid work and advice of Katya Smundak. Her analysis and questions were stimulating and helpful. Thanks also to my friend Udi for useful comments and ideas. Many thanks to Laura Hughes, whose help, advice, and attention to detail was invaluable in bringing this project to fruition. Finally I would like to thank my mother for the love of reading, history, investigation, and critical thinking she instilled in me. Last but not least, I would like to thank my wife. This project was my second job and thus took too much of our free time. Thanks for being accommodating and supportive, as you have been many times in the past. This page of acknowledgments is not complete without a special thank you note to all Indiegogo supporters and, of course, you, dear readers, for investing your time and money and trusting me with telling this story.

Palo Alto, California,
February 2015